Anonymous

The Desk Hong List

A General and Business Directory for Shanghai and the Northern and River

Ports

Anonymous

The Desk Hong List

A General and Business Directory for Shanghai and the Northern and River Ports

ISBN/EAN: 9783337372675

Printed in Europe, USA, Canada, Australia, Japan

Cover: Foto ©Suzi / pixelio.de

More available books at **www.hansebooks.com**

THE

Desk Hong List;

A

GENERAL AND BUSINESS DIRECTORY

FOR

SHANGHAI

AND THE

NORTHERN AND RIVER PORTS,
&c.

1884.

INDEX.

A Colored Map of China (compiled expressly for this Work), with the Provinces, the Capital Cities Chief Rivers, and the Routes of various distinguished travellers—when ordered.

Street Plan of the English and American Settlements—when ordered.

Rough Plan of District between the Defence Creek and the Bubbling Well—when ordered.

Rough Plan of the Settlement of Fusan.

Roads in American, English and French Settlements.

English and Chinese Calendar.

Fixed and Moveable Festivals, &c.

Jewish Calendar.

Mohammedan Calendar.

Shanghai Hong List 1-3
Chefoo Hong List 37-3
Chinkiang Hong List 40-4
Foochow Hong List 43-4
Hankow Hong List 48-5
Ichang Hong List 52
Kiukiang Hong List 53-5
Newchwang Hong List 55-5
Ningpo Hong List 57-5
Peking List—Legations at Peking 59-6
Tientsin Hong List 62-65
Wenchow Hong List 66
Wuhu Hong List 67
Corea Directory 68-7
Who's Who (An Alphabetical List of Foreign Residents at Shanghai, Foochow, Ningpo, Northern and Reverine Ports, etc.) 72-1
Ladies' Directory (An Alphabetical List of Lady Residents at Shanghai, Foochow, Ningpo, Northern and Reverine Ports) 103-114

British Treaty with Corea 156-1
Chamber of Commerce Tariff 134-135
Chinese Government Departments at Peking 116-117
Chinese Land Measure ....
Chinese Names of Eighteen Provinces ....
Customs' Trade Regulations—
Contraband Goods; and Goods which were formerly contraband, but trade in which is now permitted under certain restrictions 141-1
Duty-Free Goods 142
Tariff on Imports 143-14
Tariff on Exports 144-148
Unenumerated Goods 149
Diplomatic and Consular Service in China (H.B.M.'s)... 115
Events connected with China 167-17
Exchange Tables 197-21
Gold and Silver Coins Table 193
Harbour Regulations for the Port of Shanghai, &c. 150-15
High Provincial Authorities of the Chinese Empire (List of) 118-11
Insurance Offices in Shanghai—Marine and Fire 121-125
Letter Pillars—Local Post Office 133
List of Coast and Riverine Steamers 33-36
List of Foreign Hongs (Alphabetically arranged according to Chinese pronunciation) 179-19

Mail Tables—(P. & O. Co.'s) 126
" " (M. M. Co.'s) 127
Masonic Lodges 122-123
Money Order Rates—British Post-Office 129
Naval Squadrons in China and Japan (H.B.M. and U.S.) 158-166
Postage, Rates of—British Post-Office 128-129
" " French Post-Office 130
" " Japanese Postal Agency 131-132
" " Local Post-Office 132
Telegraphic Rates—(Great Northern Telegraph Co.) 136-138
" " (Eastern Extension Telegraph Co.) 139
" " (Reuter's Tel. Co.) 140
" " (Imperial Chinese Telegraphs) 140
Thermometer Table—Comparative Ranges (Reaumur, Centigrade and Fahrenheit) 193
Tide Table—Shanghai 196
Weights and Measures, Foreign and British 194-195
Woosung Rules: I, Anchorage; II, Sea-going Vessels; III, Cargo-Boats 153-155
Yang-tsze-kiang—Distance between Towns on 196
Advertisements 214-216

DESK HONG LIST:

A GENERAL AND BUSINESS DIRECTORY

FOR

SHANGHAI

AND THE NORTHERN AND RIVER PORTS, &c., FOR 1891.

ROADS. ENGLISH SETTLEMENT.

NORTH AND SOUTH.

E.

Yang-tsze Road (or Bund)	黃浦灘	揚子路
Yuen-ming-yuen Road, Lower		下圓明園路
Do. do. Upper		上圓明園路
Szechuen Road	二洋涇橋路	四川路
Kiangse Road	三洋涇橋路	江西路
Honan Road	老巡捕房路	河南路
Shantung Road	打狗橋路	山東路
Shanse Road		山西路
Chihli Road		直隸路
Fohkien Road		福建路
Hoopeh Road		湖北路
Chekiang Road		浙江路
Quangse Road, Lower		下廣西路
Do. do. Upper		上廣西路
Yunnan Road		雲南路
Lloyd Road		勞合路
Thibet Road (or Defence)		西藏路

W.

EAST AND WEST.

S.

Sung-kiang Road	洋涇浜	松江路
Pakhoi Road		北海路
King-hong-ka (or Woo-woo Road)		金隆街
Canton Road	五馬路	廣東路
Swatow Road		汕頭路
Si-king Road		泗涇路
Foochow Road	四馬路	福州路
Albany Road		阿百弼內路
Hankow Road	三馬路	漢口路
Kiukiang Road	二馬路	九江路
Nanking Road	大馬路	南京路
Tientsin Road	後馬路	天津路
Taiwan Road		臺灣路
Ningpo Road		寧波路
Woo-sieh Road		無錫路
Chefoo Road		芝罘路
Peking Road		北京路
Hongkong Road		香港路
Amoy Road		廈門路
Newchwang Road		牛庄路
Soochow Road		蘇州路

N.

AMERICAN SETTLEMENT (HONGKEW.)

NORTH AND SOUTH

W.

North Honan Road	河南北路
" Kiangse Road	江西北路
" Szechuen Road	四川北路
Chapoo Road	乍浦路
Woosung Road	吳淞路
Broadway (and part in E. & W.)	百老滙
Astor Road	禮查路
Woochang Road	武昌路
Ming-hong Road	閔行路
Old China Street	老中涨街
Nanzing Road	南潯路
Tsingpoo Road	青浦路
Boone Road	文監師路

S.

NORTH TO SOUTH.—*Continued.*

Fearon Road	斐倫路
Dixwell Road	狄思威路
Taiping Road	太平路
Kee-chang Road	旗昌路
Yuen-fong Road	元芳路
Wah-kee Road	華記路
Chaou-foong Road	兆豐路
Dent Road	寶順路
Kung-ping Road	公平路
Quinsan Road	崑山路

E.

EAST AND WEST.

S.

North Yangtsze Road	洋子北路
Whang-poo Road	黃浦路
Broadway (part runs in N. & S.)	百老滙
Seward Road	西華德路
Tiendong Road ... 旂東街	天潼路
Miller Road	密勒路
Hanbury Road	漢璧禮路

N.

FRENCH SETTLEMENT.

NORTH TO SOUTH.

French Bund	法蘭西地界
Quai du Wampou	黃浦灘
Quai de France	天妃宮橋南沿黃浦
Quai des Remparts	金利源後面城河浜
Rue la Guerre	永安街
Rue Montauban	新北門外天主堂街
Rue de la Mission	興聖街
Rue Petit	吉祥街
Rue Durun	適隨街
Rue du marché Français	寶興街
Rue Discry	紫來街
Rue de la Porte du Nord	老北門大街
Rue Protêt	恒德當街
Rue de l'Administration	新街
Rue du Moulin	火輪磨坊街
Rue Tourane	陳家木橋街
Rue Hué	西馬路新橋街
Rue des Pères	自來火行街
Rue de Saigon	自來火行西街
Rue Palikao	八里橋路
Rue du Wampou (Quartier de l'Est)	洋行街
Rue des Poissons do.	彤繁街
Rue Chin-chew do.	同桂街
Rue Transversale do.	裕興街
Passage du Consulat	東永興
Passage du Yang-king-pang	西永興
Passage Colbert	天一衖
Passage de l'Administration	捕房西北衖
Passage Montigny	

EAST TO WEST.

Quais du Yang-king-pang et Confucius	洋涇浜路
Quais de la Pagode, des Fossés et de la Brèche	天后宮橋城河浜
Rue du Consulat	法蘭西大馬路
Rue Colbert	永安街東西路
Rue du Weikwé	寗興街
Rue de Ningpo	寧波馬路
Rue Formose (Quartier de l'Est)	金利源西衖
Rue Chousan do.	舟山路
Rue Takou do.	大沽路
Rue du Fokien do.	福建路
Rue de la Paix do.	協碑路
Rue Ming-hong do.	閔行路
Rue de la porte de l'Est do.	東門路
Passage Nesiang do.	南翔路

English and Chinese Calendar

1884.

(Chinese Cycle 甲申.)

47th & 48th Years of H. M. QUEEN VICTORIA.

9th & 10th Years of H. I. M. KWANG SÜ 光緒

Jany.	12 & 1 Chinese Moons.	Feby.	1 & 2 Chinese Moons.	March.	2 & 3 Chinese Moons.	April.	3 & 4 Chinese Moons.	May.	4 & 5 Chinese Moons.	June.	5 & 5 Int. Chinese Moons.
1 Tu	4	1 F	5	1 S	4	1 Tu	6	1 Th	7	1 Sun	8
2 W	5	2 S	6	2 Sun	5	2 W	7	2 F	8	2 M	9
3 Th	6	3 Sun	7	3 M	6	3 Th	8	3 S	9	3 Tu	10
4 F	7	4 M	8	4 Tu	7	4 F	9	4 Sun	10	4 W	11
5 S	8	5 Tu	9	5 W	8	5 S	10	5 M	11	5 Th	12
6 Sun	9	6 W	10	6 Th	9	6 Sun	11	6 Tu	12	6 F	13
7 M	10	7 Th	11	7 F	10	7 M	12	7 W	13	7 S	14
8 Tu	11	8 F	12	8 S	11	8 Tu	13	8 Th	14	8 Sun	15
9 W	12	9 S	13	9 Sun	12	9 W	14	9 F	15	9 M	16
10 Th	13	10 Sun	14	10 M	13	10 Th	15	10 S	16	10 Tu	17
11 F	14	11 M	15	11 Tu	14	11 F	16	11 Sun	17	11 W	18
12 S	15	12 Tu	16	12 W	15	12 S	17	12 M	18	12 Th	19
13 Sun	16	13 W	17	13 Th	16	13 Sun	18	13 Tu	19	13 F	20
14 M	17	14 Th	18	14 F	17	14 M	19	14 W	20	14 S	21
15 Tu	18	15 F	19	15 S	18	15 Tu	20	15 Th	21	15 Sun	[illegible]
16 W	19	16 S	20	16 Sun	19	16 W	21	16 F	22	16 M	[illegible]
17 Th	20	17 Sun	21	17 M	20	17 Th	22	17 S	23	17 Tu	[illegible]
18 F	21	18 M	22	18 Tu	21	18 F	23	18 Sun	24	18 W	25
19 S	22	19 Tu	23	19 W	22	19 S	24	19 M	25	19 Th	26
20 Sun	23	20 W	24	20 Th	23	20 Sun	25	20 Tu	26	20 F	27
21 M	24	21 Th	25	21 F	24	21 M	26	21 W	27	21 S	28
22 Tu	25	22 F	26	22 S	25	22 Tu	27	22 Th	28	22 Sun	29
23 W	26	23 S	27	23 Sun	26	23 W	28	23 F	29	23 M	1
24 Th	27	24 Sun	28	24 M	27	24 Th	29	24 S	30	24 Tu	2
25 F	28	25 M	29	25 Tu	28	25 F	1	25 Sun	1	25 W	3
26 S	29	26 Tu	30	26 W	29	26 S	2	26 M	2	26 Th	4
27 Sun	30	27 W	1	27 Th	1	27 Sun	3	27 Tu	3	27 F	5
28 M	C. N. Y.	28 Th	2	28 F	2	28 M	4	28 W	4	28 S	6
29 Tu	2	29 F	3	29 S	3	29 Tu	5	29 Th	5	29 Sun	7
30 W	3	..	..	30 Sun	4	30 W	6	30 F	6	30 M	8
31 Th	4	..	..	31 M	5	..	..	31 S	7	..	..

July.	5 Int. & 6 Chinese Moons.	Augt.	6 & 7 Chinese Moons.	Sept.	7 & 8 Chinese Moons.	Oct.	8 & 9 Chinese Moons.	Nov.	9 & 10 Chinese Moons.	Dec.	10 & 11 Chinese Moons.
1 Tu	9	1 F	11	1 M	12	1 W	13	1 S	14	1 M	14
2 W	10	2 S	12	2 Tu	13	2 Th	14	2 Sun	15	2 Tu	15
3 Th	11	3 Sun	13	3 W	14	3 F	15	3 M	16	3 W	16
4 F	12	4 M	14	4 Th	15	4 S	16	4 Tu	17	4 Th	17
5 S	13	5 Tu	15	5 F	16	5 Sun	17	5 W	18	5 F	18
6 Sun	14	6 W	16	6 S	17	6 M	18	6 Th	19	6 S	19
7 M	15	7 Th	17	7 Sun	18	7 Tu	19	7 F	20	7 Sun	20
8 Tu	16	8 F	18	8 M	19	8 W	20	8 S	21	8 M	21
9 W	17	9 S	19	9 Tu	20	9 Th	21	9 Sun	22	9 Tu	22
10 Th	18	10 Sun	20	10 W	21	10 F	22	10 M	23	10 W	23
11 F	19	11 M	21	11 Th	22	11 S	23	11 Tu	24	11 Th	24
12 S	20	12 Tu	22	12 F	23	12 Sun	24	12 W	25	12 F	25
13 Sun	21	13 W	23	13 S	24	13 M	25	13 Th	26	13 S	26
14 M	22	14 Th	24	14 Sun	25	14 Tu	26	14 F	27	14 Sun	27
15 Tu	23	15 F	25	15 M	26	15 W	27	15 S	28	15 M	28
16 W	24	16 S	26	16 Tu	27	16 Th	28	16 Sun	29	16 Tu	29
17 Th	25	17 Sun	27	17 W	28	17 F	29	17 M	30	17 W	[illegible]
18 F	26	18 M	28	18 Th	29	18 S	30	18 Tu	1	18 Th	[illegible]
19 S	27	19 Tu	29	19 F	1	19 Sun	1	19 W	2	19 F	[illegible]
20 Sun	28	20 W	30	20 S	2	20 M	2	20 Th	3	20 S	[illegible]
21 M	29	21 Th	1	21 Sun	3	21 Tu	3	21 F	4	21 Sun	5
22 Tu	1	22 F	2	22 M	4	22 W	4	22 S	5	22 M	6
23 W	2	23 S	3	23 Tu	5	23 Th	5	23 Sun	6	23 Tu	7
24 Th	3	24 Sun	4	24 W	6	24 F	6	24 M	7	24 W	8
25 F	4	25 M	5	25 Th	7	25 S	7	25 Tu	8	25 Th	9
26 S	5	26 Tu	6	26 F	8	26 Sun	8	26 W	9	26 F	10
27 Sun	6	27 W	7	27 S	9	27 M	9	27 Th	10	27 S	11
28 M	7	28 Th	8	28 Sun	10	28 Tu	10	28 F	11	28 Sun	12
29 Tu	8	29 F	9	29 M	11	29 W	11	29 S	12	29 M	13
30 W	9	30 S	10	30 Tu	12	30 Th	12	30 Sun	13	30 Tu	14
31 Th	10	31 Sun	11	..	..	31 F	13	..	..	31 W	15

1885.

Jan.—11th & 12th Chinese Moons.						Feb.—12th & 1st Chinese Moons.				
1 Th	16	11 Sun	26	22 Th	7	1 Sun	17	12 Th	28	
2 F	17	12 M	27	23 F	8	2 M	18	13 F	29	
3 S	18	13 Tu	28	24 S	9	3 Tu	19	14 S	30	
4 Sun	19	14 W	29	25 Sun	10	4 W	20	15 Sun	1	C. N. Year.
5 M	20	15 Th	30	26 M	11	5 Th	21			
6 Tu	21	16 F	1	27 Tu	12	6 F	22			
7 W	22	17 S	2	28 W	13	7 S	23			
8 Th	23	18 Sun	3	29 Th	14	8 Sun	24			
9 F	24	19 M	4	30 F	15	9 M	25			
10 S	25	20 Tu	5	31 S	16	10 Tu	26			
..	..	21 W	6	..	..	11 W	27			

FIXED AND MOVEABLE FESTIVALS.

January.
1 T., Circumcision.
6 Sun., Epiphany.
13 i. Sunday after Epiphany.
20 ii. Sunday „ „
27 iii. Sunday „ „

February.
2 S., Purf. B. V. M.
3 iv Sunday after Epiphany.
10 Septuagesima Sun
14 Th., St. Valentine
17 Sexagesima Sun.
24 Quinquagesima S.
27 Ash Wednesday.

March.
1 S., St. David.
2 i. Sunday in Lent.
9 ii. Sunday „
16 iii. Sunday „
17 M., St. Patrick's D.
23 iv. Sunday in Lent.
25 Tu., Annun. V. M.
30 v. Sunday in Lent.

April.
6 Palm Sunday.
11 Good Friday.
13 Easter Sunday.
20 Low Sunday.
23 W., St. George.
25 F., St. Mark.
27 ii. Sun. af. Easter.

May.
1 Th., St. Philip and St. James.
4 iii. Sun. af. Easter
11 iv. Sun. „ „
18 Rogation Sunday.
22 Th., Ascension Day.
25 Sunday aft. Ascen.

June.
1 Whitsun Day.
8 Trinity Sunday.
11 W., St. Barnabas.
12 Th., Corpus Christi
15 i. Sun. af. Trinity
22 ii. Sun. „ „
24 Tu., St. John Bapt.
29 iii. Sun af. Trinity St. Peter.

July.
6 iv. Sun. af. Trinity
13 v. Sunday „ „
20 vi. Sunday „ „
25 F., St. James.
27 vii. Sun. af. Trinity

August.
3 viii. Sun. af. Trinity
10 ix. Sunday „ „
17 x. Sunday „ „
24 xi. Sun. af. Trinity St. Bartholomew.
31 xii. Sun. af. Trinity.

September.
7 xiii. Sun. af. Trinity
14 xiv. Sunday „ „
21 xv. Sunday „ „ St. Matthew.
28 xvi. Sun. af. Trinity

October.
5 xvii. Sun. af. Trinity
12 xviii. Sunday „ „
18 S., St. Luke.
19 xix. Sun af. Trinity
26 xx. Sunday „ „
28 Tu., St. Simon and St. Jude.

November.
1 S., All Saints
2 xxi. Sun. af. Trinity All Souls.
9 xxii. Sun. af. Trinity
11 Tu., St. Martin.
16 xxiii. Sun. af. Trinity
22 S., St. Cecilia.
23 xxiv. Sun. af. Trinity
30 Advent Sunday; St. Andrew.

December.
7 ii. Sunday in Adv.
14 iii. Sunday „ „
21 iv. Sunday in Adv. St. Thomas.
25 Th., Christmas Day
26 F., St. Stephen.
27 S., St. John.
28 i. Sun. aft. Chris.

CHRONOLOGICAL NOTES.

Golden Number	4	Dominical Letter	FE
Epact	3	Roman Indiction	12
Solar Cycle	17	Julian Period	6597

JEWISH CALENDAR.

1884.					5644.
Jan.	1	Tu	Fast of Tebet	Tebet	3
„	28	M	New Moon	Sebat	1
Feb.	27	W	New Moon	Adar	1
Mar.	10	M	Fast of Esther	„	13
„	11, 12	Tu W	Purim	„	14, 15
„	27	Th	New Moon	Nisan	1
Apr.	10, 11	Th F	Passover	„	15, 16
„	25	F	New Moon	Yiar	1
May	9	F	Second Passover	„	14
„	13	Tu	33 of the Homer	„	18
„	25	S	New Moon	Sivan	1
„	30, 31	F S	Sebuot	„	6, 7
June	24	Tu	New Moon	Tamuz	1
July	10	Th	Fast of Tamuz	„	17
„	23	W	New Moon	Ab	1
„	31	Th	Fast of Ab	„	9
Aug.	22	F	New Moon	Elul	1
					5645.
Sept.	20	S	New Year	Tisri	1
„	22	M	Fast of Guedaliah	„	3
„	29	M	Kipur	„	10
Oct.	4, 5	S S	Tabernacle	„	15, 16
„	10	F	Hosana Raba	„	21
„	11, 12	S S	Feast of the 8th Day	„	22, 23
„	20	M	New Moon	Hesvan	1
Nov.	19	W	New Moon	Kislev	1
Dec.	13	S	Hanuca	„	25
„	19	F	New Moon	Tebet	1
„	28	S	Fast of Tebet	„	10

MOHAMMEDAN CALENDAR.

1884.	1301.	1884.	1301.
Jan. 1	Rabia 2	July 25	Shawal
„ 30	Latter Rabia	Aug. 23	Dulkadah
Feb. 28	Gomada	Sept. 22	Dulhagea
Mar. 29	Latter Gomada		1302
Apr. 27	Rajab	Oct. 21	Muharrem
May 27	Schaban	Nov. 20	Saphar
June 25	Ramadân	Dec. 19	Rabia

The year 5645 of the Jewish Era commences on September 20, 1884.
Ramadân (Month of Abstinence, observed by the Turks) commences on June 25, 1884.
The year 1302 of the Mohammedan Era commences on October 21, 1884.

LIST
OF
HONGS AND RESIDENTS
AT
SHANGHAI, 1884.

A

行洋剌白埃
E bo-la Yung Hong.
704, Nanking Road, opposite the Racquet Court.
ABDOOLA, A., & Co.,
Abdoola, Abrahim, *Mngr.*
Seleman, Aboobucker.
Ahmed, Carsem

記祥 *Zeang-che.*
0, Szechuen Road.
ABDOOLALLY EBRAHIM & Co.
Esoofally, Bhaynin, *Manager.*
Dawoodbhoy, Abdoolally

豐華 *Wa-fung.*
Corner of Kiangse and Kiukiang Roads.
Residence—Canton Road.
ABRAHAM, A. E. J.
Moses, E. J.

祥天 *T'ien-seang.*
4, Yangtsze Road.
ADAMSON, BELL & Co.
Bell, F. H.
Grant, C. Lyall (absent)
Youd, F. M. do.
Dodwell, G. B.
Meuser, Otto
Carlill, A. J. H.
Burgoyne, J. W. H.
Piper, G. S.
Webster, Sydney H.
Law, D. R.
Senna, C. M. de
Aquino, J. C. d'
Botelho, J. M. D.

喇加呵 *Ah-ka-leh.*
6, Kiukiang Road.
AGRA BANK, LIMITED.
Lemarchand, F. W., *Mngr.*
Campbell, R. M., *Acting Accountant.*
Cock, A. C., *Assistant.*
Tweedie, Wm. L., *do.*
Senna, E. F. de, *Clerk.*

8, Seward Road.
ALVARES, DR. EUGENIO M., *Physician and Surgeon.*

AMATEUR DRAMATIC CLUB OF SHANGHAI
Little, R. W., *Hon. Sec.*
Hay, Drummond, *Hon. Trea.*

A

會經聖國美大
Da-mé-kwoh-shêng-king-hwey.
18, Peking Road.
AMERICAN BIBLE SOCIETY'S AGENCY.
Gulick, Rev. Luther H., *Agent.*
Wills, Rev. W. A., *Assistant.*

生茂 *Mow-sing.*
11A, Szechuen Road.
AMERICAN CLOCK AND BRASS Co.
Sole Agents for "The American Waltham Watch Co.," Waltham, Mass., U.S.A.
Vale, T. Harold, *Agent.*
Dunne, J. J.

館書華美
Mei-hwa-shu-kwan.
18, Peking Road.
AMERICAN PRESBYTERIAN MISSION PRESS
Holt, Rev. W. S., *Supt.*
Office of the *Chinese Recorder and Missionary Journal*; Agency for the Chinese School and Text Book Series' Publications; Depository for the Chinese Publications of the Religious Tract Society, London.

The Club.
AMOORE, H. E. (absent)

和協 *Hip-wo.*
11, Peking Road.
ANDERSON, ROBERT & Co.
Anderson, Robt. (absent)
Anderson, J. H. „
Tritton, E. W. „
Grant, P. McGregor
Allen, A. E. (K'kiang)
Styan, F. W.

Near French Gas Works.
AMOW & Co.,
General Storekeepers, Fancy Goods Importers, Furniture Dealers, &c.
Amow, O.
Letah, M., *Manager.*
King, P., *Asst. do.*
Stan-sho, K., *Clerk.*

A B C D E F G H I J K L M N O P R S T U V W Y Z

A.

院書西中 *Chung-si-shu-yuen.*
Nos. 9, Woosung Road,
and 13 and 14, Quinsan Road.
ANGLO-CHINESE COLLEGE.
Allen, Rev. Y. J., D.D.
Royall, Rev. W. W.
Loehr, Rev. G. R.
Minglcdorff, Rev. O. G.
Allen, Miss M.
Muse, Miss A. C.

館書華英 *Ying-hwa-shu-kwan.*
10, Upper Yuen-ming-yuen Rd.
ANGLO-CHINESE SCHOOL.
Lanning, George
Chinese Assistant.

爬順 *Zung-che.*
ARIEL, British Ship.
Croal, R. W., *Commander.*
Xavier, L. A., *Purser.*

記瑞 *Sooy-che.*
10, Nanking Road.
ARNHOLD, KARBERG & Co.
Arnhold, Ph.
Beurmann, C.
Sachsé, G.
Suldter, L., *Silk Inspector.*
Encarnação, F. X.
Agents for Hamburg-Magdeburg Fire Insurance Co.;
La Grande Compagnie Société Anonyme d'Assurances Maritime de Paris;
Fortuna Allgemeine Versicherungs Actiengesellschaft Berlin;
Straits Insurance Co., Ld.

發泳新 *Sing-yoong-fah.*
ASHLEY, C. J., *Sailmaker,*
80 to 83, Tsingpoo Road,
Hongkew.
Residence—10, Woosung Rd.

查禮 *Le-zo.*
11, Whangpoo Road, Hongkow.
ASTOR HOUSE HOTEL.
Jansen, D. C., *Proprietor.*
Delouk, M. F., *Manager.*
Braine, Joseph, *Cook.*

場身操 *Tsao-shen-ch'ang.*
ATHLETIC CLUB AND GYMNASIUM (SHANGHAI.)
Comline, C., *Hon. Sec.*

B

利悟 *Bay-lee.*
7, Commercial Chambers,
24, Nanking Road.
BAILEY, JNO., *Accountant, Land, House and Estate Agent.*
Stiles, Geo. W.

隆泰 *Tai-loong.*
Paking Road.
BARLOW & Co.
Darling, D. A.
Pellitt, J. S.

B

噸吧 *Ba-ton.*
BARTON, Captain Z.,
Surveyor to H.M. Registry Office of Shipping.
Surveyor for Bureau Veritas and Local Insurance Offices.
Office—No. 7, Canton Road.

門治平 *Pen-zz'-men.*
17, Yangtsze Road.
BENJAMIN, B. D.

衛德畢 *Be-tah-way.*
BIDWELL, H. S., *Merchant.*
Bidwell, H. S.
Yang, J. F.

行洋泰乾 *Ch'ien-ta.*
4, Canton Road.
BIELFELD, ALEX.,
Auctioneer, General Broker and Commission Agent.
Bielfeld, Alex.
Bielfeld, Franz, *(Signs per procuration.)*
Holdinghausen, F.
Rangel, J. M.

畢斯碧 *Be-sz'-be.*
4, Quai du Yang-king-pang,
and Shanghai Club.
BIGSBY, W. E. D.,
Bill and Bullion Broker.

和平 *Bing-oo.*
3, Honan Road.
BIRT, W., & Co.
Waste Silk Inspectors and Commission Merchants, Hydraulic Pressers and Packers, Hide Brokers and Inspectors.
Birt, W.
Liddell, C. Oswald
Harris, Wilmer
Purcell, G. H.
Agents and General Managers Birt's Wharf Co.;
Agents and Secretaries Chinese Glass Works Company.

BIRT'S WHARF COMPANY,
Hide Skin, Wool, etc., Preparing Godowns,
Birt's Wharf, Hongkew,
and 3, Honan Road.
Corner, G. R., *Trustee.*
Birt, W., & Co., *Gen. Mngrs.*
Liddell, C. O., *Inspector.*
Whitfield W., *Wharfinger.*
Tong Wai-sing, *Asst. do.*

利長 *Chang-le.*
16, Canton Road.
BISSET, J. P., & Co.
Land Agents, Share Brokers, &c.
Buchanan, Jas.
Buchanan, W.
Ure, C. W.
Cushny, Alex., Jnr.

威播 *Foo-tong.*
20, Kiangse Road.
BOVET, BROTHERS & Co.
Bovet, A. (absent.)
Malherbe, R. do

38, Nanking Road.
BOWLING ALLEY (SENIOR)

B

生祥 *Zeang-sung.*
Pootung.
BOYD & Co., *Engineers.*
Grant, P. V.
Robertson, Wm.
Risch, John
Hay, C. W.
Johnston, Jas.
Prentice, John
Mackenzie, Jas.
MacCallum, A.
Liddell, A.
Ford, John
Wilson, Jno.
Rawsthorne, F. W.
Barry, R.
Scott, R.
Ord, J. Wallace
Howes, J. H.
Holmes, G. N.
Roberts, A.
Adrian, I.
Shinagawa, H.
Cano, Geo.
Edwards, W. J.
Lent, R. L.
Agents and Owners New Dock.

32, Chapoo Road.
BRAGA, J. M.,
Piano Tuner and Repairer.

源義 *E-yuen.*
10, Yangtsze Road.
BRAND, BROTHERS & Co.
Brand, David
Brand, William
King, C. H.
Wingrove, G. R. (absent)

泰來学 *Beh-lay-t'a.*
40, Nanking Road.
Address—Shanghai Club.
BRANDT, O.,
Bill, Bullion & General Broker and Accountant.

15, Nanking Road.
BRAHN, L.,
Commission Agent.

39, Whangpoo Road.
BRITISH & FOREIGN BIBLE SOCIETY.
Dyer, S., *Agent.*
Murray, D., *Sub-Agent.*

外城坭 *Nee-ch'ing-nga.*
BUBBLING WELL COTTAGE.
Yoh Chang-hsiau, *Proprietor*

生瑞 *Deay-sung.*
1, Ningpo Road.
BUCHHEISTER, J. J.
Stepharius, C.

頓巴係生醫之培生醫
Pei-tsih E-sung.
Riverbank, 71, Broadway,
Hongkew, next the Camp Hotel, Yang-tsze-poo Creek.
BURGE, FREDERICK JOHN,
L.R.C.Phys. Lond., M.R.C.S.E., L.M., A.K.C.

行洋泰復 *Vooh-t'a.*
5, Siking Road.
BURJORJEE, D., *Broker.*

B

茂祥 *Zeang-mau.*
3, Kiukiang Road.
BURKILL, A. R.,
Public Silk Inspector.

利派新 *Sing-pai-li.*
15, Canton Road.
BURN, J., *Merchant.*

瑞昌 *Soey-chong.*
11, Szechuen Road.
BUTLER, GEORGE,
Public Tea Inspector.

古太 *T'a-koo.*
5, Kiukiang Road.
BUTTERFIELD & SWIRE.
Lang, William
Scott, J. H.
Aubert, F. B.
Brown, J. L.
Burrows, A.
Cano, Alex.
Dowley, E. B.
Endicott, H. B.
Fonceca, J. B.
Ford, T.
Hall, James
Nesbitt, D.
Noronha, A. J.
Robinson, W. J.
Smith, H.
Tomlin, K.
Agents—Ocean Steam Ship Co.;
British and Foreign Marine Insurance;
Royal Exchange Fire Assurance of London;
China Navigation Company (Limited);
London and Lancashire Fire Insurance Co.

C

和廣 *Kwang-ho.*
7, Foochow Road.
CALDBECK, MACGREGOR & Co.
(late Geo. Smith & Co.),
Wholesale & Retail Wine & Spirit Merchants.
Caldbeck, E. J.
Macgregor, J. (London)
Rae, T. F.
Gaude, J. W.
Agents:
Chinkiang—
Messrs. Gearing & Co.
Hankow—
Alex. Price, Esq.
Foochow—
Messrs. Newman & Co.
Amoy—
T. G. Harkness, Esq.
Hongkong—
Messrs. Norton & Co.
Nagasaki—
Messrs. Holme, Ringer & Co.
Kobe—
H. E. Reynell, Esq.
Yokohama—
Alex. W. Glennie, Esq.

London Address:
Macgregor, Caldbeck & Co.,
"Leadenhall House,"
101, Leadenhall Street, E.C.

南盛 *Kieang-nay.*
35, Kiangse Road.
CAMAJEE, D. N. & SON.
Camajee, H. D. (absent)

C

會總禮 *Le-tsoong-way.*
CAMP HOTEL.

The Club.
CANCE, W.

和禮 *Le-woo.*
19 and 20, Kiukiang Road.
CARLOWITZ & Co.
Krause, A.
Joergens, R.
Blasky, P.
Holm, Adolf
Ruff, Th.
Agents of Hamburg, Bremen Fire Insurance Company; Florio & Rubattino's Steamer lines.

和中 *Chung-woo.*
24, Kiangse Road.
CARTER & Co., *Silk Brokers.*
Carter, W. H. (absent.)
Dalgliesh, W. H. (absent)
Westall, Alfred C.
Lamond, Wm.
Little, W. D.
Agents—Phœnix Fire Office; Lancashire Fire and Life Office; Jules Mumm & Co.

生利合 *Ha-lee-sun.*
Rue du Consulat, near the French Bund.
CARTER, J., *Auctioneer, Storekeeper and General Agent.*
Carter, J.
Agent for Upper Yangtsze Pilots.
Pilots.
Hickley, P. S.
McCappin, A.
Robinson, J.
Clough, B.
Thompson, C.
Carter, J.
Brun, J.
Peterson, P. M.
Popp, B.

會演正 *Chung-yung-wei.*
Rue Montauban, Fr. Con.
CATHOLIC CIRCLE (SHANGHAI.)

昌廣 *Kwang-ts'ang.*
3, Yang-king-pang, Fr. Con.
CAWASJEE, PALLANJEE & Co.
Rustomjee, C.
Cooverjee, P.
Khan, Sorabjee C.
Domanjee, F.
Owners of R.-S. *Ariel.*

源晋 *Tsing-yuen.*
31A, Nanking Road.
(Old Tung-fu.)
CELESTIAL EMPIRE AND SHANGHAI COURIER OFFICES.
Thirkell, Jno. Geo., *Lessee.*

Thirkell, Jno. Geo., } *Editors and Mngrs.*
Macfarlane, W., }
Colgan, T. H., *S'ping Reporter*
Martins, R. F., *Print. Mngr.*
Rosario, Aug. X., *Foreman.*
Rosario, F. P., *Compositor.*
Rosario, Art. do, *do.*
Silva, F., *do.*
Aquino, A. M. d', *do.*
Passos, M. D., *do.*
And Chinese Staff.

C

The *North-China Advertiser* is also published every morning in conjunction with the *Shanghai Courier* and the *Celestial Empire.*

中滙 *Way-choong.*
Corner of Yangtsze and Nankin Roads.
CENTRAL HOTEL.
Reilly, F. E., *Manager.*

行車商總 *Tsoong-shang-chie-hong.*
20, Foochow Road.
CENTRAL STABLE.
Symons, Sewjee & Co., *Proprietors.*
Zwarg, R., *Manager.*

明和 *Wo-ming.*
10, Szechuen Road.
CHAMBER OF COMMERCE, SHANGHAI GENERAL
Corner, Geo. R., *Secretary.*

利加麦 *Mah-ka-le.*
21, Bund.
CHARTERED BANK OF INDIA, AUSTRALIA AND CHINA.
Inverarity, A. J. M., *Mnger.*
Macinorran, J., *Actg. Acct.*
Skottowe, E. B., *Sub-Acct.*
Diniz, Adelino, *Clerk.*
Diniz, S. J. *do.*
Almeida, A. F. d', *do.*

利有 *Yuh-le.*
15, Yangtsze Road.
CHARTERED MERCANTILE BANK OF INDIA, LONDON & CHINA.
Robilliard, W. S., *Manager.*
Murray, G. S., *Acct.*
Rozario, J. B.
Boyol, H.

合祥廣 *Kwang-seang-heh.*
Corner of Hongkew and Minhong Roads.
CHEAP JACK & Co.
Ship Chandlers & Storekeepers
Cheap Jack, K. L.
Ah-ming, Stevedore.
Waters, W., Ship's Runner.

祥晋 *Chin Tsiang.*
507, Nanking Road.
CHIN TSIANG, *Silk Merchant.*

院書文洋 *Yang-vang-shoo-yuen.*
1, Upper Yuen-ming-yuen Road
CHINA BRANCH OF THE ROYAL ASIATIC SOCIETY
Drew, E. B., *President.*
Haas, Jos., *Vice-President.*
Hirth, F., PH.D., *do.*
Smithey, T. S., *Hon. Sec. and Treasurer.*
Robinson, K., *Hon. Librarian.*
Wilson, J. H., *Curator.*
Morrison, G. J., *Councillor.*
Kingsmill, Thos. W., *do.*
Sheyegh, Max, *do.*
Deighton-Braysher, C., *do.*

C

裕豐 *Foong-yuh.*
2, Sunkiang Road.
CHINA & JAPAN TRADING Co. (Limited).
Importers of and Dealers in General Merchandise, Commission Agents and Auctioneers.
Head Office—New York.
Branches in China, Japan and London.

Shanghai Branch.
Haskell, F. E., *Manager.*
Eastlack, W. R.
Gordon, H. L.
McKeige, F.
Baird, J.
Silva, A. M.
Nunes, J. C. S.
Haskell, F. H.
Britto, J.
Jones, James

局總商招船輪 *Lun-ch'uen-ch'au-shang-tsung-kiuh.*
Head Office—
N1 and 2, Hankow Road.
CHINA MERCHANTS' STEAM NAVIGATION Co.
Tong King Sing, *Gen. Mngr.*
Tong Mow-chee, *do.*
Chu Yu Chee, *Manager.*
Chang Su Ho, *Asst. do.*
Ching To Chai, *do. do.*
Tong Ping E
Chun Fai Ting
Wong Yeng Ching
Chung Oi Tong
Li Sung Wan
Chow Sow San
Chun Chiu Tung
Kum A-yean
Yip Kum Cho
Yip Min-chi
Fok Wai Kit
Kwan Sou Ping
Tsai Shou-kie
Foreign Staff.
Bolton, C. J., *Marine Supt.*
Weir, Thomas, *Supt. Eng.*
Butler, G. A., *Agent.*

局商招險保 *Pao-tien-ch'ou-shang-kiuh.*
Agents for China Merchants' Marine and Fire Insurance Company.
Ho Shun Chee, *Secretary.*

司公船輪古太 *Ta-koo-lung-zen kung-sz'.*
French Bund.
CHINA NAVIGATION COMPANY, LIMITED.
Butterfield & Swire, *Agents.*

司公紙造興天 *Tien-shin.*
Office—14, Szechuen Road.
Mill—Yang-tsze-poo, below Water Works.
CHINA PAPER MILL COMPANY.
Doyle, Wm. H., *Supt. and Agent.*

甯保 *Pao-ning.*
7, Nanking Road.
CHINA TRADERS' INSURANCE COMPANY (LIMITED.)
Reding, J. E., *Agent.*
Noel, W. W.
Botelho, R.

C

局總務礦平開 *Kai-ping-kwang-wu-tsu-kiuh.*
N 1, Hankow Road.
CHINESE ENGINEERING AND MINING COMPANY.
Tong King Sing, *Gen. Mngr.*
Tong Mow-chee, *do.*
Lanng G. Wong, *Prin. Sec.*
Tong Yin-chan, *Agent.*

院書心清 *Tsing-sing-shoo-yuen.*
CHINESE ILLUSTRATED NEWS AND CHILD'S PAPER (both in Chinese.)
Farnham, D.D., Rev. J. M. W., *Editor.*

院書致格 *Ké-tsz'-su-yuen.*
CHINESE POLYTECHNIC INSTITUTION AND READING ROOMS.
Corner of Quangsi and Hoopoh Roads.
Drummond, W. V., *Chairman.*
Hau-hsueh-taun, *Hon. Treas.*
Fryer, John, *Hon. Secretary.*
Hwa-joh-ting, *Res. Curator.*

記順老 *Laou Zung-che.*
1089a, Broadway, Hongkew.
CHING CHONG.
Ching-chong, Y.
Hong-dow, Y.
Liping, W. S.

記順南 *Nan-sung-che.*
13B, Canton Road.
CHING CHONG, W.

記順新 *Sing-sung-che.*
Broadway, Hongkew—Corner of Bridge.
CHING CHONG, Y., *Ship-Chandlers and General Storekeeper.*

3, Sunkiang Road.
CITY BOWLING SALOON.

拉刻 *Ka-lah.*
3, Canton Road.
CLARK, J. D., *Commission Merchant, Valuer and Broker.*
Agent for American Mail Export Journal; Paper Trade Journal; American Stationer; The Miller's Journal.

Outside the South Gate.
CLASSICAL AND SCIENTIFIC BOARDING SCHOOL.
(*For Chinese Boys.*)
Smith, Rev. J. N. B., *Supt.*

吉泰 *Wei-che.*
Nos. 48, 50 & 52, Rue Montauban.
CLETAND, J. & Co., *General Commission Agents and General Wine Depôt, &c.*
Cletand, J.

D E F G H I J K L M N O P R S T U V W Y Z

C

房子彈路馬五
Wu-ma-loo-dan-tsz-vong.
10, Canton Road.
CLUB CONCORDIA.
Committee:
Hubbe, P. G., *President.*
Heurmann, C., *V.-President.*
Telge, H., *Hon. Treasurer.*
Sauhan, G., } *Working*
Holm, A., } *Committee.*
Sievogt, M., *Librarian.*

Peterson, J., *Steward.*

會總橋新
Sin-kiu-tsoong-way.
Bubbling Well Road.
CLUB, COUNTRY
Hay, Drummond, *Hon. Sec.*

20, Whangpoo Road.
CLUB, CUSTOMS'

會總矩規
Kwei-chü-tsung-kwei.
(Square Compasses Club.)
30, Yangtsze Road.
CLUB, MASONIC
Holland, C. J., *Secretary.*

會總洋西
Se-yang-tsoong-way.
1, Chapoo Road.
CLUB PORTUGUEZ.
Danenberg, J., *Hon. Sec.*

會總 *Tsoong-way.*
3, Yangtsze Road.
CLUB, THE SHANGHAI
Ashton, J., *Secretary.*
Williams, F. T., *Assist.*
Redonnet, J., *Steward.*

明精 *Ching-ming.*
8, Kiukiang Road.
COMINS, C.

行銀西蘭法
Fah-lan-se-ning-hong.
20, Yang-tsze Road.
COMPTOIR D'ESCOMPTE DE PARIS.
Vouillemont, E. G., *Manager.*
Arranger, J., *Acct.*
Inchbald, C. C., *Act.-Acct.*
Hincelni, F., *Asst. Acct.*
Jorge, H.
Xavier, J. P.
Placé, F. L.
Simoens, J. R.
Xavier, J.
Blum, M., *Agent,* H'kng.
Fitz-Henry, D., *do.*, Y'hma.
Cochinard, F., *do.*, F'chow.

Consulates.

AUSTRO-HUNGARY—
領加馬旗奥大
門衙事
Da Au Ling-sz' Yamên.
20, Peking Road.
Kreitner, Lieutenant Gustav Chevalier de, in charge of the Consulate.
Hsia I-ni, *Linguist.*
Zoelius, C., M.D., *Physic.*

BELGIUM—
領國時利比大
館公事
Da Pe-le-sz' Yamên.
1, Balfour Buildings.
Serruys, Hubert, *Consul-General.*

BRASILIAN—
Martins, João A. Rodrigues, *Consul-General.*
Pontes, Jr., Manuel da S., *Vice-Consul.*
Martins, José
Souza, Alfredo M. de, *Interpreter.*

DENMARK—
館公國丹大
Da Tan Koong-kwan.
27, Yangtsze Road.
Paterson, W., *Acting-Consul.*
Keswick, James J., *Acting Vice-Consul.*

FRANCE—
總國西蘭法大
門衙事領
Da Fah-lan-se Yamên.
The Bund—French Concession.
Lemaire, G., *Consul-Général.*
Frandon, *Chancelier.*
——, *Interprète.*
Lobel-Mahy, R. de, *le Commis*
Rélabre, Marquis Lionnel de, *2e Commis.*
Clément, C., *Clerk.*

GERMAN EMPIRE—
署事領總國德大
Ta-tê-kuo-tsung-ling-shi-shu.
26 & 27, Whangpoo Road.
Lührsen, J., Dr. jur., *Consul-General.*
Gabriel, H., Dr. jur., *Vice-Consul.*
Streich, K., *Interpreter.*
Kölling, W., *Secretary.*
Kock, M., *Constable.*
Su Yo-ling, *Writer.*

Zacharias, V., M.D., *Physician.*

GREAT BRITAIN—
門衙事領英大
Da-ying-ling-sz' Yamên.
Hughes, P. J., *Consul.*
Giles, H. A., *Vice-Consul.*
Carles, W. R., *Acting Vice-Consul.*
Ford, Colin M., *1st Assistant.*
Tratman, J. N., *Acting Assistant.*
Fulford, H. E., *Acting Assistant.*
Mortimore, R. H., *Acting Assistant.*
Rivero, E. T., *Linguist.*
Zuw Koo-woo, *do.*

REGISTRY OFFICE OF SHIPPING FOR CHINA AND JAPAN.
Hughes, P. J., *Registrar of Shipping.*
Barton, Z., *Government Surveyor.*

BRITISH CONSULAR GAOL.
Barnes, Alfred, *Chief Constable.*
Bowman, J., 2nd *do.*

C

ITALY—
事領國利大意大
門衙
Da E-ta-le-ling-sz' Yamên.
Kiukiang Road.
Nocentini, Lodovico, *Acting-Consul.*
Nembrini-Gonzaga, Marquis C. de

JAPAN—
門衙事領國本日大
Da Jipen-ling-sz' Yamên.
13, Whangpoo Road.
Shinagawa, E., *Consul-General.*
Go, S., *Interpreter.*
Matsunobo, O., *Secretary.*
Murasé, T., *do.*
Okura, K., *do.*
Dan, S., *do.*

NETHERLANDS—
門衙事領國蘭和大
Da O-lan Ling-sz' Ya-mên.
1, French Bund.
(For Shanghai and River Ports)
Jantsen, Carl, *Consul.*

PORTUGAL—
領總國洋西大
館公事
Da Se-yang Koong-kwan.
Ferreira, Leonelo, *Acting Consul-General.*
Olveira, F. M. d', *Chanc.*

RUSSIA—
門衙國斯羅俄大
Da Ngoo-loo-sz' Yamên.
7, Nanking Road.
Rodlug, J. E., *Consul.*
Chen-chang-shen, *Chinese Secretary.*

SPAIN—
國亞尼巴斯日大
館公
Da Zeh-sz'-pa-ne-ya Koong-kwan.
At the prolongation of North Szechuen Road.
Toda, Ed., *Consul* (absent)
Ginart, Manuel, *Act.-Consul.*
Oliveira, A. M. de, *Interpreter.*
Yu Cha-tung, *Chinese Secy.*

SWEDEN AND NORWAY—
總國威哪典瑞大
門衙事領
Da Sui-tan-na-wei-kwo Tsung-ling-shih Yamên.
7, Yangtsze Road.
Lagerheim, O. de, *Vice-Consul p.i.*, in charge of the Consulate-General.

UNITED STATES—
事領總國美大
門衙
Da-mê-kwoh-tsung-ling-sz Yamên.
The Bund, Hongkew.
Denny, O. N., *Consul-General* (absent.)
Cheshire, F. D., *Vice-Consul General and Interpreter, in charge.*

Coffey, J. J., *Deputy Consul-General and Clerk of Shipping.*
Shufeldt, Geo. A., *Marshal and Clerk of the Consular Court.*
Macleod, Neil, M.D., *Physician.*
O'Neil, John, *Jailer.*
Hsiu Shih Chun, *Chinese Writer.*
Wong Soong Dong, *Compdr.*

克可四密 *Me-sz' K'oh-ka.*
A 315, 316, 317, Broadway, Hongkew.
COOK, M. H., *Sail Maker, Rigger and Ship-Chandler.*
Schiller, E. G.

Foochow Road.
CO-OPERATIVE CARGO BOAT COMPANY OF SHANGHAI, THE
Lewis & Hopkins, *Managers.*
Hopkins, W. B.
Souza, M. de
Sham-hai
Woo

源信 *Sing-nyuen.*
CORE A, R. S.
Law, W. C., *Commander.*
Castillo, S. P., *Purser.*
Wade, John J., *Mate.*
Roberts, C., *2nd do.*
Sassoon, E. D., & Co., *Agents.*

明和 *Wo-ming.*
19, Szechuen Road.
CORNER, GEO. R., *Public Accountant.*

和同 *Doong-oo.*
1, Kiukiang Road.
CORY, J. M., A.R.I.B.A., *Architect.*
Marshall, F. L.

Bubbling Well Road.
COUTTS, GEORGE W.

昌法 *Fa-tsang.*
8, Yang-king-pang, Fr. Con.
Successeurs de LACROIX COUSINS & CIE,
COZON & GIRAUD.
Bluntschli, G.
Girard, U.
Lajeat, G.
Campos, A. P. de
Agents for—
La Foncière Assc. Maritime.
La Foncière Assc. Feu.
Compagnie Nationale de Navigation.

場球拋內場馬跑
Bau-mo-zang-noi-p'au-jeu-zang.
CRICKET CLUB, SHANGHAI
Tottie, W. H., *Hon. Sec.*

昌公 *Kung-chang.*
3, Kiukiang Road.
CROMIE, C., *Public Silk Inspector.*

名錦 *King-ming.*
3, Siking Road.
CUMINE & CO.
Cumine, Chas. (absent)
Cumine, Alex. G. T.
Cooper, John
Valentine, J.

C

處冊造司務稅總 *T'sung-shui-wu-ssŭ Tsao-ts'ĕ-ch'u.*

Customs.
Inspectorate General of, Statistical Department.

9, Peking Road.

STATISTICAL OFFICE.

Drew, E. B. (Commissioner), *Statistical Secretary.*
Hirth, F. (Deputy Commissioner), *Assistant Statistical Secretary.*
Dulberg, F. W. E., *Clerk.*

PRINTING OFFICE.

Palamountain, R., *Printing Office Manager.*
Bright, Wm., *Proof Reader.*
Merrilees, A. G., *do.*

—

關海南江 *Kiang-nan Hai-kuan.*

Customs.
Imperial Maritime.

Glover, Geo. B., *Commissioner.*
Sidford, H. Æ., *Deputy Com.*

1st Class Assistants:
Markwick, R.
Hough, R.
Holwill, E. T.

2nd Class Assistants:
King, P. H.
Merrill, H. F.
Taylor, F. E.

3rd Class Assistants:
Rochor, E.
Nully, R. de

4th Class Assistants:
Galembert, P. M. G. de
Kerr, J. A.
Carl, F. A.
Clayson, F.
Waldman, H. E.

Assistants:
May, F N.
Lent, R. J.

Clerks:
Donovan, J. P. (Postal Dept.)
Pearson, J. T. (Trans. Dept.)
Becks, A. J.
Poli, G. D.
Porcoboi̇s, D.

Consulting Surgeon:
Jamieson, R. A., M.A., M.D.

Medical Attendants:
Pichon, L., M.D.
Zacharia, V., M.D.

—

RETURNS OFFICE.

Bernières, A. M. de, *Deputy Commissioner.*

Clerks:
Smith, E. J.
Lowie, A.

—

OUT-DOOR STAFF.

Howard, W. C., *Chief Tidesurveyor.*
May, J. H., *Tidesurveyor.*

Assistant Tidesurveyors:
Illand, A.
Ballard, T. J.

Boat Officer:
Andrews, J. W.

Chief Examiner:
Tolliday, T.

Examiners:
Laigre, J.
Ross, J.
Godwin, A. A.
Pinnott, P. W.
Schmoluffel, H.
Purcell, P. H.
Dolestre, J. E.
Eckhold, M.
Bailey, O. E.

Assistant Examiners:
Boyol, J. R.
Bartolini, A.
Killeen, C.
Roberts, J.
Martel, A.
Cornelli, J.
Tonkin, C.

Tidewaiters,
1st Class:
Carr, R. P.
Luce, G. W.
Kahler, W. S.
Laidler, T. W.
Bernard, E.

2nd Class:
Felton, E.
Carr, R. A.
Smith, O. W.
Smith, E. R.
Tregillus, E. C.

3rd Class:
Belbin, R.
Wilson, W.
Teichert, C. W. P.
Hegnat, F. J.
Milhe, E.
Leach, A. W.

Watchers:
Bonneau, E.
Osborne, H.
Roberts, E. A.
Lorentsen, J. C.
Kahler, W. F.
Strong, J. P.
Nightingale, J. H.
Bond, W.
Van der Stegen, L.
Hopkins, F.
Citti, G.
Cronon, A. B.

Supernumerary Watchers:
Clark, J.
Theissen, A.
Schultze, V.

—

廳船理 *Li-ch'uan-t'ing.*

HARBOUR MASTER'S OFFICE.

Bisbee, A. M., *Coast Inspector and Harbour Master.*
Deighton-Brayshar, C., *Asst. Harbour Master.*
Southey, T. S., *Clerk.*
Carlson, W., 1st *Berthing Officer.*
Kraul, W. H., 2nd *do.*
Paterson, J. W., 2nd *do.* *(at Woosung.)*
Sangster, T., | *Signalmen.*
Villanova, C., |

—

捕巡水 *Shui Hsun-pu.*

RIVER POLICE.

Howell, J., *Inspector.*
Luther, C. F., *Sergeant.*
McKay, A., *Constable.*
Mitchell, T., *do.*
Vizenvinovich, M., *do.*

—

LIGHTS DEPARTMENT.

Lightships in Shanghai District.

"TUNG-SHA."

Crighton, R. T., *Captain.*
Hills, J. C., *Lightkeeper.*
Hartmann, H. U., *do.*

"KIUTOAN."

Osborn, E., *Actg. Captain.*
Schlur, A. A., *Lightkeeper.*
Rayner, E., *do.*
Rasmussen, P. W., *do.*

—

Lighthouses in Shanghai District.

North Saddle, Gutzlaff, West Volcano, Shaweishan, Bonham Island, Steep Island.

Chief Lightkeepers:
Smerdeley, N.
Hayden, G. W.

2nd Class:
Coffin, F. M.
Cunningham, T.
Bond, C. W.
Antonio, L.

3rd Class:
Penzig, A. F. C.
Anderson, F. T.
Johnson, H.
Theege, A.
Klein, A.

4th Class:
Rodrigues, J.
Luz, L. J. A. da
Collaço, J. M.

—

處造營 *Ying tsao-ch'u.*

ENGINEER'S OFFICE.

Henderson, D. M., *Engineer-in-Chief.*
Loan, W. B., *Clerk.*
Chaumont, M., *do.*
Mason, A., *Mechanic.*
Roberts, Jno., *Diver.*
Wilson, W., *do.*
Gram, Chas. C., *Godown-keeper.*

R.-CRUISER "KWA-BSING."

Andersen, N. P., *Commander.*
Chenoweth, R., 2nd *Officer.*
McKechnie, A., 3rd *do.*
Shaw, H. W., *Engineer.*

D

Bubbling Well Road.

DALLAS, BARNES, *Bill and Bullion Broker.*

—

昇日 *Zeh-sung.*

33, Szechuen Road.

DALY, S.

—

記福 *Fo-chee.*

c80, Honan Road.

D'ENCARNAÇÃO & SON.
D'Encarnação, Albino
D'Encarnação, Cesar
D'Encarnação, J.

—

D'Encarnação, C. C.

—

順寶 *Pau-zung.*

16, Yangtsze Road.

DENT, ALFRED & CO.
Dent, Alfred (absent)
Hearn, H. R.
Wheeley, Edward (absent)
Buckley, H. P.
Silva, J. P. da
Agents—Norwich Union Fire Insurance Society; Royal Exchange Assurance Corporation, Marine Branch; North Borneo Co., Limited.

—

1, Canton Road.

DONALDSON, C. M.

—

福生同 *Dong-sung-fou.*

DONG SANG,
DONG FOOK,
Metal Brokers and Merchants.

—

廉威陶 *Tan-wei-lien.*

21, Foochow Road.

DOWDALL, W. M., A.R.I.B.A., *Architect.*

文扣 *Tai-wun.*

4, Balfour Buildings.

DRUMMOND, LATHAM & LEACH
Drummond, W. V., *Barrister-at-Law.*
Latham, T., *Barrister-at-Law.*
Leach, A. J., *Barrister-at-Law.*
Lo Cheng-yee, *Clerk.*
Kwan Chi-ming, *do.*
Cheng Ying-kwei, *do.*

—

行興德 *Teh-hsing.*

6, Canton and Szechuen Roads.

DRYSDALE, RINGER & CO.
Ringer, J. M.
Danenberg, J.
Agents—London & Provincial Marine Insurance Co., Ltd.; The Positive Government Security Life Assurance Co., Ltd.
Secretaries—Shanghai Waterworks' Co., Limited.

—

3, Nanking Road.

DUDGEON, C. J., *Secretary,*
The Perak Tin Mining and Smelting Co.;
The Perak Sugar Cultivation Co.;
The Selangor Tin Mining Co. of Shanghai.

—

昌延 *Yue-tsung.*

7, Upper Yuen-Ming-Yuen Road.

DUFOUR BROTHERS & CO.
Schmoers, A.
Bohnen, C.
Ghisi, E.

—

34, Nanking Road.

DUNMAN, W.

—

信惇 *Tun-sin.*

1A, Kiukiang Road.

DYCE & CO.
Dyce, C. M.
Burman, A.
Allanson, Wm.
Matthews, C. A.
Agents for the Scottish Imperial Insurance Co., for Life.

E

行綫電 *Deen-seen-hong.*

The Bund.

EASTERN EXTENSION AUSTRALASIA & CHINA TELEGRAPH CO., LIMITED.
Judd, Walter, *Superintendent.*
Cole, C. J., *Clerk in charge.*
Uren, C. J., *Operator.*
Bartley, A., *do.*
Webster, L. *do.*
Gilby, H. H., *do.*
Cordeiro, P. A., *Clerk.*
Braga, J. C., *do.*
Rocha, A. C. A., *do.*

—

利巴八 *Pah-po-le.*

29, Ta-lay Buildings, French Bund.

EBRAHIMBHOY PABANEY,
Soomar, Mawjee, *Manager.*

D E F G H I J K L M N O P R S T U V W Y Z

E

司禮愛 *E-lee-sec.*
6, Szechuen Road.
EILERS, AUG., *General Merchant and Commission Agent.*

利安 *E-li.*
18, Kiukiang Road.
ELLIOTT & Co.
Wallace, Thos. (England.)
Scott, J. W. do.
Coulson, Chs.
Ameluxen, E. A. von
Kock, Chs.
Head Office:
J. H. Elliott & Co., Birmingham.

EMPIRE STEAM BREWERY AND AUTOMATIC AERATED MINERAL WATER WORKS.
Evans, H., & Co.
Evans, H.
Pappa, W.
James, W.

隆英 *Ying-loong.*
Corner of Kiangse and Nanking Roads.
ENGLAND, C. R.,
Commission Agent, Auctioneer, Appraiser, and General Dealer.

店頭饅凡埃
Ev an Man-doo-tien.
6, Ming-Hong Road, Hongkew.
EVANS & Co.
Ship Chandlers, Bakers, &c.
Evans, H.
Pappa, Wm.
James, W.
Town Depot, 3, Nanking Road.
Evans, H.

和寶 *Pau-wo.*
5, The Bund.
EVANS, PUGH & Co.
Evans, J. H. (absent)
Pugh, W. do.
Hawes, J. A.
Fonseca, F. V. da
Letchford, R. H.
Walter, W. (Hankow)
Agents for Universal Marine Insurance Co., Limited;
The City of London Fire Insurance Co., Limited.

F

棚牛英大
Da-ying-neu-bang.
Opposite the Race Course.
FARM, THE
Dasilva, J. P. N.
Souza, D. M. do
Private address—
Dasilva, J. P. N.,
"Poverty Hall."

松耶 *Ya-soong*
14, Broadway, Hongkew; and Old Dock, Pootung Dock, and Lower Dock.
FARNHAM, S. C. & Co.
Shipwrights, House-builders, Engineers & Boiler-makers, Dock-proprietors.
Simpson, James
Gallus, F. W.
Gallus, G.
Knowles, John
Dick, James
Webster, A.
Robertson, A.
Mathieson, A.
Högemann, A. H.
Black, D. T.
Armstrong, O.
Cranston, D.
Gillanders, A.
Johnston, D. M.
Oswald, R. R.
Smith, James
Giles, J.
Johnsford, W.

昌發 *Fau-chung.*
Opposite Old Dock, Hongkew.
FAU CHUNG & Co.,
Iron and Brass Founders, Engineers and Blacksmiths, Steam Launch Builders and Engineers Storekeepers.
Fau Chung.
Tai Yung, F.
Darko, G. T.

隆協 *Yah Loong.*
20, Foochow Road.
FEARON, LOW & Co.
Fearon, J. S.
Low, E. G.
Fearon, R. I. (New York)
Cunningham, J. K. (Japan)
Kerr, C. D.
Fearon, C. H.
Figueiredo, H. C. V. de
Agents—General Fire Assurance Co.
New Zealand Fire Insur. Co.

"FEI YUEN" (STR.)
Wigton, R. H., *Master.*

行琴利德 *Teh-le-fin-hong*
1, Szekiang Road.
FENTUM, CHAS. B.,
Professor of Music, Piano Tuner and Repairer.

Office, Nanking Road (Messrs. Sassoon's New Buildings.)
FERGUSSON, JOHN C., C.E.,
Consulting Engineer.

所公龍水海上
Se-loong-Koong-so.
FIRE BRIGADE, SHANGHAI
Ashley, C. J., *Chief Engineer.*
Glass, D., *Engineer* for District No. 1, Hongkew Settlement.
Moore, L., *Engineer* for District No. 2, English Settlement.
Guieu, L., *Engineer* for District No. 3, French Settlement.
Kite, W., *Engineer.*

理地會 *Way-de-le.*
14F, Foochow Road and 1, Quangse Terrace.
FISLER, L. F. & Co.,
Photographer and Dealer in Photographic Goods.
Fisler, L. F.

興泰新 *Sin-t'a-hsing.*
9, Foochow Road,
FLOUR MILL, SHANGHAI STEAM
Wilson, John, *Agent.*

F

館番旅國
Kwang-yih Shi-kun.
13, Peking Road.
FONSECA & Co.
Fonseca, A. A.
Costa, F. C. da

泰萬 *Van-tah.*
6, Foochow Road.
FORRESTER & Co.
Forrester, Wm.
Nail, Chas. H.
Agents—Lion Fire Insurance Co., Limited.

茂英 *Ying-mow.*
10, Peking Road.
FRANCIS, R., & Co.
Francis, Robert

泰豐 *Foong-t'a.*
7, Kiukiang Road.
FRAZAR & Co.
Frazar, Everett (absent)
Wetmore, W. S.
Lindsley, J. (Yokohama)
Eastlack, R. F.
Souza, M. G. de
Agents—Java Sea & Fire Insurance Company.
Queen Fire Insurance Company of Liverpool.
National Marine Insurance Co. of South Australia.
New York Board of Underwriters.
Boston Board of Underwriters.
American Ship Masters Association.

行興鴻 *Fung-hing-hong.*
37, French Bund.
FONG HING HONG.
L. Kong-yam, *Manager.*
L. Sack Long, *do.*
T. W. Song
T. Lian Bee
F. Tsoo-chang
T. Yat-chong
K. Y. Wong
S. P. York
Agents for the On Tai Insurance Co., of Hongkong.

G

房病法 *Fah-ping-fang.*
Corner of Peking and Kiangse Roads.
GALLE & PICHON.
Pichon, L., M.D. Paris.

記京新 *Sing-king-che.*
20, Foochow Road.
GAMMAN, EDWIN, & Co.
Gamman, Edwin

房火來自英大
Da Ying Ze-lay-hoo-vong.
GAS COMPANY, SHANGHAI
Yoo, Geo. J., *Eng. & Secy.*
Rogerson, J. M., *Foreman.*
Borchardt, F.
Schuppelmann, C.
Goodfellow, W.
Tredd, A. B.
Thistle, J. M.
Works and Offices at the Junction of the Soochow River and Defence Creek.

G

行火來自西蘭法
Fah-lan-se-ze-lay-hoo-hong.
Yang-king-pang, Fr. Concession
GAZ DE LA CONCESSION FRANÇAISE DE SHANGHAI, COMPAGNIE DU
Schonhard & Co., *Agents.*
Deck, A., *Directeur, Chef de l'exploitation.*

Yang-king-pang Creek.
GERMAN AND SCANDINAVIAN SAILORS' HOME
Williams, J. C., *Proprietor and Shipping Master.*

泰順南 *Nay-zung-tai.*
60, French Bund.
GESSEIT, A.,
Broker and General Commission Merchant.
Gesseit, F. A.
Chow, H. C.

行洋和公 *Koong-woo.*
9A, Hankow Road.
GILMOUR, DAVID, (absent)
Public Silk Inspector.
Anderson, Arthur
Ross, Claude A.

記仁 *Zung-che.*
22, Yangtsze Road.
GIBB, LIVINGSTON & Co.
Wood, A. G.
McLeod, Alex.
Daniel, H. W.
Sharp, C. S.
Sheppard, H.
Halton, Jr., Eldred
Kinnear, H. R.
Ozorio, E. C.
Agents—Eastern and Australian Steam-Ship Co., Ltd.;
China Fire Insurance Company (Limited);
Imperial Fire Insurance Co.;
Lloyds;
The Merchant Shipping and Underwriters' Association of Melbourne;
Italia Societá d'Assicurazioni Marittime, Fluviali et Terrestri in Genova;
Assicurazioni Generali in Triest;
Commercial Union Assurance Co. (Life Department);
Italia and Helvetia Marine Insurance Companies (Limited);
The Underwriting and Agency Association London, (composed of Underwriting Members of Lloyds only.)

隆興 *Hsing-loong.*
4 & 5, Szechuen Road.
GIPPERICH & BURCHARDT.
Gipperich, E.
Burchardt, Fr. A. (absent)
Mordhorst, O.
Klein, W.
Agents for the
Prussian National Insurance Co. of Stettin;
General Marine Insurance Co., Dresden.

芝葛 *Ku-che.*
25, Kiangse Road.
GOERTZ, A., *General Broker.*

H

昌公 *Kung-chang.*
3, Kiukiang Road.
HAGART & Co.
Cromie, C., *Agent.*

泰德 *Tuck-tai.*
Corner of Szechuen and Hankow Roads.
HAGUE, F.

生醫馬星龍
Loong-sing-mo-e-sung.
Rue des Pères, French Concession.
HALL, H. E.,
Veterinarian & Shoeing Smith.

35, Nanking Road.
HALL, J. WARD,
Doctor of Dental Surgery.

利福 *Fuh-le.*
Nanking and Szechuen Roads.
HALL & HOLTZ *(in liquidation),*
General Storekeepers, Furniture Manufacturers, &c.
Everall, H., *Liquidator.*
Stewart, J. Alexr.

司公利福
Fuh-le-kung-see.
HALL & HOLTZ CO-OPERATIVE CO., THE,
Provision Dealers, Bakers, Naval Contractors, Jewellers, Outfitters, Tailors, Wine & Spirit Merchants, Furniture Manufacturers, Drapers, Complete House Furnishers, Upholsterers, Artistic Decorators.
Stores—Nankin and Szechuen Roads.
Steam Factory—S'chow Road.
Bakery—Szechuen Road.

Everall, H., } *Managers.*
Short, W. H., }
Dyer, H. J., }
Byrne, E., }
Clifford, W. W., *Secretary.*
Hayward, W., *Clerk.*
Quick, Jno. C., do.
Carion, F. F., do.
Souza, M., do.
Remedios, S.B. *(Shipping.)*
Merchandise Department:
Rawlinson, C. J.
Gurney, James
Stewart, Chas. J.
Wine Department:
Dallas, F.
Outfitting Department:
O'Rourke, D.
Palin, W. G.
Tailoring Department:
Bowman, A. B.
Drapery Department:
Cottam, J. P.
Groves, L. J.
Furnishing Department:
Grayston, B. R.
Factory:
Wilson, John
Compradore:
Soo U-hin.
Agents for—
Shanghai Pilot Co.
Taylor, J. T., *Bonita.*
Art Union of London.
Sole Agents for—
Jaunay's Champagnes;
Salt's Burton Ales;
Brandeburg's Clarets;
Sazerac's Brandies.

H

廳船理 *Li-ch'uan-t'ing.*
HARBOUR MASTER AND COAST INSPECTOR'S OFFICE.
Bisbee, A. M., *Coast Inspector and Harbour Master.*
Deighton-Brayshor, C., *Asst. Harbour Master.*
Southey, T. S., *Clerk.*
Carlson, W., *1st Berthing Officer.*
Kraul, W. H., *2nd Berthing Officer.*
Patersson, J. W., *2nd Berthing Officer* (in charge Woosung Inner Bar Station.)
Sangster, T., *Signalman.*
Villanova, C., do.

東夏 *Ha-tung.*
5, Hankow Road.
HARDOON, E. A.

太華 *Wah-ta.*
21, Kiukiang Road.
HARRIS, GOODWIN & Co.
Goodwin, Oliver
Callaway, J. W.
Luther, C. A.

行洋味哈 *Hah-fe.*
28, Kiangse Road.
HARVIE, J. ALEX.
Merchant & Commission Agt.
Harvie, J. Alex.
Harvie, W. M.
Agent Reliance Marine Insurance Co.

生醫柏 *Pah E-sung.*
5, Hongkong Road.
HENDERSON, EDWARD, M.D., F.R.C.S., Edin.
Municipal Surgeon & Health Officer.
(Henderson & Macleod.)

利波 *Poo-le.*
HERMITAGE, THE, Sicaway.
Höflich, Mrs. Anna, *Propri.*
Bowman, Miss B.

行洋昌裕 *Yu-Chong.*
8, Peking Road.
HEWETT, W., & Co.
Hewett, W., Jnr. (London.)
Hewett, F., do.
Such, H. J.
Grose, F.
Such, F. W.
Silva, E. da

HILL, CHARLES E.,
9, Hotel des Colonies, Shanghai;
Care of Pethick, Maclay & Co., Tientsin.

昌永 *Yung-Chang.*
1, Nanking Road.
HIRSBRUNNER & Co.,
Watchmakers and Jewellers; Agents for Messrs. Negretti & Zambra.
Hirsbrunner, John
Macgregor, John
Hodge, James

H

茂增 *Tsun-mow.*
7, Siking Road, corner of Honan Road.
HIRSBRUNNER, JAMES,
General Merchant and Commission Agent
Hirsbrunner, James
Brunner, Chs. A. (Tientsin
Knopp, Ernest G.

15, Nanking Road.
HÖFLICH, JOSEPH,
Commission Agent.

豐兆 *Chaou-foong.*
10, Peking Road.
HOGG, E. JENNER

記義 *Ne-che.*
19, Foochow Road.
HOLLIDAY, WISE & Co.
Holliday, Chas. J.
Anderson, F.
Williamson, J. W. L.
Nichol, F. E.
Ross, A.
Barretto, L.
Rozario, A. D.
Souza, S. A. de
Agents to the—
London Assurance Corporation;
Manchester Fire Assurance Office;
Manchester Underwriters Association, Limited.

Broadway.
HONGKEW HOTEL
Holmes, J. H., *Manager.*

廠器機昌均
Kwan Cheong.
1113 & 1114, Broadway, Hongkew.
HONGKEW IRON WORKS.
Kwan Cheong & Co., *Propr., Engineers, Shipbuilders, Contractors, and Dealers in Engineer's & Ship's Stores.*

院醫英大口虹
Hong-kew Da-ying-e-yuen.
3c, Whangpoo Road.
HONGKEW MEDICAL HALL.
Mactavish, J. W.
Meldrum, E. D., *Manager* (Chemist by examination.)

Broadway, opposite Astor House.
HONGKEW TOILET CLUB.
Klampermeyer, Fr., *Proprietor.*
Three assistant Barbers.

院書英 *Yung-su-yön.*
15, Boone Road, Hongkew.
HONGKEW SCHOOL.
Martin, Mrs. *Superintendent.*

行銀豐匯 *Way-foong.*
12, Yangtsze Road.
HONGKONG AND SHANGHAI BANKING CORPORATION.
Cameron, Ewen, *Manager.*
Veitch, Andrew, *Sub-Manager* (absent.)
St Croix, G. C. de, *Acting Sub-Manager.*
Bevis, H. M., *Accountant* (absent)

H

Balfour, L. C., *Act Account.*
Wilson, Robert (absent)
Jackson, David
Byres, G. M.
Moffat, J.
Smith, J. R. M.
Hunter, H. E. R.
Browne, T. McC.
How, G. T.
Hillier, E. C.
Nicol, A. J.
Ruttonjee, B.
Dinis, Anto. Jé.
Gutterres, D. M.
Souza, B. de
Rangel, S. J.
Soares, E. E.
Souza, J. Thos.

件亮 *K'o-chien.*
Foochow Road
Hovkins, G. G., *Broker.*

庄肉羊牛顺德
Teh-sung-niew-yung-nioh-tsong.
Corner of Szechuen and Ningpo Roads.
Hopkins, Lavinia, *Butcher.*

飛龍 *Loong-fe.*
Near Race Course.
Horse Bazaar, Shanghai
Symons, Sewjee & Co., *Proprietors.*
Symons, H.
Sewjee, P. T.
Valentine, B. A.

館醫濟仁
Zâng-tse-e-kwan.
6, Shantung Road.
Hospital, Chinese
Johnston, James, M.D., *Medical Officer.*

院醫濟公海上
Shanghai Kung Che E-Yuan.
1, North Soochow Road.
Hospital, Shanghai General
Little, L. S., M.D., *Physician*
Thurburn, A., *Secretary.*

館醫仁同
Doong-zung-e-kwan.
14, Seward Road.
Hospital, St. Luke's
Boone, H. W., M.D., *Superintending Surgeon.*
Jamieson, R. A., M.D., *Visiting Surgeon.*

里采密 *Mih-ts'ay-le.*
72, Rue Montauban.
Hôtel des Colonies
Soisson, A., & Co.
Soisson, A.
Brown, Ch.
Vidaau, U.
Raynaud, F., *Assistant.*
Bruins, Jh.
Décoppe, *Steward.*

行洋理華 *Wa-lee.*
1, Hongkong Road.
How, A. J.

行洋泰亨 *Hang-ta.*
46, Kiangse Road.
Hunt, W. E., *Public Silk Inspector and Commission Agent.*

H

館報滬 *Hu Pao Kuan*
15, Hankow Road
"Hu Pao" Office
Pickwood & Co., *Proprietors.*

師鎮海 *Ho-ching.*
12, Peking Road.
Hutchison, C. H., *General Broker and Commission Agent.*

行洋源生 *Sing-yuen*
17, Peking Road.
Hyde, Hertz & Co.
Hyde, Wm. W. (absent)
Hertz, Henry
Craven, T.
Forushew, Ernest
Genin, Paul
Agents—The London and Provincial Fire Insurance Co., Limited.

I

行琴普宜
Ye-poo Chin Hong.
19, North Soochow Road Hongkew.
Ibuno, J. C. H., *Professor of Music.*

Ice Association, Shanghai
Mackenzie & Co., *Secretaries.*

茂公老 *Lau-kung-mow.*
2, Kiukiang Road.
Ilbert & Co.
Ilbert, A. (absent)
Beattie, Joseph
Walker, Samuel
Machado, J. M. R.
Kwong Chiu-wing

局報電國中
Chung-kwok-tin-pau-kuk.
Imperial Chinese Telegraphs.
Sheng Hung-shuen, *Director General.*
Ching To-chai, *Director.*
King Ling-shan, *Manager.*
Zeār Sui-chee, *Asst. do.*
Bojesen, C. C., *Engineer-in-chief.*
WongTsz-yuan, *Translator*
Chu Pau-fay, *Clerk-in-charge.*
Sew Shan-chow, *Account.*
Chung Lin-chih, *Clerk.*
Wong Yan-taung, *do.*
Tong Yun-chain, *do.*
Se Ching-dong, *Instrument Maker.*

Independent Order of Good Templars.
Wilson, E. G., *District Deputy for China.*

堂學女瑟若聖
Shen-ya-hsi-ne-ho-dong.
24, Rue Montauban, French Concession.
Institution St Joseph.
Mother Mary of St. Dominique, *Superior.*
Mother Mary of St. Vincent, and others.

I

平公 *Kung-ping.*
13, Nanking Road.
Iveson & Co.
Iveson, Egbert (absent)
Rankon, A. A. (London)
Artindale, Robt. H.
Ward, W. C.
Tottie, W. H.
Rex, A. B.
Ambrose, J.
Iburg, C.
Talbot, T. F.
Jansen, J. L.
Agents—Royal Insurance Co.

J

紀利 *Le-che.*
Ta-lay Buildings, French Bund
Jairazbhoy Peerbhoy, *Merchant.*
Abdulla Hassumbhoy, *Mnger.*
Mahomed Rahimtoolla (absent)

利賡 *Kiong-li.*
4, Yang king pang.
Jamieson & Co., *Commission Agents and Brokers.*
Jamieson, W. B.

生醫哲 *Tseh E-sang.*
1a, Kiukiang Road.
Jamieson, Alex., M.A., M.D., M.R.C.S. (Eng.), *Consulting Surgeon to the Customs.*

生大 *Da-sang.*
28, Nanking Road.
Jansen, J. E.

和怡 *E-wo.*
27, Yangtsze Road.
Jardine, Matheson & Co.
Paterson, W.
Keswick, J. J.
Clarke, B. A. (absent)
Ward, E. do.
Kenney, E. H.
Allum, W. E.
Allan, H. T.
McKie, James
Yvanovich, A.
Couto, E. J. do
Sá, A. F. de
Tavares, L. A.
Sá, Lino J.
Roustan, Laurent
Macgregor, R.
Reynell, A. E.
Bell-Irving, J. J.
Maitland, H.
Veitch, G. T.
Blair, E. T.
Hough, T. F.
Gatti, C.
Kennedy, R.
McEwen, J. T.
Aitchison, W.
Cousins, E. (Tientsin)
Inglis, R. (Hankow.)
Agents for
Banks—
Russian Bank for Foreign Trade, St. Petersburg.
Insurance, Marine—
Canton Insurance Office Limited;

J

Triton Insurance Company;
Alliance Marine Insurance Company.
Insurance, Fire—
Hongkong Fire Ins. Company, Limited;
Alliance Fire Insurance Company.
Steam—
Indo-China Steam Navigation Company, Limited;
Glen Line of Steamers;
Drage, Z. D., *Marine Superintendent.*
Buchanan, Colin, *Marine Supt. Engineer.*
Receiving-Ship *Yuen-Fuh,*
Dobie, W., *Commander.*
Vieira, U. A., *Purser.*
General Agents for—
Shanghai and Hongkew and Jardine's Assd. Wharves.

生醫張 *Tsang E sang.*
2, Shantung Road
Johnston, James, M.D., Edin. L.R.C.S.E., *Medical Officer, H.B.M.'s Consulate, Surgeon Chinese Hospital.*

康復 *Fook-hong.*
6, Nanking Road.
Joseph, J.

大成 *Zung-da.*
13, Szechuen Road.
Judkins, H., *General Broker, Commission Agent and Auctioneer.*

威有 *Yu-way.*
7, Siking Road.
Juvet, Leo (absent), Importer of Watches and Musical Boxes of all descriptions.
Hirsbrunner, James, *Agent.*

K

發別 *Bih fah.*
The Bund, next door to Hongkong & Shanghai Bank.
Kelly & Walsh, *Publishers, Music Sellers, Booksellers, Printers, Stationers, News Agents & Tobacconists.*
Brown, Thomas
Brinkworth, B. J. S.
West, John
Smith, John T.
Brinkworth, George
Xavier, C. A.

Nanking Road.
Kelly & Walsh's Printing Office
Morris, John, *Manager*

利開 *Kai-lee.*
16, Kiukiang Road.
Kelly Brothers, *General Brokers and Commission Agents*
Kelly, K. S.
Kelly, M. S.

I J K L M N O P R S T U V W Y Z

K

號二路潼天 *Tien-dong-lu-ne-haou.*
2, Tiendong Road.
KENNELLY, T. F.

廟昌高 *Kao-chang-miaou.*
局總造製南江
KIANGNAN ARSENAL.
Principal Director:
Pan-ta-jen 人大潘
Second Director:
Chai Lao-ya 爺老蔡
Third Director:
Njo-ta-jen 人大聶

Allan, J. M., *Superintendent Engineer and Teacher of Engineering Science.*
Mackenzie, John, *Superintendent of Gun Factory.*
Newton, W., *Superintendent of Foundry.*
Donnan, William, *Naval Constructor.*
Yang Cho-tang, *Interpreter.*
Stone, S. C., *do.*
Loong-hwa Branch Works.
Atkinson, John, *Superintendent Gunpowder Factory.*
Butler, Arthur, *Superintendent Cartridge Factory and Military Science Teacher.*
Translation Department.
Fryer, John.
Suvoong, V. P., M.D., B.A., B.D.
Schools for Languages.
Suvoong, V. P., M.D., B.A., B.D., *Teacher of English.*
Boyer, Edouard, *Teacher of French.*
Ku Sheng-te, *Teacher of French.*

廠水藥蘇江 *Kiang-su-yau-shue-chang.*
Soochow Creek, near Stone Bridge.
KIANG-SU ACID WORKS.
Major Bros., *Proprietary Directors.*
Maun, F., *Manager.*

恒有 *Yu-hang.*
24, Nanking Road.
KINGSMILL, THOS. W., *Civil Engineer and Architect.*
Kingsmill, T. W.
Atkinson, Brenan

利順 *Sun-lee.*
19, Kiangse Road.
KIRCHNER & BOEER.
Kirchner, A.
Böger, H. (absent)
Naulin, F.

L

館事公洋華譯繙
31, Nankin Road.
LAIDUN & Co.,
Public Translators and Interpreters.
House and Land Brokers.
Tseng S. Laidun.
Wong Tsz Yüan.

L

記利 *Le-che.*
4, Kiangse Road.
LALCACA, E. F., *General Broker.*

興泰 *Ta-hsing.*
11, Nanking Road.
LANE, CRAWFORD & Co.,
Ship-Chandlers, Outfitters, Wine and Spirit Merchants, Government Contractors and Shipping Agents.
Hewett, Wm.
Stanford, J. W.
Stauford, G. A.
Braga, F. A.
Marçal, G. F.
Sole Agents for—
Crane's Cylinder and Valve Oils;
Dick's Engine Oil;
Rahtjen's Composition for Ships' Bottoms;
Baxter's Canvas.
Fredk. Friend & Co.'s Portland Cement.
Wines—
Sole Agents for Adet Seward & Co.'s Clarets;
Agents for Gibb & Bruce Ports and Sherries;
Bulloch, Lade & Co.'s Whiskies.
John Hopkins & Co.'s "Glengarry" Whisky.
Forwarding Agency—
G. W. Wheatley & Co.'s Globe Express;
W. R. Sutton & Co.;
Elkan & Co., Continental Express;

平太 *Tae-ping.*
9, Kinkiang Road.
LAVERS & Co.
Lavers, E. H.
Limby, H. J.
Agents—Ocean Marine Insurance Co.;
London Westminster Bank, Limited, for payment of Circular Notes;
Bank of Montreal, for payment of Circular Notes;
Commercial Union Assurance Co.—Fire.

隆福 *Fook-loong.*
25, Foochow Road.
LEFFMANN, I. H.

Legations.

署公使欽國西巴大 *Ta-pa-she-kwo-ching-she-kung-shu.*
BRAZILIAN LEGATION—
Callado, H.Ex. E., *Envoy Extraordinary and Minister Plenipotentiary* (absent)

ITALIAN LEGATION—
Residence—Peking.
De Luca, Ferdinand, *Envoy Extraordinary and Minister Plenipotentiary.*

—o—

行洋信禮 *Hsin-sing.*
5, Canton Road.
LEMBKE, JUSTUS, & Co.
Lembke, Justus (Hongkong)
Bieber, Theodor (absent)
Troch, Max.
Fuhrmann, Richard

L

和德 *Teh-ho.*
1, The Bund.
LESTER, H., *Architect and Surveyor, Estate Agent.*

5, Nanking Road.
LEWIS, WILLIAM FREDERICK.

師意羅 *Lo-e-sz.*
Foochow Road.
LEWIS, GEORGE, *Ship, Freight, Coal Broker and Auctioneer.*

院書文洋 *Yang-vung shue yuen.*
1, Upper Yuen-Ming-Yuen Road.
LIBRARY, SHANGHAI
Latham, T., *Hon. Secy. and Treasurer.*
Mr. and Mrs. Gale, *Librarians.*
Open from 9 to 12 A.M., 4 to 7 P.M.

行洋興振 *Chin-hin-hong.*
48, French Bund.
LIM HO-CHEOW & Co., *British Merchants.*
Lim Ho-cheow, *Manager.*
Lim Ho-ong
Yeoh Seong-yok
Yau Kheng-yuan

德立 *Lih-teh.*
8, Kiukiang Road.
LITTLE, ARCH. J.

醫儒李 *Lee-ah-e.*
10, Kiukiang Road.
LITTLE, L. S., M.B., F.R.C.S. EDIN., B.A., Physician to the General Hospital.

家住德立 *Lih-teh-zu-chia.*
14, Yuen-ming-yuen Road.
LITTLE, ROBERT W., *Secy., Shanghai Electric Co.*

記德老 *Laou-teh-che.*
2, Nanking Road.
LLEWELLYN, J. & Co., *Manufacturing, Analytical and Family Chemists.*
Bradfield, J.
Stickler, F. M.
Watkins, G. A.
Green, A. G.

LOONG-YE CARRIAGE FACTORY.
Ashing, L., *Manager.*

LOONG-YE HARNESS FACTORY.
Ashing, L., *Manager.*

廠器機順寶 *Pau-zung-chi-ch'i-tsong.*
LOWER DOCK.
Farnham, S. C. & Co., *Proprietors.*

德厚 *Hou-teh.*
3, Hongkong Road.
LUCAS & Co.
Jacobs, Clement
Pinckvoss, J. H.
Death, John.

L

幾巳羅 *Lo-chi-e.*
142, Boone Road, Hongkew.
LUCINI, CLEOFAS, *Provisioner, &c.*

園戲樂西 *Se-loh-hse-yuen.*
8, Upper Yuen-ming-yuen Road.
LYCEUM THEATRE.
Corner, Geo. R., *Hon. Sec.*

M

生醫家波麥 *Mak-du-chu E-sung.*
Care of Hirsbrunner & Co.,
1, Nanking Road.
MACDOUGAL, Dr. A. MASON, F.R.C.S., L.R.C.P., L.S.A. LOND., &c. (absent)

茂隆 *Loong-mow.*
4, Foochow Road.
MACKENZIE & Co.,
Wine Merchants, Storekeepers, Auctioneers, and Hydraulic Press Packers.
Mackenzie, Robert
Poate, W. H.
Fowler, James
Allen, J. W.
Osborne, Jas. H.
Urquhart, John
Agents for
Cockburn & Co.'s Wines and Spirits;
A. & F. Pears' Soaps;
Lafitte & Co.'s Clarets;
De Gorson & Co.'s Clarets;
Delbeck & Co.'s Champagne;
Pellisson & Co.'s Brandy;
Auction Department.
Wallace, T.
Rosario, F. H.

隆申 *Sun-loong.*
25, Yangtszo Road.
MACKINTOSH, DUDGEON & Co.
Mackintosh, L. (absent)
Beauchamp, H. L.
Kranes, A. A.
Gutterres, L. M.
Senna, V.
Agents—Caledonian Fire and Life Insurance Office.
Union Marine Insurance Co. (Limited.)
Merchants Marine Insurance Company (Limited.)

林葛麥 *Ma-ka-ling.*
1, Foochow Road.
MACLEAN, PETER

盛裕 *Yü-sung.*
6, Canton Road.
MACLEAN, P. & Co.
Lindsay, G. A.
Watson, W.

生醫百新 *Sing Pah E-sung.*
9, Kiangse Road.
MACLEOD, NEIL, M.D., &c., Ed. (Henderson & Macleod.)

Care of Messrs. Adamson, Bell & Co.
MACOMBER, W. H.

M

院醫英大 *Da ying-i-yueng.*
Fogg's Buildings,
1, The Bund.
MACTAVISH & LEHMANN,
Chemists, Druggists and Aërated Water Manufacturers.
Mactavish, J. W.
Rueens, W. S.
Meldrum, E. D.
Twigg, P. O'B. E.

利麥 *Moh-lee.*
Yangtze Road, The Bund.
MACTAVISH & LEHMANN,
Merchants and Commission Agents.
Mactavish, Jas. W.
Emens, W. S.
Kit Fook, D.

司登麥 *Ma ting-sze.*
25, Whangpoo Road, Hongkew.
MAERTENS, AUG. H.,
Manager of the Kung ping Silk Filature.

行洋美長 *Chang-mae.*
41, Rue Montauban.
MAITLAND, J., & Co.
Maitland, John

芳元 *Yuen-fong.*
1, Hankow Road.
MAITLAND & Co.
Maitland, J. Andrew (abst.)
Purdon, J. G.
Noel, O. W.
Cole, Chas.
Webb, E. G. C.
Maitland, Frank
Church, W.
Purdon, Jr., James
Pereira, E. P.

Thorne, Cornelius

查美 *Mei-cha.*
14, Hankow Road.
MAJOR BROS.
Major, Frederick
Major, Ernest
Findlay, John
Pereira, H. A.
Proprietary Directors—
Kiang-su Acid Works;
"Shun-pao" Chinese Newspaper;
Tien-shih-chai Photo-lithographic Works;
Sui-chang Match Factory;
Shun-chong Publishing Business.

和信 *Sing-wo.*
MAJOR BROS. (Hankow.)
Major, Ernest
Major, Frederick

記源新 *Sin-yuen-kee.*
77, French Concession.
MALCAMPO & Co.,
General Merchants and Commission Agents.
Malcampo, Joquim (absent)
Keong Soon, K.
Tai Sum, O. Y.
Teng Liong, O. Y.
Saw Kheng, C.
Chu Dong, W.

會公機理海航
Hang-hai le-che-kung wey.
36, Kiangse Road.
MARINE ENGINEERS' INSTITUTE.
Kennedy, F., *President.*
Campbell, W. H., *Vice Pres.*
Mathieson, A., *Hon. Trea.*
Gillanders, A., *Hon. Sec.*
Clifton, F., *Librarian.*
Committee:
McGregor, D.
Sinclair, A.
Astill, R. W.
Buchanan, C.
Robertson, A.
Ferrier, J.

堂矩規 *Kway-chü-dong.*
30, Yangtsze Road.
MASONIC HALL.
Merritt, Chas., *Tyler.*

行洋邊麥
Ma-pin-yang-hong.
French Bund.
McBAIN, GEORGE.
McBain, George
Almeida, F. A. M. d'
Silva, Elias da
Yop fong, *Chinese Clerk.*
Office for strs. *W. C. de Vries,* and *Saul*

行洋時最美
Mei-che sz'.
French Bund.
MELCHERS & Co.
Jantzen, Carl
Michaelsen, St. C.
Thyen, Joh.
Lücke, G.
Korff, A.
Haupt, H.
Rodrigues, P. V.
Almeida, I. E. d'
Agents — Chinese Insurance Company, Limited;
Austrian Insurance Company "Donau," Vienna;
Marine Insurance Company of Basel;
General Insurance Company, "Helvetia";
"Rhenania" Insurance Company of Cologne;
"Providentia" Frankfurt Insurance Company, Frankfurt o/M;
Badische Schifffahrts-Assecuranz Gesellschaft, Mannheim;
Bremen Underwriters;
North German Fire Insurance Company, Hamburg;
Fire Insurance Association, Limited;
Germanic Lloyd;
Austro Hungarian Lloyd Steam Navigation Co.;
London and Lancashire Life Assurance Company.

司公船輪火國法大
Da-fah-kuo-ho-lun-su-kong-sz.
MESSAGERIES MARITIMES,
(COMPAGNIE DES)
French Mail Company.
Shanghai Agency.
Bund, French Concession.
Chapsal, J., *Agent.*
Lalanssiere, E.
Porte, R.
Campos, F. N. P. de

M

18, Nanking Road.
MERCANTILE MARINE OFFICERS' ASSOCIATION.
Hamlin, W. P., *Hon. Sec.*

臨全順 *Zung-zeen-loong.*
15, Canton Road.
MEYERINK, WM., & Co.
Meyerink, Wm.
Tiefenbacher, Max. (absent.)
Rohde, M.
Pereira, J. O.

羅㒲 *Me-lo.*
4, Yang-king-pang, French Concession.
MILLOT, E. & Co.,
Importers of French Goods, Wines and Spirits and General Commission Agents.
Millot, E. (absent)
Teillol, A.
Almeida, C. M. de
Agents for A. Grenot, and Remi de Montigny.

Missionaries, Churches, &c.

會經聖國美大
Da-mé kwoh-sheng king-hway.
18, Peking Road.
AMERICAN BIBLE SOCIETY'S AGENCY.
Gulick, Rev. Luther H., *Agent.*
Wills, Rev. W. A., *Assistant.*
Copp, A., *Colporteur,* C'kiang.
Bagnall, B., *do.* Peking.
Taylor, J. R., *do.* Canton.
Ware, J., *do.* Shanghai.

AMERICAN PRESBYTERIAN MISSION (South.)
Stuart, Rev. J. L., (H'chow.)
Kirkland, Miss H., do.
Painter, Rev. G. W. (absent)
Randolph, Mrs. A. E., do.
DuBose, Rev. H. C., (S'chow.)
Davis, Rev. J. W., (S'chow.)
Safford, Miss A. C., do.
Sydenstricker, Rev. A., (Hangchow.)
Woodbridge, Rev. S. J., (Chinkiang)
Johnson, Rev. J. F., (Hangchow.)
P. O. address, care of American Presbyterian Mission Press, 18, Peking Road, Shanghai.

Union Church.
BAMFORD, REV. A. J., B.A.

BOARD OF FOREIGN MISSIONS OF THE PRESBYTERIAN CHURCH, U.S.A.
Farnham, Rev. J. M. W., D.D.
Farnham, Miss L. (absent.)
Holt, Rev. W. S.
Smith, Rev. J. N. B.
Fitch, Rev. Geo. F., (S'chow)
Hayes, Rev. J. N., (N'king)
Judson, Rev. J. H. (H'chow.)
Mills, Rev. F. V., (H'chow)
Leaman, Rev. C. (Nanking.)
Allen, H. N., M.D.
Stubbert, J. E., M.D. (Ningpo)
Abbey, Rev. R. E. (Nanking.)
Chapin, Rev. O. H. (N'king)
Butler, Rev. J. (Ningpo)
McKee, Rev. W. J., do.
Warner, Miss S. A. do.
Address: care of Am. Presbyterian Mission Press, 18, Peking Road.

29, Whangpoo Road.
BRITISH & FOREIGN BIBLE SOCIETY.
Dyer, S., *Agent.*
Murray, D., *Sub-Agent.*

堂拜禮大
Ta Li pai T'ang.
CATHEDRAL, THE,
Bishop—Right Rev. George E. Moule, D.D. (Address, care of Local Post Office.)
Dean—Very Rev. Charles H. Butcher, D.D. (absent)
Chaplain—Rev. F. R. Smith, M.A.
Archdeacon — Ven. A. E. Moule, B.D.
Canon—Rev. Thomas McClatchie, M.A. (in England)
Trustees—F. W. Lemarchand, F. H. Bell.
Treasurer—Walter C. Ward.
Organist.—G. B. Pentuto.
Sextoness—Mrs. P. O'B. Twigg

房二第路德華西
Se-wa-tuk loo-te-yé-vong.
Office—2, Seward Road.
CHINA INLAND MISSION.

生先徐會地內
Nei-ti way-tu sien-sang.
Dalziel, J.

Office, 18, Peking Road.
CHINESE RECORDER AND MISSIONARY JOURNAL.
Happer, Rev. A. P., D.D., *Editor.*

院書心清
CHINESE RELIGIOUS TRACT SOCIETY.
Happer, Rev. A. P., D.D., *Pres.*
Farnham, Rev. J. M. W., D.D., } *Cor. Secretaries.*
Yen, Rev. Y. K., M.A., }
Wills, Rev. W. A., *Treas.*
Bankers—Hongkong & Shanghai Bank.

堂主天口虹
Hong-kew-tien-chu-dong.
Hongkew.
CHURCH OF SACRED HEART OF JESUS.
Guillen, R. F., S.J.

堂拜禮口虹
Hong-kew le-pa-dong.
Broadway, Hongkew.
CHURCH OF OUR SAVIOUR.
Clergy in charge Foreign Services:
Appleton, Rev. G. H.
Sayres, Rev. W. S.

生先藍 *Lau-sien-sang.*
South. Meth. Mission.
42, Kiangse Road.
LAMBUTH, REV. J. W., D.D., and family.
LAMBUTH, W. R., M.D.

圈家麥 *Mah-ka-ch'uen.*
3, Shantung Road.
LONDON MISSION.
Muirhead, Rev. Wm.
Stonehouse, Rev. Joseph

N O P R S T U V W Y Z

M

昌 茂 *Mo-chang.*
Chikiang Road.
MAHOMEDAN CHURCH
Goolamally Mahomed Ajum, *Mahomedan Priest.*
Abdoorahoman Goolamally
Abdoolajis Goolamully

MISSION OF THE AMERICAN PROTESTANT EPISCOPAL CHURCH, U.S.A.
生先施濟家吳 *Wu-ka-tsan Se-sien-sang.*
St. John's College.
Schereschewsky, Rt. Rev. S. I. J. (absent.)
Schereschewsky, Mrs. S. I. J. (absent.)
生先湯 *Tang-sien-sang.*
Thomson, Rev. E. H.
Thomson, Mrs. E. H.
生先文 *Wen-sien-sang.*
Boone, Rev. W. J.
Boone, Mrs. W. J.
Harris, Miss C. W.
生先聊 *Hsieh-sien-sang.*
Sayres, Rev. W. S.
Sayres, Mrs. W. S.
Appleton, Rev. G. H.
Appleton, Mrs. G. H.
Bruce, Miss M.
Lawson, Miss S. R.
Spencer, Miss E. A.

4, Ming-hong Road and at St. Luke's Hospital.
Boone, H. W., M.D.

圖家麥 *Mak-ka-ch'uen.*
4, Shantung Road.
OLSSON, A., British and Foreign Bible Society.

堂普首 *Cheou-chen-tang.*
PROCURE DES LAZARISTES, French Concession, Rue Laguerre.
Meugniot, Ph.
Barrière, Ch.

堂德三 *San-tuh-dong.*
PROCURE DES MISSIONS ETRANGERES.
Quai de France, above S.S.N. Co.'s Godowns, No. 29.
Martinet, Rev. J. B., *Procurator.*

堂主天 *Tien-tchu-tang.*
French Concession, Rue Montauban.
ROMAN CATHOLIC MISSION.
Garnier, Monseigneur V., S.J., Bishop of Titopolis, Vicar Apost. of Kiang-nan.

St. Joseph's Church and St. Xavier's School.
Basuiau, R. F., S.J., *Supr.*
Desjacques, R. F., S.J.
Formmil, R. F., S.J., *proc.*
Pittar, R. F.; S.J. *Lyen. Manager of St. Xavier's School.*
Twedy, R. F.; S.J.
Boucher, D., S.J.
Lanning, H., S.J.
Le Cornec, L., S.J.
Lonall, J.
Van Hesselaere, J., S.J.

M

Gauchef, P., S.J.
Templet, J., S.J.
Jouzeur, P., S.J.

Zi-ka-wei Observatory.
Dechevrens, R. F., S.J., *Direct.*
Zi-ka-wei Museum.
Heude, R. F., S.J.

會公理監
Kan-li-kung-wei.
9, Woosung Road and 23 & 24, Quinsan Road.
S. M. E. MISSION.
Allen, Rev. Y. J., D.D., *Supt.*
Lambuth, Rev. J. W., M.D.
Royall, Rev. W. W.
Loehr, Rev. G. R.
Mingledorff, Rev. O. G.
Allen, Mrs. Y. J. (in U.S.A.)
Lambuth, Mrs. J. W.
Royall, Mrs. W. W.
Mingledorff, Mrs. O. G.
Allen, Miss
Muse, Miss

SEAMEN'S CHURCH, POOTUNG. (Closed at present.)

St. Catherine's Bridge, beyond West Gate.
SEVENTH DAY BAPTIST MISSION.
Davis, Rev. D. H.
Davis, Mrs. S. G.
Swinney, Ella F., M.D.

生先祝 *Chuh-sien-sang.*
12, Woosung Road.
SHANGHAI BAPTIST CHURCH, *Worships in the Masonic Hall.*
Pastor, G. H. Judd

記禮 *Li-chi.*
13, Hankow Road, The Deanery.
SMITH, Rev. F. R., M.A.

SOUTHERN METHODIST BOARD OF FOREIGN MISSIONS, U.S.A.
Allen, Rev. Young J., D.D., LL.D., *Superintendent.*
Lambuth, Rev. J. W., M.D.
Royall, Rev. W. W.
Loehr, Rev. Geo. R.
Mingledorff, Rev. O. G.
Allen, Miss M.
Muse, Miss Anna J.
Nantsiang.
Anderson, Rev. D. L.
Rankin, Miss L.
Rankin, Miss D.
Soochow.
Parker, Rev. A. P.
Reid, Rev. C. F.
Lambuth, Rev. W. R., M.D.
Park, W. H., M.D.

堂主眞敎太猶
Yu-t'ai-chiaou-chen-chu-tang.
24, Foochow Road.
SYNAGOGUE "BETH EL"
Working Committee,
Moore, L., *President.*
Gubbay, R. A., *Vice-President.*
Ezekiel, J. S.
Nathan, S. A.
Moses, M. M., *Hon. Treas.*
Sopher, M. A., *Hon. Secy.*
Dyan, J. M., *Reader.*

堂拜禮路東山
Shantung-loo-le-pa-dong.
1, Shantung Road.
UNION CHURCH.

M

Bridgman Home.
WOMAN'S UNION MISSION.
Pruyn, Mrs. Mary
Burnett, Miss M. A.
Kirkby, Miss Annie E.
Reifsnyder, Elizabeth, M.D.

Missionary of the Southern Baptist Convention, U. S. A.
生先晏 *Yen-sien-sang.*
YATES, Rev. M. T.
Rue du Consulat, 2 Blocks West of French Municipal Hall.

MITCHELL, J. F., *Ship-builder, Pootung.*

司公船輪菱三本日
Ji-pen-san-lin-lang-zay-kung-sz.
MITSU BISHI MAIL STEAMSHIP COMPANY.
Duer, Yeend, *Agent.*
Sylva, Henry
Ekstrand, T. A.
Agents for Takashima Colliery; Tokio Marine Insurance Co.

井三 *Sang-ching.*
11a, Szechuen Road.
MITSUI BUSSAN KAISHA.
Wooyeda, Y.
Fukuhara, Y.
Soyeshima, O.
Hasuba, N.
Ishida, N.
Momonoi, Y.
Oui, Y.
Agents for The First National Bank, Tokio;
The Imperial Miike Coal Mine;
The Union Steam-ship Company (str. *Kiyodo-Unyu-Kaishia.*)

賜賚 *Lay-sz.*
Fogg's Buildings, The Bund.
MÖLLER, NILS, *Ship-owner, Freight & General Commission Agent.*
Möller, Nils
Oberg, G., *Capt. Super.*
Möller, Christopher
Oelkers, H., *Foreman Shipwright.*
Agent—
The Shanghai Shipping Co.;
The Twin-Screw Tug *Heron* (call flag T);
The Svenges Allmanna Marine Insurance Co., Ltd., of Gothenburg.

禮吉孟 *Meng-chi-li.*
16, Szechuen Road.
MONCRIEFF, A. L. M., *Merchant.*
Down, S.
Agent for Shaw's Godowns, Pootung and Shanghai.

摩師意穆 *Loo-e-sz-mo.*
4, Siking Road, and 11, Canton Road.
MOORE, L., *Broker, Auctioneer and Commission Agent.*
Moore, L.
Gale, S. R.

M.

師立馬 *Ma-li-sz.*
Quai du Yang-king-pang.
MORRIS & CO. *Commission Agents, Ship Owners, and Agents.*
Morris, John
Hammond, J. L.
Ollerdessen, H.
Agents for
Shanghai Tug Boat Association;
Foochow Dock Yard;
China Shipowners' Association;
The Chinese Salah Land Farming Co.;
S.S. *Waverley*;
S.S. *Greatham Hall.*

MORRIS & FERGUSSON, *Bill and Bullion Brokers.*
Bubbling Well Road.
Morriss, Henry
Fergusson, Robt.

孫禮瑪 *Ma-li-sun.*
1, Kiukiang Road.
MORRISON, G. JAMES, M. INST. C.E., A.SOC. T.E., *Civil Engineer.*
Gratton, Fredk. M., A.R.I.B.A.
Davies, W.

利美 *May-lee.*
30, Kiangse Road.
MOSES & ELIAS, *General Brokers*
Moses, M. J.
Elias, E. E.

吉用堂善種
Chung-shen-tang-yung-chi.
21, North Soochow Road.
MOTOMIYOSHI, S., M.D.

利得謀 *Mow-teih-le.*
28, Kiangse Road.
MOUTRIE, SYDENHAM, *Pianoforte & Music Warehouse.*
Moutrie, Sydenham
Mansfield, J. J.
Harris, W. F.

館公默 *Mo Kung-kwan.*
32, The Bund.
MOWAT, R. A., *Assist. Judge, H.B.M. Supreme Court.*

13, Boone Road, Hongkew.
MOXHAM, W. E.

Club Concordia.
MULLER, C. E., *Broker.*

起美 *Mei-che.*
21, Nanking Road.
MÜLLER, H. & Co. *Watch, Clock & Chronometer Makers.*
Pfaff, L.
Isaner, C.

院物博 *Po-wu-yuen.*
1, Upper Yuen-ming-yuen, above the Shanghai Library.
MUSEUM, SHANGHAI
Wilson, J. H., Ph.C., *Curator.*

M

隆晉 *Ching loong.*
9a, Nanking Road.
MUSTARD & Co.,
California Store and General Agency, Commission Agents
Mustard, R. W.
Bennett, C. C. (absent)
Fritz, J.
Rosa, F. da
Bennett J. W.
Agents for the Pilot Company.
Lanman & Kemp, Florida Water, New York;
Southard, Robertson & Co., Stoves & Grates, N. York;
Tarrant & Co., Seltzer Aperient, New York;
Fellows Compound Syrup of Hypophosphites, London and New York;
Seeley & Howell, New York,
Perry Davis & Son, Pain Killer, Providence, R.I.;
E. W. Vail, Chairs, Worcester, Mass;
Dr. Scott's Electric Brushes;
Standard Soap Company, San Francisco, Cal;
S. Foster & Co., San Francisco, Cal.;
F. V. Nicholls & Co., Harness and Saddlery, London, S.W.;
Morel, Brothers, Specialities, London, W.

易高 *Kaou-yih.*
21, Foochow Road.
MYBURGH & DOWDALL.
Myburgh, Alex., *Barrister-at-Law.*
Dowdall, Chas., *Solicitor.*
Lindsay, Geo.
Chubing, L.
Ah-mow.
Yih-chung.

Municipal Council

(For the Foreign Settlements) North of the Yang-king-pang.

Andrew Burnan, Esq
Ph. Arnhold, Esq.
J. M. Cory, Esq
J. J. Keswick, Esq.
C. J. Holliday, Esq.
Robt. Mackenzie, Esq.
E. Major, Esq.
Alex. Myburgh, Esq
E. O. Vouillemont, Esq.

COUNCIL OFFICES,
23, Kiangse Road.
部工 *Kung-boo.*
SECRETARIAT,—
Thorburn, R. F., *Secretary.*
Pond, J. A., *Accountant*
Hart, G. M., *Assistant.*
Fabris, E. A., ,,
Johnsford, A., *Collector and Overseer of Rates.*
Skinner, G. L., *Asst Tax Collector.*
Gould, J., do.
Schmidt, F., do.
Christiansen, A., do.
Smith, C., do.
Chang Sang, Z., *Linguist.*

SANITARY DEPARTMENT.
Henderson, Dr. E., *Officer of Health.*
Howes, J., *Inspector of Nuisances, &c.*
Weed, James A., *Asst. Insp. of Markets, &c.*

M

Davies, G. W., *Assistant to Inspector of Nuisances.*
Peters, F., do. do.
Jordan, M., do. do
Roberts, W., do. do.

MUNICIPAL GENERAL STORE,
Hankow Road.
房棧部工
Kung-boo-dzan-vong.

MUNICIPAL COUNCIL ARMOURY,
18, Honan Road
Merritt, C., *Armourer*

SURVEYOR'S OFFICE,
Kiangse Road.
務工理管部工
房字寫
Kung-boo-sia-zz-vong.
Clark, C. B., *Surveyor.*
Dallas, Arthur, *Clerk.*
Beckhoff, James, *Overseer.*
Kitter, G., *Overseer.*
Wong Yuen foo, *Office Writer.*
Yung Kiang, S., *Tracer.*

Henderson, Dr. E., *Surgeon.*
Bishop, J. D., *Telegraph Contractor.*

MUNICIPAL POLICE STATIONS.
房廳捕巡
Dang-boo-ting-vong.
CENTRAL STATION.
Penfold, C. E., *Superintendent.*
Fowler, W., *Inspector.*
Eveleigh, J., do.
Mack, A., *Detective Inspector.*
Wilson, A., *Inspector* (on leave.)
HONGKEW STATION.
Kluth, O., *Inspector.*
Charters, James, do.
LOUZA STATION.
Howard, George, *Inspector.*
FOOCHOW ROAD STATION.
McCarthy, J., *Inspector.*

CENTRAL STATION.
Sergeants:
Smyth, William
Hardy, Rodrick
Keeling, Fredrick
Canning, Thomas
Smith, Robert L.
Constables:
Buttenshaw, John
Ommundsen, Antoin
Growloff, Nicholas
Hamilton, Henry
Taylor, Sydney
Drickosen, Peter
Drew, Henry
Leich, Thomas
Garwood, Francis
Lawrence, Samuel
Eddie, Alexander
McDonald, Alexander
Wilson, Thomas
HONGKEW STATION.
Sergeants:
Reid, Joseph
Clarke, William A.
Plumbley, Richard
Hall, Nathaniel
Constables.
Wirry, William
Bennett, William G.
De Costa, Henry J.
Rae William
Mills, Henry
Ramsay, John

M

Bourke, Ralph
Surley, Peter
Jones, Henry
Storey, Thomas
Wells, James
Speed, George
Purse, Edward
Stuckey, Charles
Belharry, Alexander
Morrison, George
McLean, James
Harmer, William
Mason, William J
LOUZA STATION.
Constable.
Cox, Edwin

Conseil d'Administration Municipale de la Concession Francaise.

J. Oriou, *Président.*
C. Dowdall, *Vice-Président.*
C. Guieu, *Conseiller.*
C. Jantzen, ,,
H. Lester, ,,
Ph. Meugniot, ,,
J. H. Scott, ,,
A. Teillol, ,,
Bonabeau, James, *Secrétaire.*
BUREAUX DU SECRETARIAT.
部工國法大
Fuh-lan-se Koong-boo.
Bonabeau, James, *Secrétaire.*
Giudicelli, T., *Contrôleur-Comptable.*
Bottu, A., *Expéditionnaire.*
Romanet, E., *Percepteur.*
Ricco, E., ,,
Portier, E., ,, (abt.)
BUREAUX DES TRAVAUX.
Lagerheim, O. de, *Ingénieur.*
Bastien, Ed., *Surveillant*
Duval, V., *Inspecteur de la Salubrité.*

POLICE MUNICIPALE.
房廳捕巡國法大
Fuh-lan-se Zing-boo-vong.
Binos, J., *Chef de la Garde (en congé.)*
Berthelot, C., *Sous-Chef, do.*
Collomb, F., *Sergent attaché aux écuries.*

SERVICE MEDICAL.
Pichon, Dr., *Médecin de la Municipalité.*
Un Médecin Chinois pour la Vaccine.

INSPECTEUR DES MARCHES ET DES ECURIES.
Collomb, F., *Inspecteur.*

Poste Central à l'Hôtel Municipal, Rue du Consulat.
Sergents Adjudant — Chaigneau, J., Fortamp, A., Courbon, M.
Agents—Bourlier, A., Bastion E., Pavletich, N., Pariset, J., Sigalas, C., Urosu, H., Courbon, H., Lachelard, Féro, A., Crar, G., Hugues, C., Dufour, H., Annoi, J., Coroeveanu, A., Houllegate, F., Revest, J. P.

---

2 Interpreter Chinois, 2 Agents Secrets Chinois, 15 Agents Chinois.

Poste de l'Est, Quai de France.
Berthelot, C., *Sous-chef, Chef de Poste.*
Sergents—Benlanlet, J., Jégo, L. M.

M

Agents—Laurent, F., Tonnier, J. A., Orsoni, A., Dourcongar, Allène, J., Tuèleau, C., Piol, D., Campana, D., Lanusse, A.

---

1 Interprete Chinois, 6 Agents Chinois

Poste de l'Ouest, fin de la Rue du Consulat.
Sergents—Pichon, G., Jaune, P.
Agents—Neuciolt, A., Trolliet, E.

---

1 Interprete Chinois, 6 Agents Chinois.

N

NATIONAL BANK OF INDIA, LIMITED.
Turner & Co., *Agents.*

普飛 *Nai-poo.*
4, Peking Road.
NEUBOURG, A., & Co.,
Merchants and Commission Agents.
Neubourg, A.
Baessler, Joh.

昌和 *Wo chang.*
41, Rue Montauban, French
NICKELS, M. G.
Ship, Coal & General Broker.

館紙森望
Vong-yuh-tse-Loon.
12, Canton Road.
NORONHA & SONS,
Printers and Stationers.
Noronha, L. (absent)
Pereira, T. S.
Aquino, J. F. d'
Botelho, J. M.
Carion, L. F.

院醫華英
Ing-woo-e-yuen.
Broadway (opposite Astor House.)
NORTH-CHINA DISPENSARY.
Strachan, B.

林字 *Tsz lin.*
15, Hankow Road.
NORTH CHINA HERALD AND S. C. & C. GAZETTE,
NORTH-CHINA DAILY NEWS.
Pickwood & Co., *Proprietors.*
Balfour, Frederic H., *Editor and Co-Proprietor.*
Greathead, Ashlo, *General Manager.*
Maclellan, J. W., *Commercial Editor.*
Gowing, L. F., *Sub-Editor and Shorthand Reporter.*
Kahler, W. R., *Shipping and General Reporter.*
Ferris, F. F., *Clerk*
Printing Office:
Oliveira, F. X., *Superintd.*
Tavares, P. J
Costa, J. C. da
Sanches, C. A.
Senna, R. M.
Nunes, F. S.
And Chinese.

N O P R S T U V W Y Z

N

行家保 *Pau-chu-hong.*
9, Hankow Road.
NORTH-CHINA INSURANCE CO. (LIMITED.)
Davis, J. Kennard, *Secretary.*
Starkey, Regd D., *Assistant Secretary.*
Pardon, Walter
Clifton, A. S. T.
Price, H. J.
Rozario, J. F.
Warburg, C. J., *Marine Surveyor.*
London Branch, 25, Cornhill, E.C.—Herbert S. Morris, *Agent.*
Hongkong Branch,
Ross, Alex., *Agent.*
Beauchamp, R. H.
Yokohama Branch—
Gray, B. C. T. *Act. Agent.*
Singapore Branch—
Rayne, W. O., *Agent.*
Agents for Commercial Union Assurance Co., 19 and 20, Cornhill London, E.C., (Marine Branch).

司尼那 *No-ne-sze.*
12, Canton Road.
NUNES, G., *General Printer and Bookbinder.*

O

古太 *Tà-koo.*
5, Kiukiang Road.
OCEAN STEAM SHIP CO.
Butterfield & Swire, *Agents.*

署總部工英大 *Da Ying-kung-pùo Tsung-za.*
1, Yuen-ming-yuen Road.
OFFICE OF WORKS, H.B.M.'s, FOR CHINA, JAPAN AND SIAM.
Marshall, F. Julian, *Surveyor*
Donaldson, C. P. M.

倉大 *Ta-chong.*
22, Kiangse Road.
OKURA & CO.
Akabe, S. N., *Manager.*
Ninomiya, K., *Clerk.*

廠船老 *Laou-zen-tsang.*
OLD DOCK FOUNDRY AND SHIP YARD.
Farnham, S. C., & Co.

棧順華 *Whu Zung-zlang.*
OLD NINGPO WHARF.

和怡 *E-wo.*
Jardine, Matheson & Co., *Agents.*

烝立頓 *Mee-lee-ton.*
Middleton, Osborne, *Mngr.*
Ramsay, Thos. C., *Act. Acct.*

茂泰 *Tai-mow.*
5, Peking Road.
OLIVER, GEORGE, & CO., *Merchants.*
Oliver, George (London)
Pinel, John, do.
Allen, J. H. B.,
Easterbrook, S. T. F.

O

Bubbling Well Road.
OLIVER'S HOTEL
Thornley, Mrs. H. M.

如麗 *Le-zu.*
18, Yang-tsze Road, The Bund.
ORIENTAL BANK CORPORATION.
Burns, B. H., *Actg. M'ger.*
Taylor, H. Howard, *Acct.*
Haggitt, J. R., *Asst. Acct. and Cashier.*
Carvalho, P. M. de, *Clerk.*
Pereira, J. L., *do.*

發順 *Suun-fat.*
Macao Buildings, Yuen-ming-yuen.
OVERBECK & CO.
Overbeck, H (Europe)
Overbeck, Chas.
Siegfried, G. W.
Timm, O. F.

P

店頭剃國法 *Fa-kuo-t'i-t'ou-tien.*
4, Nanking Road.
PARISIAN SALOON.
Magnan & Co.
Parisod, A.
Magnan, B.
Gillard, F.

裕宏 *Hong-yu.*
French Concession.
PAUL, R., YU-DING, } *Compradores.*

行司公船輪火英大 *Da-ying-koong-sz-ong.*
24, Yangtsze Road.
P. & O. S. N. Co.'s OFFICE.
Lind, Adam, *Agent.*
Joseph, H. H., *Chief Clerk.*
Ritchie, H. A., *Clerk.*
Hewett, E. A., *do.*
Fryer, H., *Gunner.*
Barris, T.

The Marine Insurance Company, Limited, Head Office, 20, Old Broad Street, London, Shanghai Branch—
Lind, Adam, *Agent.*

生醫盛興 *Chin-sing-e-sang*
1, Kiukiang Road.
PERKINS & COE, *Dent. Surg.*
Perkins, H. Mason, D.D.S.
Coe, F. E., D.D.S.

和遂 *Sue-wo.*
Corner of Kiangse and Tientsin Roads, next to Messrs. Cama,jee & Son.
PESTONJEE, R., *General Broker.*
Pestonjee, Ardeshir R.

房藥發科 *Ko-fa Yo-fong.*
29, Corner of Nanking and Kiangse Roads.
PHARMACIE DE L'UNION.
Voelkel, S., *Proprietor.*
Wilson, J. H.
Schroeder, A.
Grenard, Louis

P

PHIPPS, W. T.
Agent—Standard Life Assurance Co.;
Sun Fire Office.
Care of Messrs. Turnbull, Howie & Co.

房病法 *Fah-ping-fang.*
16, Corner of Peking and Kiangse Roads.
PICHON, L., M.D. Paris.
French Municipal Surgeon & Health Officer, & Customs Medical Attendant.

喇筆 *Pe-la.*
9, Upper Yuen-ming-yuen Rd.
PILA, ULYSSE, & CO.
Pila, Ulysse (absent)
Pila, Louis
Bancal, E.

PILOTS (*Licensed*)—
Andersen, R. A. J.
Bain, W. B.
Braud, E.
Brun, J.
Burr, W. A.
Cameron, H.
Campbell, D. C.
Coates, J. E.
Corbach, W. van
Dalrymple, S. O.
Deville, W. N. (Reserve)
Gutley, A.
Hjunsbery, E. H.
Hunt, J. H.
Jurgensen, J.
Knott, R.
Kofod, F. A. A.
Martin, D (Reserve)
McCaslin, R. J.
Meldrum, A.
Muller, B. J.
Nelson, M.
Pike, J.
Smith, A. (absent)
Snowdon, A.
Taylor, J. T.
Thomas, J.
Vaughan, J.
Williams, R.

隆晉 *Ching-loong.*
Nanking Road.
PILOT COMPANY.
Mustard & Co., *Agents.*
Pilot Sch. *S. C. Farnham.*
" " *C. P. Blethen.*
" " *Syren.*
" " *Ruby.*

戶船渡家黃東浦 *Poo-tung, woong-ka-doo-zay-oo.*
POOTUNG DOCK SHIPYARD.
Farnham, S. C., & Co.

Post-Offices:—

館信書英大 *Da-ying Su-sing-kwan.*
7, Peking Road.
BRITISH—
Machado, F. G., *Postmaster.*
Pereira, A. M., *Clerk.*

館信書國法大 *Fah-kuo-ss-en-sing-kwan.*
81, Rue Montauban.
FRENCH—
Orion, J., *Principal Postmaster.*
Berthon, L., *Assistant.*

P

JAPANESE—
13, Whangpoo Road.
Shinagawa, E., *Consul-General and Postal Agent.*
Wooyena, T.
Inayama, K.

館信書部工 *Kung-boo Su-sing-kwan.*
12, Hankow Road.
LOCAL—
Jones, A. E., *Postmaster.*
Rimner, A., *Assistant.*
Open Daily 8 A.M. to 6 P.M.
Sundays 9 to 10 A.M., and 3 to 4 P.M.

局信書門衙國美 *Mei-kuo Yamên Su-sing-jooh.*
The Bund, Hongkew.
UNITED STATES—
Denny, O. N., *Postal Agent,* (absent.)
Coffey, J. J., *Deputy Postal Agent.*

寶昇 *Sing-Paon.*
5, Yuen-ming-yuen.
PRIMROSE & CO., *Commission Merchants.*
Primrose, W. M.
Anderson, W. H.
Llewellyn, J.
Agents—
South British Fire and Marine Insurance Co. of New Zealand.

PUBLIC BAND, SHANGHAI
Ward, W. C., *Chairman,* } *Committee.*
Brunat, P.
Corner, Geo. R.,
Nachtrieb, A.,
Scott, J. L.,
Vouillemont, R. G.,
Fabris, E. A., *Secretary.*
Vela, M., *Band-Master.*
And 25 Musicians.

R

RACE CLUB (SHANGHAI)
Dallas, Barnes, *Secretary.*

場球拋 *P'au-jeu-zan.*
Malon.
RACQUET COURT.
Joseph, H. H., *Hon. Sec.*

棗子彈理修記趙 *Zau-chee.*
2, Boone Place, Hongkew.
RAGO & CO.,
Billiard Sellers & Repairers.
Chew Quay-chin, *Manager and Foreman.*

發立 *Lih-fah.*
8, Kiukiang Road.
RAPHAEL, E. S.
Elias, R. H.
Soojaw, C. Y.

泰履 *Le-t'a.*
3, Peking Road.
REID, EVANS & CO.
Evans, M. P.
Arbuthnot, E. O.
Macdonald, T. J.
Samson, J.
Wrightson, C. W.
Perrott, E. S.

R

和泰 *Ta-wo.*
7, Hankow Road.
Brown & Co.
Kalb, M.
Adler, M.
Percival, R. H.
Crutch, S. J.
Souza, V. B. de

名利 *Le-ming.*
4, Yang-king-pang, on the French Concession.
REMI DE MONTIGNY,
Montigny, Rémi de (absent)
Millot, E., & Co., *Agents.*

明和 *Wo-ming.*
10, Szechuen Road.
REUTER'S TELEGRAM CO. (LIMITED.)
Corner, Geo. R., *Agent.*
Souza, Jr., J. F. de

行洋因來 *Lae-yin.*
43, Rue Montauban.
RUBIN, G., *Storekeeper.*

茂新 *Sing-mow.*
2, Yangtsze Road.
RICE, E. W.

行洋順源 *Neuen-sung.*
3, Canton Road, & 3, Bubbling Well Road.
RIVINGTON, CHARLES, *Share Broker,*
Agent for McClean's Telegraphic Bureau, London.

Office—Club Chambers.
ROBERTS, JOHN P., *Mar. Surveyor.*
For—American Shipmasters' Association; Record of American and Foreign Shipping; Germanic Lloyds; New York, Boston, San Francisco and Bremen Underwriters; The Chinese, China Traders', Java Sea, and Fire, National Marine of North Australia, Insurance Companies.

生皮樂 *Loh-be-sung.*
1, Yuen-ming-yuen Buildings.
ROBINSON, A., *Solicitor.*
Encarnaçho, L. d', *Clerk.*

活愛樂 *Loh-a-wer.*
2, Yuen-ming-yuen Buildings.
ROBINSON, EDWARD, *Barrister-at-Law.*
Cher-sui-fong, *Clerk.*

威化阿 *Ah-hwo-way.*
3, Hongkong Road.
RODEWALD & CO.
Rodewald, J. Fred.
Young, J. M.
Huchting, F.

順和 *Wo-tung.*
Corner of Szechuen and Foochow Roads.
ROSENBAUM, JOS., & CO., *Dealers in Cigars and Smoker's Goods.*

R

ROWING CLUB, SHANGHAI
Dudgeon, C. J., *Hon. Sec.*

飂板杣頭下
Ao-dou-sampan-tsang.
Lower Boat-house—Soochow Creek.

飂板杣頭上
Sang-dou-sampan-tsang.
Upper Boat-house—Soochow Creek.

克履 *Li-k'é.*
Shanghai Club.
RUKOG, E., *General Broker.*

昌旗 *Ke-chung.*
6, Yangtsze Road.
RUSSELL & CO.
Forbes, H. de C. (absent)
Hitch, F. D.
Wheeler, G. H.
Ballard, J. A.
Brunat, Paul
Bush, L. L.
Green, F. J.
Gouilloud, L.
Hunter, A. C.
Jackson, W. S.
Lubeck, H. C.
Lubeck, L. A.
Maher, J. M.
Mur, J. M.
Silva, P. da
Simoens, N.
Stone, E.
Thorburn, J. D.
Wintle, V. D'O.
Secretaries Yangtsze Insurance Association, Limited.
Agents North British and Mercantile Insurance Company (Fire Branch.)
Pootung Wharf and Godown Co.

局繅絲昌旗關老
Lao-ca-ke-chong-chao-sz-kuh.
North Soochow Creek.
RUSSELL & CO.'S SILK FILATURE.
Brunat, Paul
Riva, A.
Rey, P.
Perotta, Mme. M.
Castelnovo, Mlle. E.
Rossi, Mlle E.
Calderola, Mlle. A.

S

順豐 *Foong-rung.*
20, Broadway, Hongkew.
SAILORS' HOME.
Huoy, B. E., *Superintendent.*

遜沙老 *Laou So-sung.*
23, The Bund.
SASSOON, DAVID, SONS & CO.
Ezekiel, J. S.
Moses, M. M.
Michael, J. R.
Sophor, M. A.
Sopher, J. A.
Judah, R. S.
Rahamim, A. J.
Isaac, R. Michael
Agents for R. S. *Wellington.*
Parker, J. H. P., commander.

S

遜沙新 *Sing-so-sung.*
20, Bund.
SASSOON, E. D. & CO.
Sassoon, E. E.
Nathan, S. A.
Gubbay, Y. A.
Joseph, S. S.
Moses, J.
Perry, M. S.
Ezra, E. M.

館像泰森
Sång-t'a Zeung-kway.
3, Whangpoo Road, Hongkew,
SAUNDERS' PHOTOGRAPHIC STUDIO.
Saunders, W.
Douglas, R.

司公厘些
Say-le Kvong-sz.
Nanking and Szechuen Roads, & Victoria Exchange, H'kong.
Linen Drapers, Silk Mercers, Tailors, &c.
SAYLE & CO., Executors of the late Robt. Sayle (England)
Sayle, T. H., *Manager.*
Wheen, E.
Latty, E. R.
Jeffrey, T.
Buck, H.
Neilson, J. R.
Morgan, G.
Hickens, F. D.
Mason, J.
Prentice, A.
Hope, E. R.
Bell, R.

Sayle, Mrs. T. H.
Wheen, Mrs.

亨元 *Yuen-hang.*
French Bund.
SCHELLHASS, E. & CO.
Beyer, Ludwig (absent)
Buschmann, R. (Hongkong)
Harling, G. (absent)
Seip, F.
Körner, F.
Bramann, M.
Schweng, B.
Agents—Transatlantic Marine Insurance Company, (Limited), Berlin.
Lubeck Fire Insurance Co.
Consolidated Marine Insurance Companies of Berlin.
Magdeburg General Insurance Co., Limited.
Rhenania Versicherungs Actien Gesellschaft in Cöln a Rh.
The Fire Insurance Co. of 1877, Hamburg
Saghalien Coal Co. (o Doue.

四狄爹，門的雷耶
Chi-lai-ti-mên, Ma-tek-see.
14a, Foochow Road.
SCHLICHTMANN & MADAUS, *Milliners, Dress and Mantle Makers.*

S

生戴新 *Sing-tai-sung.*
27, Rue Colbert, Fr. Con.
SCHMIDT & CO.
Burmeister, Ed. (Hamburg.)
Schmidt, Chs. (Tientsin)
Burmeister, Emil
Ellert, Arnold
Moritz, A
Schmidt, John (Tientsin)

行洋泰滙
Hui-tai-yang-hang.
33, Rue du Consulat, opposite French Consulate General.
SCHMIDT, J. MEINHARD
Public Accountant, Bill Collector & Commission Agent

昌泰新 *Sin Ta-ts'ang.*
6, Kiangse Road.
SCHONHARD & CO.
Nachtrieb, A.
Nachtrieb, C. (absent)
Fourael, J.
Rozario, F. do

士亞地 *Di-a-sz.*
8, Szechuen Road.
SCHULTZ, H. M. & CO.
Schultz, H. M.
Gebhardt, F.

1, Broadway, Hongkew.
SEAMAN'S HALL AND READING ROOM.

豐德會 *Way-tuh-foong.*
Ta-lay Buildings, French Bund.
SHANGHAI CARGO BOAT CO.
Wheelock & Co., *Agents.*

易高 *Kaou-yih.*
21, Foochow Road.
SHANGHAI DOCK COMPANY.
Myburgh & Dowdall, *Secretaries & Legal Advisers.*

司公氣電
Deen-ch'i-kung-sz.
Central Station, 41, Chapoo Road, Honekew.
Office—8, Kiukiang Road.
SHANGHAI ELECTRIC CO.
Little, R W., *Secy.*
Brown, A. D., *Supt.*
Dorsick, G., *Engineer.*

昌利 *Lee-chang.*
30, Kiangse Road.
SHANGHAI EXCHANGE OFFICE.
Robins, M., & Co.
Robins, M.
Rosenstreich, M.

司公險保燭火海上
Shung-hai ho-chok-pao-sien-kung-sz.
21, Foochow Road.
SHANGHAI FIRE INSURANCE COMPANY, LIMITED.
枝茂唐
Tong Mow Chee, *Chairman.*
坪秋李
Lee Chu Ping, *Gen. Manager.*
純子黃
Wong Tsze Shun, *Clerk.*

S T U V W Y Z

S

祥和公 *Kung-woo-tsang.*
SHANGHAI AND HONGKEW AND JARDINE'S ASSOCIATED WHARVES.
Glass, D., *Manager.*
Hamlin, W. P., *Sub.-Mgr.*
Law, R., *Accountant.*
Poignand, W., *Wharfinger.*
Cooper, H. *do.*
Moore, Bernard, *Clerk.*
Severin, A. B., *do.*
Evans, A. E. M., *do.*
York, W. C., *do.*

會仁輔友文 *Wên-yu-fu-jên-hui.*
SHANGHAI LITERARY AND DEBATING SOCIETY.
Bright, Wm., *President.*
Bamford, B.A., Rev. A. J., *Vice-President.*
Wainewright, R. E., *Vice-President.*
Such, F. W., *Hon. Sec.*
Osburne, Jas. H., *Hon. Treas.*
Drew, E. B., } *Committee.*
Hart, G. M., }
Latham, T., }
Moule, Ven. Arch., B.D., }
Robinson, Ed., }

SHANGHAI MARINE ENGINEERS' MUTUAL INSURANCE SOCIETY, LIMITED, THE
Wilmer Harris & Co., *General Agents.*
Office, care of Marine Engineer's Institute, Kiangse Road.

記德老 *Laou-teh-che.*
2, Nanking Road.
SHANGHAI MEDICAL HALL.
Llewellyn, J. & Co. *Manufacturing, Analytical and Family Chemists.*
Bradfield, J.
Stickler, F. M.
Watkins, G. A.
Green, A. G.

匯文 *Wen-wei.*
3, Canton Road.
SHANGHAI MERCURY.
Rivington, Charles
Clark, J. D., *Business Manager.*
——— *Accountant.*
Navario, A., *Reporter.*
Xavier, F. P.
Portaria, V. P. M.
Rozario, L.
Tavares, A. G.
Pereira, A.
Maher, F.
Maher, D.
And Chinese Staff.
Sloan, R. J., M.D., *Med. Attend.*

局紙造器機 *Che-ch'i-tsao-che-chok.*
Yang-tse-poo Road.
SHANGHAI PAPER MILL Co.
Tso Tsze-lai, *Manager.*
Li Shou-chi
Lan Yau-pan
Chai Shun-hin
Waters, Thos. J., *Consulting Engineer.*
Maitland, W., *Superintendent.*
Melvin, A., *Paper-maker.*

房藥大氏臣屈 *Wa-sun-sz Tai-yeuk-fong.*
24, Nanking Road.
SHANGHAI PHARMACY,
A. S. Watson & Co., *English & Foreign Chemists and Agents for the Hongkong Aërated Waters.*
Humphreys, J. D. (London)
Davey, John, *Manager.*
Wilkins, E.
Agents for Morgan's Patent Plumbago Crucibles.

SHANGHAI VOLUNTEER CORPS.
Commandant:
Major C. J. Holliday.

Surgeon-Major R. Henderson

Sergeant-Major C. Merritt.

Light Horse:
Captain Keswick.
Lieut. B. A. Clarke.
Surgeon H. M. Perkins.
1 Sergeant.
2 Corporals.
16 Troopers.
Sergeant T. F. Hough, *Instructor.*

Artillery:
Captain R. Dallas.
Lieut. G. W. Noel.
„ A. B Rex.
Surgeon R. J. Sloan.
2 Sergeant.
2 Corporals.
36 Gunners.

No. 1 Company:
Captain G. J. Morrison.
Lieut. D. Glass.
„ J. Buchanan.
4 Sergeants.
61 Privates.

No. 2 Company:
Captain J. A. Harris.
Lieut. W. H. Anderson.
„ W. Bright.
3 Sergeants.
2 Corporals.
44 Privates.

No. 3 Company:
Captain G. Lanning
Lieut. J. W. H. Burgoyne.
4 Sergeants.
1 Corporal.
1 Bugler.
23 Privates.

No. 4 Company:
Lieut. F. N. P. de Campos.
„ C. M. Souza.
4 Sergeants.
1 Bugler.
56 Privates.

SHANGHAI WATERWORKS' Co., LIMITED.
McLeod, A., } *Members of the Committee.*
Hearn, H. R., }
Mackenzie, R., }
Ringer, J. M., }
Drysdale, Ringer & Co., *Secretaries.*
Hart, J. W., *Engineer-in-chief.*
Campbell, O., *Pipe-layer.*
Antill, R. W., *Foreman Eng.*
Clifton, F., *Foreman Plumber.*
Wallace, T., *Storekeeper.*

S

16, Szechuen Road.
SHAW'S GODOWNS, POOTUNG AND SHANGHAI.
Benjamin, B. D., *Proprietor.*
Moncrieff, A. L. M., *Agent.*

館報申 *Shun Pau Kwan.*
14, Hankow Road.
SHUN-PAU DAILY NEWS.
Major Bros., *Proprietary Directors.*
Pereira, H. A., *Mngr. & Ed.*
Tsien Hing-peh, *Sub-Editor.*
Shun Pau-shau, *do.*
He Kuei-sung
Chau Yih-jon, *Chinese Mngr.*

昌時 *Tsi-tsang.*
2, Hankow Road.
SIEBER-WASSER
Baumann, A.
Rudolph, Chs.
Costa, G. G. da
Agents of "la Suisse" Company Assurances Maritimes.

臣稱 *Zay-zhang.*
28, Yangtsze Road.
SIEMSSEN & Co.
Hibbin, P. G.
Wasserfall, A.
Ottomeier, P. A. W.
Siemssen, Alfred
Mottel, L.
Müller, Joh. F.
Börner, H.
Agents—Globe Marine Insurance Company Limited of London;
Samarang Sea and Fire Insurance Company;
Transatlantic Fire Insurance Company Limited of Hamburg;
Düsseldorf Universal Marine Insurance Company, Limited;
Verein Hamburger Assecuradeure;
German Lloyd Marine Insurance Company, Limited;
"Fonciere" Pester Versicherungs-Anstalt Buda-Pest.

Carter Road.
SILAS, D. H.

行洋昌義 *Ne-chang.*
25, Szechuen Road, Corner of Pekin Road.
SKEGGS, C. J., & Co., *Public Silk Inspectors and Commission Agents.*
Skeggs, C. J.

福天 *Tien-foo.*
23, Szechuen Road.
SLEVOGT, MAX.
Slevogt, Max.
Schlichting, H.

生醫羅賜 *Sz-loo E-sung.*
47, Kiangse Road.
SLOAN, ROBT. J., M.D.

密司熙 *Se-sz-me.*
37, Nanking Road.
SMITH, C., *General Storekeeper, Commission Agent and Auctioneer.*

和盛老 *Lao-kwang-ho.*
SMITH, GEO., & SON, *Wine and Spirit Merchants.*
Smith, Geo.
Smith, A. G.

福祥 *Tsiang-foo.*
6, Foochow Road.
SMETHLAGE, H., *General Broker and Commission Agent.*

康榮 *Yoong-kong.*
15, Szechuen Road.
SOLOMON BROS., *Merchants and Commission Agents.*
Solomon, R. J.
Solomon, S. J.

722, Broadway, Hongkew, opposite the Astor House.
SONNENBLICK, J., *Tobacco and Cigarette Factory.*

悅昌號 *Yat-chaong-hou.*
42, Yang-king-pang, French Concession, 3rd Bridge.
SORABJEE JEEWANJEE GUZDAR, *Dealer in Indian and European Goods.*
Sorabjee Jeewanjee Guzdar
Loganjy, J.

外門西住生倫沙 *Sa-lun-sang-zi Si-mên-wei.*
Outside the West Gate.
SORENSEN, H. B.

STAR IN THE EAST
Published at 3, Canton Road.
Clark, J. D., *Publisher.*

生華 *Hwo-sung.*
4, Kiukiang Road.
STEWART, MRS., *Millinery Show Rooms.*
Stewart, Mrs.

局昌燧 *Sui-chang-chu.*
Soochow Creek, near Stone Bridge.
SUI-CHANG MATCH FACTORY.
Major Bros., *Proprietary Directors.*
Chai Tong-ben, *Managing* ——— *Compradore.*
4, Pekin Road.
SULLIVAN, JNO. A., *Share Broker.*

門衙司使鑾刑英大 *Da-ying hsing-ch'ien shih-sz ya-mên.*
SUPREME COURT FOR CHINA AND JAPAN, H.B.M.'S
33, Yangtsze Road, or Bund.
Sir Richard T. Rennie, Kt., *Chief Justice.*
Mowat, R. A., Esq., *Assistant Judge.*
Smith, T. G., *Chief Clerk and Private Sec.*
Jones, Malcolm, *Clerk* (Civil Department.)
Percival, W. S., *Clerk* (Sum. Civil and Criminal)
Hore, T., *Usher* (absent)

Wilkinson, H. S., Esq., *Crown Advocate.*

S

德寶 *Pau-teh.*
27, Nanking Road.
SWEETMEAT CASTLE,
Pastry Cook, Confectioner, French Baker.
Poitevin, L., *Proprietor.*
Poitevin, Mrs. V. L.
Brown, R., *Assistant.*

T

屋代田 *Tia-toi-wu.*
1, Soochow Road.
TASHIROYA,
Dealers in Japanese Porcelains, Lacquer Wares, Curios, &c.
Kaneko, Kenjiro, *Manager.*
Kaneko, Tauesabro, *do.*

興庚 *Kang-hsing.*
6, Szechuen Road.
TATA & Co.
Tata, C. B.
Tata, Kakaus M.

豐廣 *Kwang-foong.*
10A, Foochow Road.
TAUMEYER & Co., *Merchants and Commission Agents.*
Taumeyer, Ernst
Nölting, Joh.
Wortmann, R.

行洋來泰 *T'a-lay.*
Ta-lay Buildings, French Bund.
TELGE, R.
Telge, R.
Fock, O.
Lieder, P...
Mandl, H.
Agents of the Hanseatic Fire Insurance Co. of Hamburg.

堂會酒戒
Ka-tsiu-hwui-dong.
18, Nanking Road.
TEMPERANCE HALL.
Muirhead, Rev. W., *President*
Macleod, Neil, M.D., *Vice-President.*
Lanning, G., *Hon. Secretary.*
McKiego, F., *Hon. Tre.*
Moheby, G., *Librarian.*
Grimmer, J., *Manager.*
Darnell, D.
Committee—Very Rev. Dean Butcher, Capt. C. J. Bolton, J. G. Purdon, Esq., C. Thorne, Esq., D. Cranston, Esq., Rev. W. S. Holt, and J. M. Rogerson, Esq.

紙聞新酒戒
Ka-tsiu-sin-wen-chi.
31, Kiangse Road.
TEMPERANCE UNION.

茂義 *Ne-mow.*
8, Foochow Road.
THURBURN & DUNN,
Stock and Share Brokers.
Thurburn, A.
Dunn, C. A. L.

易都 *Tu-e.*
TOZO, R. E.,
Bill and Bullion Broker.

T

齋石點 *Tien-shih-chai.*
Corner of Peking and Chekiang Roads.
TIEN-SHIH-CHAI PHOTO-LITHOGRAPHIC PUBLISHING WORKS.
Major Bros., *Proprietary Directors.*
Wong Chü-jen, *Managing Compd.*

利波 *Poo-le.*
Nanking Road.
TOILET CLUB, SHANGHAI
Polite, George, *Proprietor.*
Olive, P.
Tobe, John
Turakishi, M.
Kotaro, S.

TUGS—SHANGHAI TUG-BOAT ASSOCIATION.
Morris & Co., *Agents.*
Superintendent.
Captain C. McCaslin.
Captains.
J. Roberts, Grandon, Johnson, Garrett, Latham.
Engineers.
Jas. Bannerman, *Chief.*
Thomas, W. A., *Assistant.*
Tugs,
Fuh-le, Rocket, Samson, Fokelin, Titan.

泰祥 *Zeang-t'a.*
16, Kiukiang Road.
TURNBULL, HOWIE & Co.
Turnbull, William A. (abt.)
Howie, Wm.
Harding, J. W.
Scott, J. L.
MacGregor, A. P.
Smith, F. A.
Agents—Liverpool and London and Globe Insurance Co.

記華 *Wha-kee.*
13, Yangtsze Road.
TURNER & Co.
Cheetham, J. F.
Shewan, A.
Plant, J. L.
Agents—Northern Assurance Company.

茂松 *Soong-mow.*
39, Szechuen Road.
TWIGG, Mrs. P. O'B.,
Undertaker and Municipal Sextoness.

U

安保 *Pau-an.*
17A, Yangtsze Road.
UNION INSURANCE SOCIETY OF CANTON, LIMITED.
Jones, Douglas, *Agent.*
Keston, A. J.
Bago, A. de
Agents for Home and Colonial Marine Insurance Company (Limited.)
Head Office Hongkong—
Eda, N. J., *Secretary.*
London Branch, 9, Royal Exchange—
Jukes, M. P., *Agent.*

V

立威 *Ve-la.*
9, Miller Road.
VELA, M.

園花泰森在得未
Vi-ta Tse-sen-tah-wa-yuen.
6, Whang-poo Road.
VITA, ARTURO, *Professor of Music and Languages.*

利達亨 *Hang-dah-le.*
36, Nanking Road.
VRARD, L., & Co.
Storekeepers, and Watch and Clock Makers.
Sillem, H.
Laidrich, A.
Pfaff, Rud.
Grandguillaume, A.

W

和永 *Yung-ho.*
12, Szechuen Road.
WADE, H. T.,
Public Tea Inspector and General Commission Agent.

托華哈 *Hah-wo-t'oh.*
3, Balfour Buildings.
WAINEWRIGHT, R. E.,
Solicitor.
Harwood, H. G., *Clerk.*
Rowland, E. J. O., *do.*
Char Gno-kee, *do.*

勒華 *Wah-lah.*
9, Nanking Road.
Address—Shanghai Club.
WALLER, LL. EUE,
Public Buyer and Inspector of Strawplait, Share and General Broker.

記和 *Wo-che.*
34, Nanking Road.
WATERS & DALE,
Architects and Land & Estate Agents.
Waters, T. J., C.E., F.R.G.S.
Dale, Herbert W.

房藥大氏臣屈
Wa-son-se Tai-yeuk-fong.
24, Nanking Road.
WATSON, A. S., & Co.,
English & Foreign Chemists and Agents for the Hongkong Aërated Waters
Humphreys, J. D. (London.)
Davey, John, *Manager.*
Wilkins, E.
Agents for Morgan's Patent Plumbago Crucibles.

記葉 *Wee-kee.*
41, Kiangse Road, and 5, Ningpo Road.
WEEKS, T., & Co.
Drapers, Outfitters, Dry Goods Importers and Silk Mercers.
York, G. E.
Barkham, T. W.
Trueman, T. E.

W

茂新 *Sing-mow.*
2, The Bund.
WELD, DANIEL, (absent)
Gen. Broker & Auctioneer.

源開 *K'ay-neuen.*
WELLINGTON, Br. Barq.
Parker, J. H. P., *Commander.*
Stonehold, Hy., *Assistant.*
Fonseca, V. P., *Purser.*
Rowland, T. J., *Clerk.*

豐宜 *Ne-fung.*
23, Nanking Road.
WENNMOHS & Co.,
Successor to Ludage & Oelke.
Wennmohs, E.
Ramsay, A. C.

豐德會 *Way-tuh-joong.*
Ta-lay Buildings, French Bund
WHEELOCK & Co.
Auctioneers, Ship and Coal Brokers.
Wheelock, T. R.
Sharp, John
Hay, D.
Pemberton, T.
Gove, Frank
Gray, A. T.
Agents for The Shanghai Cargo Boat Company.

膺中 *Tsoong-yoong.*
32, Nanking Road.
WHITE & MILLER.
White, Augustus
Miller, John Irwin
Pak Choo, W.

泰謙 *Heim-ta.*
16, Canton Road.
WHITE & WELCH,
Public Tea Inspectors & General Commission Merchants.
White, William
Welch, Joseph
Bois, Edward

Sentance, W. V.
Agents for Scottish Union and National Insurance Co.

昌景 *King-chang.*
26, Nanking Road.
WILCK & MIELENHAUSEN,
Tailors and Outfitters.
Wilck, C.
Mielenhausen, J. W.
Birck, V.

和信 *Sing-wo.*
6, Peking Road.
WILKINSON & Co.
Stokes, Frank
Thompson, A. F.
Bury, A. J.

生金威 *Way-king-sun*
2, Balfour Buildings.
WILKINSON, H. S.,
H.B.M.'s Crown Advocate, Barrister-at-Law.

興泰新 *Sing-t'a-hsing.*
9, Szechuen Road.
WILSON, JOHN, *Merchant and General Commission Agent.*
Wilson, John
Adam, A., *Assistant.*

T U V W Y Z

W

記榮 *Wing-kee.*
1116, Broadway, Hongkew.
WING KEE & Co.,
Ship-Chandlers, Compradores and Storekeepers.
Young Jack, *Stevedore, and Ballast supplied all kinds.*

生醫牙 *Nga E-sung.*
2, The Bund.
WINN, H. H.,
Doctor of Dental Surgery.

孚同新 *Sin Doong-foo.*
11, Szechuen Road.
WINNER & Co., *General Commission Merchants.*
Winner, John H.
Seaman, J. F.
Davis, Edward ;
Botelho, B. M.
Agents for Guardian Assurance Co.

行洋富華 *Wa-foo.*
6, Soochow Road.
WOLFF, MARCUS
Bill and Bullion Broker.

行洋昌啟 *Che-Chong.*
12, French Bund.
WONG, C. T., & Co.
Wong Chin Tsan
Kwok Fai Ting

Y

YACHT CLUB, SHANGHAI
Roberts, John P., *Hon. Sec.*

昌元 *Yuen-cheong.*
1255, Broadway, Hongkew.
YUEN CHEONG & Co.,
General Store-keepers.

Y

發源 *Neuen-fa.*
YUEN FAH, Br. Sh.
Dobie, Wm., *Commander.*
Vieira, U. A., *Clerk.*
Tong Kun, *do.*

棧生悅 *Yuet-sung.*
119, Honan Road.
YUET-SUNG & Co.,
General Storekeepers, Wine and Spirit Merchants, Dealers in Canton Goods, &c.

廠冰記亦
Yah-kee-ping-chang.
YUH-KEE ICE HOUSE.
Liu Ah-sang, *Agent.*

否而食以 *E-za-erh-fuh.*
42, Rue Montauban.
YZOLPHE, G. B., *French Hair-Dressing Saloon.*

Z

生醫厘架則
Tse-cha-le E-sang.
34, Szechuen Road.
ZACHARIAS, V., M.D.,
Physician to German Consulate-General and I. M. Customs' Medical Attendant.

生醫部郭新
Sin-go-bu-e-sang.
11, Kiangse Road.
ZEDELIUS, C., M.D.

LIST
OF COAST AND RIVERINE STEAMERS
TRADING TO AND FROM SHANGHAI, AND ARRANGED ACCORDING TO THE NEW CUSTOMS' SIGNAL CARD.

CHIN-TUNG (1) 東鎮
Winsor, Jr., A., captain
Wright, A. H., chief officer
Downie, Archd. R., 2nd „
Crolius, V. F., chief engineer
Heilsted, A. E., 2nd „
Brown, Geo., 3rd „

LEE YUEN (2) 遠利
Sim, C., captain
Hampshire S. F., chief officer
Williams, W. S., 2nd „
Marshall, Wm., chief eng.
Graham, J., 2nd „
Stewart, John, 3rd „

PAU-TAH (3) 大保
Patterson, M. F., captain
Stackwood, W. J., chief officer
Conner, T. W., 2nd „
Pearce, Wm., chief engineer
Shearer, Archd., 2nd „
Richardson, F., 3rd „

FUNG-SHUN (4) 順豐
Tisdall, E. W., captain
Glenck, C., chief officer
Benning, Ed., 2nd „
Bayers, Wm. B., chief eng.
Tweedie, A. C., 2nd „
Rodger, H., 3rd „

CHI-YUEN (5) 遠致
Wallace, F., captain
Williams, chief officer
Pearce, Richd., 2nd „
Russell, Thos., chief engineer
Imt, J. D., 2nd „
Kilgour, 3rd „

YEH-SIN (6) 新日
Deegan, E. J., captain
Blethen, G. C., chief officer
Monson, N., 2nd „
McLean, C., chief engineer
Brown, G., 2nd „
Smith, D., 3rd „

HAE-SHING (7) 琛海
Peterson, R., captain
Warwick, J., chief officer
Grayson, J. H., 2nd „
Ferguson, G. H., chief engineer
Leonard, J. T., 2nd „
Kidd, Geo., 3rd „

HAE TING (8) 定海
Mavor, J., chief officer
Clements, E. W., chief eng.

HAE-AN (9) 晏海
Andrew, R. M., captain
Ferlie, W. R., chief officer
Newham, R. L., 2nd „
Miller, A., chief engineer
Robertson, A., 2nd „
Ord, Robt., 3rd „

TOO NAN (10) 南圖
Marsden, G., captain
Kielseth, T., chief officer
Ray, C., 2nd „
Thomson, 3rd „
Jones, D. W., chief engineer
McElroy, Thos., 2nd „
Vernon, 3rd „

KUNG-PAI (12) 北拱
Buchanan G., captain
Brissander, F. A., chief officer
Dale, C., 2nd „
Ortwin, Wm., chief engineer
Beveridge, Robt., 2nd „
Halbornie, Peter, 3rd „

FU YEW (13) 有富
Barfoot, P., captain
Banfield, R., chief officer
Hallahan, J., 2nd „
Lamond, W., chief engineer.
McMinnamin, W., 2nd „
McWallace, H., 3rd „

YUNG-CHING (14) 清永
Andrew, R., captain
Nelson, J. N. S., chief officer
Lowe, J. P., 2nd „
Clements, Jas., chief engineer
Cromarty, T., 2nd „

MEE-FOO (16) 富美
Lunt, W., captain
Palmquist, A., chief officer
Green, C. M., 2nd „
Spears, Wm., chief engineer
McCallum, D., 2nd „
Parker, W., 3rd „

YUNG-NING (17) 寧永
Lincoln, R., captain
Clifford, C. H., chief officer
Turkington, R. H., chief eng.

FU SHUN (18) 順富
Croad, A., captain
Adkins, James, chief officer
St. John, H., 2nd „
Shearer, J., chief engineer
Brown, Wm., 2nd „
Wallace, G., 3rd „

KWONG-LEE (19) 利廣
Wells, H., captain
Graham, W., chief officer
Watt, J., chief engineer
Cairncross, A., 2nd engineer

TUNG-TING (20) 庭洞

KIANG-TEEN (21) 天江
Boswell, J. B., captain
Sutton, H. C., chief officer
Jossby, Chas., 2nd „
Ross, T., 3rd „
Wilson, J., pilot
Harvey, R. S., chief officer
Kirk, J., 2nd „
Smith, Wm., 3rd „

Kiang-yu (23) 裕江
Knights, A. E., captain
Null, R. C., chief officer
Edwards, 3rd ,,
Johnson, W. P., chief pilot
Clark, Geo., 2nd ,,
Ferrier, Jas., chief engineer
Brown, A., 2nd ,,
Mackenzie, 3rd ,,

Kiang-kwan (24) 寬江
Perkins, J. A., captain
Sandstedt, K., chief officer
Lawson, 3rd ,,
Wilson., chief pilot
Kennedy, Frank, chief eng.

Kiang-yung (25) 永江
Chang, S. C., captain
Park, S. D., chief officer
Nelson, A., chief pilot
Matzen, F., assist. ,,
Ferguson, Alex., chief eng.
McAlister, Alex., 2nd ,,
Fyffe, John, 3rd ,,

Kiang tung (26) 通江
Yankowsky, R., captain
Weise, chief officer
Carlson, chief pilot
Young, J., chief engineer
Page, David, 2nd ,,
Adams, 3rd ,,

Kiang-piau (27) 表江
Aping, chief pilot
Assi, 2nd ,,
Bernard, Chas., chief engineer

Kiang-foo (28) 孚江
Morse, A. H., captain
Wigand, Geo. V., chief officer
Crocer, John, 3rd ,,
Lindstrom, K., chief pilot
Frank, F., 2nd ,,
Prevost, F., chief engineer
McDonald, J., 2nd ,,
Air, Alex., 3rd ,,

Kiang-ping (29) 平江
Holmes, C., captain
Sanderson, W., chief eng.

Poo-chi (31) 濟普
Lancaster, M. V., captain
Dempsey, J., chief officer
Probers, G., 2nd ,,
Morrison, J., chief engineer
Sinclair, F., 2nd ,,
Ewing, Wm., 3rd ,,

Sin Nanking (41) 陵南新
Waddilove, Wm., captain
Howden, J. L., chief officer
Pearson, A. G., 2nd ,,
Good, Henry, chief engineer
Ferguson, J., 2nd ,,
Reynolds, 3rd ,,

Pechili (42) 隸直北
Hurst, H. S., captain
Aubin, F. P., chief officer
Knutsen, Peter, 2nd ,,
Klinghorn, John, chief eng.
Mensie, Edwin, 2nd ,,
Jackson, A. Jas., 3rd ,,

Taku (43) 沽大
Davies, T. L., captain
Moore, Lewis W., chief officer
Cellars, T. H., 2nd ,,
McFarlane, John, chief eng.
Thomson, William, 2nd ,,
Bannerman, 3rd ,,

Wing-sang (45) 生永
St Croix, d'A., captain
Amy, J. P., chief officer
Nainby, E. J., 2nd officer
Knipple, D. E., 3rd ,,
Law, A., chief engineer
McPhedran, D. 2nd ,,
McIntosh, W. W. 3rd ,,
Russell, R., 4th ,,

Kow-shing (46) 陞高
Webster, D. J., captain
Hankinson, R., chief officer
Wanstall, R., 2nd ,,
Sinclair, A., chief engineer
Macrae, H. J., 2nd ,,
Dunn, W., 3rd ,,

El Dorado (47) 和順
Young, W. U. M., captain
Payne, Geo., chief officer
Whiteford, Lee, 2nd ,,
Wilson, G. G., chief engineer
Laus, A., 2nd ,,
Davidson, W., 3rd ,,

Nanking (48) 陵南
Ballantine, C. R., captain
Wood, W., chief officer
Earl, P., 2nd ,,
Davidson, G., chief engineer
Sinclair, D., 2nd ,,
Kirkwood, 3rd ,,

Sze woo (49) 和時
Mitchell, J. A., captain
Mack, R., chief officer
Mengens, E. J., 2nd officer
Davie, A. A. chief engineer
Wilson, D., 2nd ,,
McIntyre, P., 3rd ,,

Kung-wo (50) 和公
Flaux, A. E., captain
Wilson, A. S., chief officer
Centerwall, C. M., 2nd ,,
Clough, H. P., 1st pilot
Maclean, D., 2nd ,,
Parlane, Jas., chief engineer
McPherson, D., 2nd ,,

Fuh-wo (51) 和福
Davis, Frederick, captain
Slessar, Joseph, chief officer
Vicino, Biagio, 2nd ,,
Brown, James, chief engineer
Kerr, John D., 2nd ,,

Tai-wo (52) 和泰
Friend, A. T., captain
Pybus, Henry, chief officer
Macallum, T. A., chief eng.
Murdoch, J., 2nd ,,
Russell, R., 3rd ,,

Fook-sang (53) 生福
Hogg, H. W., captain
Bremner, James, chief officer
Hoopes, Charles J., 2nd ,,
Buchanan, David, chief engn.
McDonald, Donald, 2nd ,,
Westcott, Ch. F., 3rd ,,

Po-sang (54) 生寶
Irvine, T. W., captain
Easson, James, chief officer
Mitchell, Alfred, 2nd ,,
Craig, R., chief engineer
Roberts, J., 2nd ,,
McFarlane, P., 3rd ,,

Kwong-sang (56) 生廣
Jackson, captain
Wilde, S., chief officer
Leask, W. U. G. 2nd officer
Lees, R., chief engineer
McIntyre, W., 2nd ,,
Murchie, J., 3rd ,,

Taisang (57) 生泰
Bamford, Thos. captain
Allason, Edwin, chief officer
Griffin, Edwd., 2nd ,,
Bradley, Robt., 3rd ,,
Maxwell, John, chief engineer
Wildridge, Alex. 2nd ,,
Jenkins, Wm., 3rd ,,
Fraser, Robert, 4th ,,

Tunsin (60) 信惇
Goodfellow, H. S., captain
Brown, Wm., chief officer
Fawcett, George, 2nd ,,
Coole, John, 3rd ,,
Mitchell, John, chief eng.
Hildreth, G. A., 2nd ,,
Bowes, John, 3rd ,,

Hankow (61) 口漢
Oxtoby, J., captain
Christie, W., chief engineer
Aird, J., 2nd ,,

Pekin (62) 京北
McQueen, R., captain
Harris, J. H., chief officer
Sell, 2nd ,,
Law, Alex., chief engineer
Miller, D., 2nd ,,
Riach, Peter, 3rd ,,

Shanghai (63) 海上
Martin, David, captain
Anderson, H. C., chief officer
Barrett, Charles, 2nd ,,
Collins, William, chief pilot
McGregor, Daniel, chief eng.
Angove, Richard, 2nd ,,
Miller, Boyd, 3rd ,,

Ngan-kin (64) 慶安
Perks, Charles L., captain
Dinnie, Frank, chief officer
Howell, C., 2nd ,,
Stevens, Thomas, chief pilot
Place, Edward, 2nd ,,
Campbell, Wm. H., chief eng.
Simpson, Stephen, 2nd ,,
Campbell, Jas. A., 3rd ,,

Ichang (65) 昌宜
Batten, H., captain
Harris, J. B., chief officer
Martinson, W., 2nd ,,
Smith, R., 3rd ,,
MacDougall, J., chief eng.
Bruce, A., 2nd ,,
Lock, G., 3rd ,,

Swatow (67) 頭汕
Gleason, E., captain
Murbeck, W., chief officer
Stenhem, 2nd ,,
Agnew, R., chief engineer
Kay, W., 2nd ,,
Snellgrove, 3rd ,,

Tientsin (69) 天津
Robinson, E. L. M., captain
Groundwater, A., chief officer
Smith, T. H., 2nd ,,
Hogg, G. S., chief engineer
Macmillan, Donald, 2nd ,,
Burton, N., 3rd ,,

Chefoo (70) 罘芝
Hutchinson, J., captain
Cottier, J., chief officer
Hogg, T., 2nd ,,
Wright, J., chief engineer
Carter, W. T., 2nd ,,
Foster, K., 3rd ,,

Newchwang (71) 莊牛
Peoples, J. S., captain
Polson, J., chief officer
Finnes, W. James, 2nd ,,
Mitchell, R., chief engineer
Wikley, J., 2nd ,,
Campbell, J., 3rd ,,

Wenchow (72) 州溫
Young, James, captain
Vallack, Geo., chief officer
Hanfrey, John, 2nd ,,
Carnie, Charles, chief eng.
Bailey, James, 2nd ,,
Barclay, Andrew, 3rd ,,

Hoihow (74) 口海
Varden, A., captain
Shepherd, A., chief officer
Banks, T., chief engineer
Ramsay, A., 2nd ,,
Macpherson, A., 3rd ,,

Keelung (75) 籠雞
Clegg, T. H., captain.
Parry, T. J., 2nd officer
Malcolm, A., chief engineer
Polson, H., 2nd engineer
Kater, T., 3rd ,,

Tamsui (76) 水淡
Wylus, W. S., captain
Crawford, A., chief officer
Dalvey, H., 2nd ,,
Ferguson, E., chief engineer
Taylor, H. J., 2nd ,,
Elder, John, 3rd ,,

Chung-king (78) 慶重
Deville, W. N., captain
Smith, John, chief officer
Shewan, 2nd ,,
Hardie, W., chief engineer
Hutchison, J., 2nd ,,
Henderson, J., 3rd ,,

Wu-chang (79) 昌武
Gyles, Thomas, chief officer
Stott, Alex., 2nd ,,
Sharples, John chief engin.
Murray, A. W., 2nd ,,
Frischling, Frank, 3rd ,,

Whampoa (80) 浦黃
Williams, J. E., captain
Smith, chief officer
Christie, J., chief engineer
Bibby, J., 2nd ,,
Pearman, W. F., 3rd ,,

Woosung (81) 淞吳
Hunt, Augustus, captain
Nelson, Robt., chief officer
Anderson, Olof, 2nd ,,
Lamb, Andrew, chief eng.
Stewart, James, 2nd ,,
Walker, Hugh, 3rd ,,

Tai wan (82) 灣臺
Cotter, W., captain
Bisby, W. J., chief officer
Machlan, J., chief engineer
Watt, R. D., 2nd ,,
Bell, Peter, 3rd ,,

Chang-chow (83) 洲漳
Whittle, J., captain
Evans, W., chief officer
Bewley, H. G., chief engin.
Neal, J., 2nd ,,
McWilliams, J., 3rd ,,

Amoy (90) 門厦
Potts, W., captain

Chinkiang (91) 江鎮
Herrmann, C., captain
D'Egville, L. H., chief officer
Smellmeh, F., 2nd ,,
Bisk, H., chief engineer
Bark, Fred., 2nd ,,
Carey, Edward, 3rd ,,

NINGPO (92) 波寧
Crawford, R., captain
Roberts, A., chief officer
Robinson, M., 2nd ,,
Main, Ed. J., chief engineer
Brown, H., 2nd ,,
Broadfoot, S., 3rd ,,

PEKING (93) 京北
Heuermann, G., captain
Köhler, R., chief officer

YANGTSZE (94) 子揚
Schultz, J., captain

NAGOYA MARU (102)
Walker, Wilson, captain
Pannocker, G., chief officer
Edwards, G J., 2nd ,,
Clarke, G. G., 3rd ,,
Robinson, J., chief engineer
Stewart, A., 2nd ,,
Scott, John Thos., purser
Spottiswoode, C. N., fr. clerk

GENKAI MARU (103)
Conner, Geo. W., captain
Fisher, Arthur, chief officer
Morris, J. A., 2nd ,,
Turner, C., 3rd ,,
Noble, E., chief engineer
Duncan, J. A., 2nd ,,
Gellifur, C. N., 3rd ,,
Wallin, A. C., 4th ,,
Dresser, C., purser
Walker, W., freight clerk

TOKIO MARU (104)
Swain, Richard, captain
Sommer F. L., chief officer
Inman, W. L., 2nd ,,
Arvidson, J., 3rd ,,
McCormick, P. J., ch. engin.
Steffan, P., 2nd ,,
Heyser, H., 3rd ,,
Keating, J., 4th ,,
Henny, Chas. T., purser
Frey, H. J., freight clerk

HIROSHIMA MARU (105)
Wynn, John, captain
Thomson, W., chief officer
Dunbar, F. A., 2nd ,,
Daniels, F., 3rd ,,
Harlow, L., chief engineer
Mitchell, W. L., 2nd ,,
Sharne, G., 3rd ,,
Meanbert, C., 4th ,,
Down, W., purser
Howard, F., freight clerk

TAKASAGO MARU (108)
Young, Chr., captain

INGO (109)
Jessolsen, J., captain
Trennt, M., chief officer

KUA HSING (121)
Anderson, N. P., commander
Chenoweth, R., 2nd officer
McKechnie, A., 3rd ,,
Shaw, R. W., engineer.
Jackson, A., 2nd ,,

W. CORNS DE VRIES (126)
Smith, W., captain
Smith, D., chief officer
Thorkle, E., 2nd ,,
Wise, W., chief engineer
Randle, W., 2nd ,,
Holmes, G., 3rd ,,

WAVERLEY (127)
Stout, captain

HIKKYOSHI MARU (128)
Black, W., captain
Death, W. H., chief officer
Huntriss, W., 2nd ,,
Bell, W., chief engineer
Roche, J., 2nd ,,

YOHITOMO MARU (129)
Gall, D. E., captain
Murray, A., chief officer
Hallstrom, P., 2nd ,,
Pritchitt, J., chief engineer
Thomas, W. E., 2nd ,,
Mooney, J., 3rd ,,

TYNE (132)
Hazard, Johnson, captain
Carr, William, chief officer
White, James, 2nd ,,
Jobling, Joseph, chief eng.
Young, Joseph, 2nd ,,
Brady, James, 3rd ,,

STORE NORDISKE (135)
Suenson, captain

WHA-ON (136)
Carosai, captain

DRUTUS (138)
Vooge, J. F., captain

SUAL (143)
Scott, A. J., captain
Newcomb, H., chief officer
Snow, P. Le, 2nd ,,
Ritchie, D., chief engineer
Scott, J., 2nd ,,

BAIKAL (145)
Danilovich, S. M. S., captain
Rostelman, A., chief officer
Rollman, Alex., 2nd ,,
Kalikanoff, N., chief engineer
Birman, Theodor, 2nd ,,

GREATHAM HALL (146)
O'Brien, Thos., captain
Christiansen, E C., ch. officer
Hill, R., 2nd ,,
Moor, Andrew, chief eng.
Tolpo, John, 2nd ,,
Rombasoff, N., 3rd ,,

CHEFOO HONG LIST,

1884.

BEACH HOTEL.
Buschendorff, A. W., Proprietor.

DEBERTON, Dr. J. G., L.M.Q.C.P., & L.C.S., Ireland.

CHEFOO FAMILY HOTEL. Too-shan.
Newman, Mrs. E.
Newman, Miss E. V.
Newman, Miss E. M.
Newman, E. S.

CHEFOO FILANDA (LIMITED.)
Anz, O., Manager.
Gipperich, G.
Becher, H., Engineer.

院書業敬
Ching-ye-shu-yuan.
CHEFOO READING ROOM FOR CHINESE.
Donnelly, A. R., Hon. Sec.
Li Allio, Hon. Chinese Sec.

記仁 *Yin-kee.*
CLARKE, HEAD & Co.
Clarke, W. J.
Head, R. L.
Agents—
Imperial Fire Insurance Company;
Marine Insurance Company, Limited.

有富 *Fu-yu.*
CONSTERDINE, H., & Co.
Fuller, W. R.
Smith, J.
Hesse, E.
Price, R. J.
Legg, W. H.

Consulates.

官事領國奥
Ao-kuo-ling-shih-kuan.
AUSTRO-HUNGARY—
Brenan, Byron, Acting-Consul.

BELGIUM—
Fergusson, T. T., Consul.

瓦得事領國丹大
門官
DENMARK—
Eckford, A. M., Acting Vice-Consul.

官事領國法
Fah-kuo-ling-shih-kuan.
FRANCE—
Brenan, Byron, V.-Consul.

官事領國德大
Ta-to-kwoh-ling-shih-kwang.
GERMAN EMPIRE—
Hagen, C., Vice-Consul.

官事領國英
Ying-kuo-ling shih-kuan.
GREAT BRITAIN—
Brenan, Byron, Consul.
Van Ess, W. A., Constable.

事領國本日大
門衙
Ta-ji-pen kwoh ling-shih-ya-men.
JAPAN—
Higashi, G., Acting Consul.
Uyeno, S., Secretary.

NETHERLANDS—
Eckford, A. M., Act.-Consul.

RUSSIA—
Fergusson, T. T., Vice-Consul.

SWEDEN AND NORWAY—
Eckford, A. M., Vice-Consul.

UNITED STATES—
Platt, Archer R., M.D., Consular Agent.

記和 *Wo-kee.*
CORNABE & Co.
Cornabé, W. A. (absent.)
Eckford, A. M.
Donnelly, A. R.
Lavers, P. F.
Seth, A. P.
Allin, L.
Agents for—
Royal Insurance Co. (Fire and Life);
Canton Insurance Office;
Yangtsze Insurance Association;
Samarang Sea and Fire Insurance Co.;
Imperial Fire Insurance Co.

典寶台烟 *Po-king.*
CRASEMANN & HAGEN.
Hagen, C.
Myers, H. S.
Oastmann, C.
Irons, F.
Agents for—
Colonial Sea and Fire Insurance Co. of Batavia;
Bremen Underwriters;
Magdeburger Allgemeine Versicherungs Actien Gesellschaft;
Oosterling Sea and Fire Insurance Co. of Batavia;
Second Colonial Sea and Fire Insurance Co. of Batavia;
Batavia Sea and Fire Insurance Co.;
Hamburg Magdeburger Feuer Versicherungs Gesellschaft;
China Navigation Co.

Chefoo.
Chinkiang.
Who's Who.

Customs
(Imperial Maritime.)

關海東 *Toong-Hai-kwan.*

Dene, I. M., Commissioner.
Campbell, S., 2nd Assist.
Yorke, R. S., 3rd do.
Pym, E. T., 4th do.
Brereton, J. O., L.R.C.P.I., Medical Officer.
Liang Ateem, Chinese Clerk.
Choong Yiu, do.
Jennings, T. C., Tide-Surveyor and Harbour Master.
Olson, A., Boat Officer.
Reeves, G., Examiner.
Campbell, T. M., Assist. do.
Roberts G., do do.
Horning, J., Tidewaiter.
Murray, G. T., do.
Dawson, C. P., do.
Marshall D., do.
Elder, A. G., do.
Betts, T., do.

—

'Chefoo' Light.
Scholimus, C. J., Light-keeper and Engineer-in-charge.
Walter, J. F., assist. Keeper and Engineer.

—

'Shantung' Light.
Amy, C. O., Light-keeper in charge.
Wiese, D., Light-keeper.

—

'Howki' Light.
Eccles, J., Light-keeper-in-charge.

—

'Shantung South East Promontory' Light.
Anderson, J., Light-keeper.

—

大滋 *Tseu-ta.*

Fergusson & Co.
Fergusson, Thos. T.
Du Jardin, F.
Thiom, E. A.
Wake, J. P.
Agents for Lloyds';
Indo-China S. N. Co. (Limited);
North-China Insurance Co.;
Chinese Insurance Company (Limited);
Merchant Shipping and Underwriters' Association, Melbourne;
North-British and Mercantile Insurance Co;
China Fire Insurance Co. (Limited);
P. & O. S. N. Co.;
Hongkong and Shanghai Bank.

—

行洋利傅
Fu-li-yang-hong.

Fuller, W. R.,
Architect and Builder.

—

Gardner, Mrs. F. E.,
Baker and Provisioner.

—

Glen Vue House.
Gardner, Mrs. F. E.
Gardner, W. A. E. (absent.)

—

Indo-China Steam Navigation Co. (Limited.)
Fergusson & Co., Agents.

Knight, W., Butcher
White Chapel Road.

—

Lyell, Thos.,
Marine Surveyor.

—

Maclean, Geo. F.
Maclean, Geo. F.
Burgoyne, Geo.
Agent—Union Insurance Society of Canton;
Hongkong Fire Insurance Company;
China Traders' Insurance Company;
Mitsu Bishi Mail Co.;
Scottish Imperial Life Insurance Co.;
London Assurance Corporation;
Japanese Consular and Postal.

—o—

Missionaries, Churches, &c.

—

丕第高 *Kaou-ti-pae.*

American Southern Baptist Mission.
Crawford, Rev. T. P., D.D.
Crawford, Mrs. (Tengchow.
Holmes, Mrs. (absent.)
Moon, Miss
Pruitt, Rev. C. W.
Pruitt, Mrs.
Halcomb, Rev. N. W.
Roberts, Miss

—

會老長國美大
Da-mei-kwoh-chiang-laou-wey.

American Presbyterian Mission.
Corbett, Rev. H.
Leyenberger, Rev. J. A.
Nevius, Rev. J. L., D.D.
Anderson, Miss (absent.)
Bainbridge, Miss
Berry, Miss
Reid, Rev. G.
Mateer, Rev. C. W., D.D., (Tengchow.)
Mills, Rev. C. R., do.
Hayes, Rev. W. M., do.
Shaw, Mrs. M. H., do.
Neal, Jas. B., M.D., do.
Laughlin, Rev. J. H., (Wehien)
Mateer, Rev. R. M., do.
Smith, H. R., M.D., (absent)
Murray, Rev. John (Chi-nan-foo)
Hunter, Rev. S. A. D., M.D. (Chi-nan-foo.)
Bergen, Rev. Paul D., do.

—

China Inland Mission.
Beller, Rev. F. W.
Beller, Mrs.
Elliston, W. L.
Pruen, W. L., L.R.C.P.
Sharland, Mrs.
Taylor, H. Hudson
Groom, Miss Annie L.
Seed, Miss
Malpass, Miss

—

Corfe, Rev. C. J., M.A.

—

Hildesley, W. S.

—

臣廉韋 *Wie-lien-ch'ên.*

National Bible Society of Scotland.
Williamson, Rev. A., LL.D., Agent.

—

Nightingale, J.

—

Roman Catholic Mission.
Schang, F. Césaire, M.O.
Lui, John

Society for the Propagation of Gospel.
Vincent, J. R.

—

United Presbyterian Church of Scotland Mission.

臣廉韋 *Wei-lien-ch'ên.*

Williamson, Rev. A., LL.D.

清永西 *Hsi-yung-ch'ing.*

Westwater, Rev. Alexander.

潤永西 *Hsi-yung-yun.*

Westwater, A. Macdonald, L.R.C.P. and S. Edin.

醫賚包 *Pao-lay-teh.*

Platt, Archer R., M.D.,
General Practitioner.

—

遜沙新 *Sing-so-sung.*

Sassoon, E. D. & Co.

—

唎哈台烟 *Ha-lee.*

Sietas, H., & Co.,
Naval Contractors and Storekeepers.
Biehl, J. C.
Hansen, Adolph
Hansen, H. A
Block, J.

Chinkiang
Foochow.
Hankow.
Ichang.
Kiukiang
N'chwang
Ningpo.
Peking.
Tientsin.
Wenchow.
Wuhu.
...orea.
Who's Who.

昌泰 *T'ai-Chang.*

WADLINGH & EMERY, *General and Commission Merchants.*
Wadliogh, E. C. (absent.)
Emory, D. A.
Yung-fung-an.
Li-chih-tai.
Yü-ching-chun.

室醫國英
Ying-kwo I-shih.

WHITE, DR. ROBERT GODFREY.

和日 *Yet-chung.*

WONG, BROTHERS & CO., *Merchants, Commission Agents, and Importers of General Merchandise.*
Wong Yu-yü, *Manager.*
F. T. Chio, *Clerk.*

FOOCHOW HONG LIST,

1884.

祥天 *Teen-cheang.*

ADAMSON, BELL & CO.
Dorner, Thomas M. (abt.)
Cave-Thomas, F.
Woodley, M.
Stewart, A.
Souza, H. B. de
Agents for Chinese Insurance Company (Limited);
Commercial Union Assurance Co., London—Fire & Marine Branches;
South Australian Insurance Co. (Limited), Adelaide;
Lancashire Insurance Co., Manchester;
Thames and Mersey Marine Insurance Co., Limited, London.

AGRA BANK (LIMITED.)
Gilman & Co., Agents.

太興 *Tai-hing.*

BATHGATE & CO., Merchants.
Bathgate, John
Pim, Tobias

興福 *Fook-hing.*

BIRLEY & CO.
Sanderson, J. L. P.
Gardiner, Geo. E. J.
Agents—Union Marine Insurance Co., Ld.;
Guardian Fire and Life Assurance Co.;
Norwich Union Fire Insurance Society.

古太 *Tai-ku.*

BUTTERFIELD & SWIRE.
Smith, H. D.
Baker, H.
Martin, G.
Agents—British and Foreign Marine Insurance Co. (Ld.);
London and Lancashire Fire Insurance Co.;
Royal Exchange Assurance;
China Navigation Co. (Ld.);
Ocean Steamship Co.

CHARTERED BANK OF INDIA, AUSTRALIA AND CHINA.
Marshall, A. C., Acting Agent.

行銀利有 *Yew-lee.*

CHARTERED MERCANTILE BANK OF INDIA, LONDON AND CHINA.
Purdon & Co., Agents.

局閩商招船輪
Chew-Seong-Koh.

CHINA MERCHANTS' STEAM NAVIGATION CO.
Tong Ying-chai, Agent
Tong Shun-ue, Sub-Agent
Loa Kok Hu, Shipping Clerk.
Lin Yek-chow, Writer.
Ho Lue-shek, Chinese Clerk.
Lin Kien-poo, do.
Ma Tang-foug, do.
Lin Sew-tu, Shroff.
Leong Lun, Godown Man.

Steam Launch "*Min.*"
Tsoi Wai-chuen, Engineer.

COMPTOIR D'ESCOMPTE DE PARIS.
Cochinard, F.

Consulates.

DENMARK—
Pollard, T., Consul.

FRANCE—
Frandon, E., Vice-Consul.
Zi, Joseph, Interpreter.
Tso, Lettré.

官事領國德大
Tai Tê Kwok ling shi kwan.

GERMAN EMPIRE—
Wingate, J. C. A., Actg. Consul.

門衙事領英大
Ta-ying-ling-shih Ya-mên.

GREAT BRITAIN—
Sinclair, Chas. A., Consul.
Allen, E. L. B., Act. Assist. and British Postal Agent.
Fraser, E. H., Act. Asst.
British Vice-Consulate, Pagoda Anchorage.
Mansfield, R. W., Vice-Consul.
Head, Thomas, Constable.

NETHERLANDS—
Pim, T., Consul.

PORTUGAL—
Frandon, E.
Pereira, B., Assistant.

RUSSIA—
Popoff, N. A., Consul.

SPAIN—
Frandon, E., Vice-Consul.
Rosa, D. da, Assistant.

SWEDEN AND NORWAY—
Simonson, G., Vice-Consul.

Foochow. Hankow. Ichang. Kiukiang. N'chwang. Ningpo. Peking. Tientsin. Wenchow. Wuhu. Corea. Who's Who.

大美國領事官

Ta Mai kwok ling -sih kwan.

UNITED STATES—
Wingate, Joseph C. A., Consul.
Cowles, Jr., John P., Vice-Consul, and Interpreter.
Hartwell, Charles S., Asst. and Acting Marshal.

—

Customs

(IMPERIAL MARITIME.)

海關 *Hai Kwan.*

Hannen, C., Commissioner.
Carrall, J. W., Acting Deputy Commissioner.
Muller, G. F., Assistant.
Touche, J. D. D. de la, do.
Lowder, E. G., do.
St. Croix, C. W. de, do.
Tai Tszo-king, Chinese Clerk.
Ho Chee-chuen, do.
Choah Leng-tee, do.
Lake Chow-leong, do.
Li Tat-chang, do.

Medical Officers.

Rennie, Dr. T., at Nantai.
Adam, Dr. T. B., „
Underwood, Dr. J. J., at Pagoda Anchorage.

Pagoda:

Parkhill, S., Tide Surveyor and Harbour Master.
Field, A. W., Assistant Tide Surveyor.

Nantai:

Jezowski, J. von, Assist. Tide Surveyor.
Smith, J. D., Examiner.
Young, S., do.
Waller, H. J., Asst. do.
Walter, W. B., „ do.
Creak, W., „ do.

Pagoda:

Cornelli, J., Tidewaiter.
Taylor, W. K., do.
Seier, J. F. J., do.
Hunter, J. M., Probationary Tidewaiter.
Galletti, N. J. B., do.
Segardal, J. N., do.
Schmidt, A., do.
Bull, E., do.

Police Force, Pagoda.

Livingston, J., Sergeant.

—

多比 *Do-bee.*

DOBIE & Co., Ship-chandlers and Coal Dealers, Pagoda Island.
Shaw, S. L., in charge.
Agents, Shanghai L.P.O.

—

ENGLAND, F. H., *Merchant.*
England, F. H.
Ramsay, R., Tea Inspector

—

FOOCHOW CLUB.
Allum, W. K., Chairman.
Hobbs, P. G., Hon. Treas.
Committee—H. A. Northey, T. Pim, J. L. P. Sanderson, G. Slade, J. C. A. Wingate.
Phillips, J., Secretary.

福州船塢 *Foochow-poo.*

FOOCHOW DOCK-YARD.
Nesbitt, J. E.

—

FOOCHOW GENERAL CHAMBER OF COMMERCE.
Angus, A. F., Chairman.
Schoenfeld, F., Vice-Chairman
Committee—T. Pollard, H. Baker.
Weeks, C. D., Secretary.

—

FOOCHOW HAIR DRESSING SALOON.
Campbell, H., Proprietor.

—

FOOCHOW HERALD.
Foochow Printing Press, Proprietors.

—

FOOCHOW HOTEL.
Brockett, G. T., Proprietor.

福州冰廠 *Ping-cheong.*

FOOCHOW ICE AND AERATED WATER Co.
Begley, C. W.
Steamers — "Alice," "Grip," "Mingan," "Nantai."

—

FOOCHOW NATIVE HOSPITAL AND DISPENSARY.
Rennie, Dr., Medical Officer.
Adam, Dr., do.

—

FOOCHOW SEAMEN'S HOSPITAL.
Pagoda Anchorage.
Underwood, J. J., M.D.
Mansfield, R. W., Hon. Sec. and Treasurer.
Orosio, F. A., Steward.

—

天裕 *Teen-ee.*

FORSTER, JOHN, & Co.
Forster, John (absent).
Sutherland, Hugh
Deacon, Herbert
Gilbert, William
Souza, Jr., B. D. de
Agents—North British and Mercantile Insurance Co.;
The Imperial Marine Insurance Co. (Limited.)

—

公易 *Koong-yek.*

GALTON and Co.
Galton, W. P.
Northey, H. A.
Postlethwaite, J. W.
Cooper, F. B.
Ellerton, H. B.
Agents—
Phœnix Assurance Co.;
Universal Marine Insurance Co., Limited;
Merchants' Marine Insurance Co., Limited;
China Traders' Insurance Co. Limited;
Austrian Insurance Company "Donau;"
Lancashire Insurance Co.;
Austro-Hungarian Lloyd's Insurance Co.

乾記 *King-kee.*

GIBB, LIVINGSTON and Co.
Tennant, H. F., Agent and Tea Inspector.
Clymo, H.
Agents—Union Insurance Society of Canton;
Home and Colonial Marine Insurance Co.;
Commercial Union Assurance Co., Life Department;
Eastern and Australian Steamship Co. (Limited);
China Fire Insurance Co. (Limited);
Oriental Bank Corporation;
New Zealand Insurance Co.

—

太平 *Tai-ping.*

GILMAN and Co.
Harton, Jr., W. H.
Slade, G.
Grant, L. M. F.
Agents for Lloyds';
Association of Underwriters of Glasgow;
Underwriters' Association of Liverpool;
Merchant Shipping and Underwriters' Association of Melbourne;
North-China Insurance Co. Limited;
Ocean Marine Insurance Co.;
London Assurance Corporation (Fire);
Imperial Fire Insurance Co.

—

興隆 *Hing Loong.*

GITTINS, JOHN & Co., Merchants.
Gittins, John (absent)
Chambers, H. J. J.
Gittins, Jr., Thomas
Pereira, J. P.
Agents—Sun Fire Office.

—

大丹國電線行

Ta-tan-kwo-teen-hsien-hong.

GREAT NORTHERN TELEGRAPH COMPANY.
Krogh, Lieut. C. H., R.D.A., Agent.

—

義利 *Ee-lee*

HEDGE and Co.,
Dunn, Thos. (absent)
Jones, Thos F.
Collie, J. A.
Churchill, H. W.
Agents, Shanghai L.P.O.

—

匯豐銀行

Wuy-fung-ngan-hong.

HONGKONG AND SHANGHAI BANKING CORPORATION.
Gardner, J. P. Wade, Acting Agent.
Banff, F. W., Assistant Accountant.

—

同祥 *Tung-cheong.*

HUNTER, W. L.
Tilley, J. W.
Graham, Wm., Tea Inspector.
Rohn, G. E., do.
Agent—Straits Insurance Company, Limited.

IMPERIAL ARSENAL AT FOOCHOW.
Giquel, Prosper, Director (abst.)
Medard, L., Secretary of the Direction, p.i.

—

School for Naval Construction.
Medard, L.
Navigation School.
Taylor, C. H.

—

義和 *Ee-wo.*

JARDINE, MATHESON and Co.
Pollard, T.
King, C.
Roza, D. da
Agents—Canton Insurance Office, Limited;
Hongkong Fire Insurance Co.;
Alliance Fire Insurance Co.;
Indo-China Steam-Ship Co., Limited;
Douglas Steam-Ship Co. Ld.;
Australasian, China, Japan & Straits S.S. Co.;
Glen Line of Steamers.

—

怡典 *Yee-hsin.*

KAW HONG TAKE AND Co., Merchants, Commission Agents, Ship Brokers.
Kaw Hong Take.
Ung Choon Tee, Assistant.
Kaw Eong Hean.
Agents for On Tai Insurance Co., Limited;
Magdeburgh General Insurance Co., Limited.

—

LOWE, R., Pagoda Anchorage.

—

Missionaries, Churches, &c.

美部傳道公會

Mêi-pu-chw'en-tao-kung-hwui.

AMERICAN BOARD OF COMMISSIONERS FOR FOREIGN MISSIONS.
Baldwin, Rev. C. C., D.D.
Hartwell, Rev. C.
Walker, Rev. J. E.
Whitney, H. T., M.D. (abt.)
Woodin, Rev. S. F.
Newton, Miss E. J.
Harris, Miss A. B.

—

美以美教會

Mi-i-mi-kau-hwui.

AMERICAN METHODIST EPISCOPAL MISSION.
Sites, Rev. Nathan (absent.)
Ohlinger, Rev. F.
Plumb, Rev. N. J.
Wilcox, Rev. Myron C.
Smyth, Rev. G. B.
Trask, Miss S., M.D.

—

安立間會

Ang Lik Kang Hui.

CHURCH MISSIONARY SOCIETY.
Wolfe, Rev. J. R.
Stewart, Rev. R. W., M.A.
Lloyd, Rev. Llewellyn
Banister, Rev. W.
Martin, Rev. J.
Shaw, Rev. C.
Gordie, Miss

館醫教聖
Shêng-chiào-i-kuan.
MEDICAL MISSIONARY HOSPITAL.
Whitney, Henry T., M.D.

昌協 *Hip Cheong.*
MORRIS, B. J., & Co.,
Merchants.
Morris, B. J.

NATIONAL BANK OF INDIA, LIMITED.
Turner & Co., Agents.

文隆 *Loong Mun.*
NEWMAN & Co.,
Public Tea Inspectors and Commission Merchants.
Newman, Walter (absent)
Fairhurst T.
Agents—City of London Fire Insurance Co., Limited.

昌裕 *Yü-cheong.*
ODELL & LEYBURN,
Merchants.
Odell, John (absent.)
Leyburn, Frank.
Pye, Charles.
Agents—Royal Insurance Company;
London and Provincial Marine Insurance Co.

茂太 *Tai-mow.*
OLIVER, GEO., & Co.,
Merchants.
Oliver, George (London.)
Pind, John do.
Crocker, E. A.
Featherstonhaugh, M. H.
Allen, Richard B.
Agents—
Queen Insurance Co. (Fire);
Scottish Imperial Insurance Co. (Life.)

記慶 *Khen-kee.*
OLLIA, D. D. & Co.
Laheir, E. S. (Hongkong.)
Ollia, D. D. (Taiwanfoo.)
Keeka, F. C.
Kohidr, C. B.
Vajifdar, J. M. (Amoy.)
Shroff, C. F. do.
Jamshedjee, D. (Takao.)
Vania, A. D. (Taiwanfoo.)

ORIENTAL BANK CORPORATION.
Gibb, Livingston & Co.,
Agents.

記和 *Wo-kee.*
PHILLIPS, JOSEPH,
Exchange Broker and General Commission Agent.
Phillips, J.

裕公 *Kung Eü.*
PHIPPS, PHIPPS and Co.
Phipps, A. L. (absent.)
Phipps, H. G.
Smith, C. D.
Agents—Liverpool and London and Globe Insurance Co.;
The Marine Insurance Co. London.

昌阜 *Fow-chung.*
PIATKOFF, MOLCHANOFF & Co.,
Merchants.
Piatkoff, M. F. (absent)
Molchanoff, J. M. (Hankow.)
Speshiloff, S. J.
Cheerkoff, S. A.
Moskaloff, A. P.
Cheredoff, P. N.

PILOTS.
Pagoda Anchorage.
Mitchell, W. J.
Oeltze, C.
Johnson, F.
Semonson, E. F.
McKay, A.
And 4 Chinese, outside pilots.

恒寶順
PONOMAREFF, P. A. & Co.
Solomonoff, A. A.
Brinoshib, N. N.

POST OFFICE—LOCAL.
Pagoda Anchorage.
Doble & Co., Agents.
Shaw, S. L., *in charge.*
Foochow.
Hedge & Co.

珍同 *Tung Chun.*
PURDON & Co., Merchants.
Maitland, J. A. (absent.)
Purdon, J. G. do.
Angus, A. Forbes, Tea Inspector.
Street, F. F.
Agents—Chartered Mercantile Bank of India, London and China;
Lion Fire Insurance Co., Limited;
The China Shippers Mutual Steam Navigation Co.

RENNIE & ADAM, DRS.
Rennie, T., M.D., M.O.
Adam, T. B., M.B., M.O.,
Honorary Medical Officers to "Foochow Native Hospital."

臣彌羅 *Lo-pi-sun.*
ROBERTSON, H. J.,
Architect & Builder.

行洋順隆
Leong-cheung-yong-hong.
ROZARIO & Co.
Commission Agents.
Rozario, D. do

昌旗 *Kee-chong.*
RUSSELL and Co.
Greig, M. W.
Pereira, D.
Agents—Yangtsze Insurance Association.

遜沙 *Sa-ning.*
SASSOON, DAVID, SONS, & Co.
Ezekiel, N. D.
Levy, S. E.

遜沙新 *Sin Sa-soon.*
SASSOON & Co., E. D.
Merchants.
Perry, J. S., Agent.
Catton, E. A.

SAUNDERS, Capt. J. C.
Marine Surveyor, Pagoda Anchorage.

記生 *Sang-kee.*
SCHOENKE, F.,
Watchmaker & Photographer.

豐裕 *Yue-foong.*
SCHÖNFELD & Co.
Schönfeld, F.
Krolın, Werner

SHAW Capt. S. L.,
Marine Surveyor, Pagoda Hill, Pagoda Anchorage.
Marine Surveyor for the Germanic Lloyds, and the Local Insurance Offices.

臣禪 *Seem-sun.*
SIEMSSEN & Co.
Siemssen, G., Tea Inspector.
Flothow, C.
Agents—Globe Marine Insurance Co. (Limited) of London;
The Dusseldorf Universal Marine Insurance Co. (Limited) of Dusseldorf;
German Lloyd Marine Insurance Co. (Limited) Berlin.

貞永 *Wing-ching.*
SILVERLOCK, JOHN, & Co.,
Merchants.
Silverlock, Jr., J.
Agents for the Fire Insurance Association, Limited.

房藥大氏臣屈
Wa-son-n Tai-yenk-fong.
THE DISPENSARY.
Watson & Co.,
Dispensing and Family Chemists, Cigar, Wine and Spirit Merchants, Aërated Water Manufacturers, &c.
Humphreys, J. D. (H'kong)
Dampney, J.

豐順 *Shoon-foong.*
TOKMAKOFF, SHEVELEFF & Co.
Shoolingin, P. N.
Molchkoff, J. M.

記華 *Wha-kee.*
TURNER and Co.
Walkinshaw, A. W.
Greaves, A. R.
Mendes, A. N.
Agents for Netherlands India Sea and Fire Insur. Co.;
Home and Colonial Marine Insurance Co.;
Northern Fire and Life Assurance Co.;
P. and O. S. N. Co.;
National Bank of India (Limited.)

生醫與大翁
Yung-tai-ng-Eeing.
Pagoda Anchorage.
UNDERWOOD, J. J., M.B., C.M., L.R.C.S.E.

和中 *Chung-wo.*
WEEKS & FRY,
Exchange & General Brokers, Commission Agents and Public Accountants.
Weeks, C. D.
Fry, F. W. (absent)

HANKOW HONG LIST,

1884.

祥天 *Teen-tsung.*

ADAMSON, BELL & Co.
Agents—Commercial Union Assurance Co.;
South Australian Insurance Co.;
Mercantile Marine of South Australia;
Thames and Mersey Marine Insurance Co., Limited.

AGRA BANK, LIMITED.
Ramsay, Hugh F., Agent.

德立 *Leih-tih.*

BEGG, C., M.B., C.M., Pres. M.M.F., In charge of Hankow Hospital.

昌亨 *Hang-chang.*

BURNETT & Co.
Burnett, J. H.

利有 *Yew-lee.*

CHARTERED MERCANTILE BANK OF INDIA, L'DON & CHINA.
Jardine, Matheson & Co., Agts.

CHINA NAVIGATION CO.
Hulks:—
Lanerfield / *Formosa* } T. Weatherstone in charge.

Consulates.

官事領國奥
Ta ao kwo ling sze kwan

AUSTRO-HUNGARY—
Alabaster, Chaloner, Consul.

DENMARK—
Alabaster, Chaloner, Consul.

事領法大
Ta-fa ling-sze.

FRANCE—
Imbault-Huart, Act.-Consul.

署事領英大
Ta Ying ling shi shu.

GREAT BRITAIN—
Alabaster, Chaloner, Consul.
Joly, H. B., Assistant.
Stephens, T., Constable.

館公蘭荷大
Ta ho lan-kung-kwan.

NETHERLANDS—
Walter, W., Vice-Consul.

署事領洋西大
Ta Se-yang-leang-kwan.

PORTUGAL—
Evans, J. H., Consul (absent.)

官事領國俄大
Ta Ho Lo kwo ling-sze kwan.

RUSSIA—
Imitreevsky, P. A., Consul.

府事領美大
Ta-mee ling-sze-kwan.

UNITED STATES—
Shepard, Isaac F., Consul for Hankow, Kiukiang and Ichang.
Jenkins, M. A., Interpreter.
—, U.S. Marshal.

Customs.

關漢江 *Kiang Hankwan.*

Indoor Staff.

Bredon, R. E., Commissioner.
Kocher, Ia., Deputy-Commissioner.
Chalmers, J. L., 2nd Assistant
Fauvel, A. A., 2nd do.
Von Kohrberg, P., 4th do.
Dent, V. E. J., 4th do.
Moorhead, J. M. 4th do.
Harris, A. H., 4th do.
Begg, Chas., M.B., Medical Officer.
Lim Chin-guan, Principal Clerk.
Sung Ying-chun, 2nd Clerk.
Woo Kwang-yin, 3rd Clerk.
Tin Ching-hsiang, 4th Clerk.
Cain King-son, Candidate Clk.

Outdoor Staff.

Moorehead, T., Tidesurveyor and Harbour Master.
Mesney, J., Boat Officer.
Mercan, J., Examiner.
Lant, T., do.
Brandon, R. F., Assist. Exam.
Liedeke, L., do.
Becke, F. G., do.
Nazer, R., 1st class Tidewaiter.
Claremont, G., 2nd do.
Freeth, G. J., 2nd do.
Green, J. T., 3rd do.
Christensen, L., 3rd do.
D. Land, F. J., 3rd do.
Seitz, C. L., 3rd do.
Lehberger, J. S. 3rd do.
Wilgaard, J. J., 3rd do.
Deane, A. G., Salt Watcher.
Sewell, T. H., do.

興德 *Teh-hing.*

DRYSDALE, RINGER & Co.
Ringer, J. M., (Shanghai.)
Wood, T.
Robertson, A. L.
Pullen, H. (Kiukiang.)
Haste, J.
Weatherstone, Thos., in charge of the Hulks.
Agents for
China Navigation Co (Limtd.);
China Traders' Insur. Co. (Ld.);
Queen Fire Insurance Co.;
Hongkong Fire Insurance Co. (Limited);
Chartered Bank of India, Australia and China.

順寶 *Paou-shun.*

EVANS, PUGH & Co.
Evans, J. H. (absent.)
Pugh, W. do.
Walter, Wm.
Agents Peninsular & Oriental S. N. Co.;
North-China Insurance Co., Limited;
Phœnix Assurance Co. of London;
Marine Insurance Co.

FISHER, E.,
Bill and Bullion Broker.

泰隆 *Loong-thie.*

GORDON BROTHERS,
Commission Merchants.
Gordon, William Grant
Agents for The Chinese Insurance Company, Limited;
Messageries Maritimes Co.;
North British and Mercantile Insurance Co.

樓波 *Po-lo.*

HANKOW CLUB.
Price, Alexander, Secretary.

HANKOW DAIRY.
Watson, J.

HANKOW GENERAL CHAMBER OF COMMERCE.
Price, Alex., Secretary.

館字印生萬
Wan sang.

HANKOW PRINTING OFFICE.
Jenkins, M. A.

房藥大氏臣和
Wat-son-si-da-yah-oong.

HONGKONG DISPENSARY.
A. S. Watson & Co.,
Dispensing and Family Chemists; Cigar, Wine and Spirit Merchants; Stationers, and Agents for Hongkong Aërated Waters.
Humphreys, J. D. (London.)
Laub, J. L., Geo.

豐滙 *Heng-foong.*

HONGKONG & SHANGHAI BANKING CORPORATION.
Leith, A., Agent (absent)
Nicholson, J. C., Asst. Acct.

號銀官稽乾
Keen-yu-kuan-yin hauh.

I. M. CUSTOMS BANK.

和怡 *E-wo.*

JARDINE, MATHESON & Co.
Inglis, R.
Agents for Chartered Mercantile Bank of India, London & China;
Canton Insurance Office;
Lloyds;
Indo-China Steam Navigation Co., Limited.

行洋泰公 *Kung-tai.*

JENKINS, M. A.

記仁 *Jin-kee.*

JEBSEN & Co.
Jebsen, F.
Bremelios, A. F. des
Agents for Gibb, Livingston Co.;
Oriental Bank Corporation;
Union Insurance Society of Canton, Limited;
China Fire Ins. Co., Limited;
Imperial Fire Ins. Co., L'don.

LODGE "STAR OF CENTRAL CHINA,"
No. 611, S.C.

Gordon, C.,	W.M.
Weatherstone, T.,	S.W.
Mesney, J.,	S.W.
Kindblad, A. W.,	J.W.
Titoushkin, N., Sec. & Trea.	
Brady, H. F.,	S.D.
Olsen, A.,	J.D.
Becke, F.	I.G.
Stephens, T.,	O.G.

德厚 *How-teh.*

LUCAS & Co.
Agents for Royal Exchange Assurance Corporation, Marine Branch.

芳元 *Yuen-fong.*

MAITLAND & Co., Merchants.
Agents—Lion Fire Insurance Co., Limited.

和信 *Sin-ho.*

MAJOR BROS.
Major, Frederick
Major, Ernest
Findley, John

Missionaries, Churches, &c.

會督監美大
Ta-mae-keen-tuh-hwuy.

AMERICAN EPISCOPAL MISSION.

生醫翟 *Tih-e-sang.*
Boon, W. A., M.D., Wuchang.

生先郭 *Kuoh-sien-sang.*
Graves, Rev. F. R., Wuchang.
Graves, Mrs.

生先蘇 *Soo-sien-sang.*
Sowerby, Rev. H.
Sowerby, Mrs.

生先羅 *Loo-sien-sang.*
Locke, Rev. A. H., Wuchang.
Locke, Mrs.
Sayers, Mrs. K. J., Wuchang.

院醫堂主天
Tien-choo-tang i-yuen.

CATHOLIC HOSPITAL FOR CHINESE, (in charge of the Sisters of Roman Catholic Orphanage.)

會地內 *Nuy-ti-hway.*

CHINA INLAND MISSION.
Andrew, G. (Yunnan.)
Andrew, Mrs., do.
Eason, A. (Chungking.)
Clarke, G. W. (Tali.)
Clarke, Mrs., do.
Broumton, J. F. (Kwei-yang.)
Broumton, Mrs., do.
Riley, W. (Chentu.)
Riley, Mrs., do.
Nicoll, Mrs. (Chungking.)
Fausset, Miss A. L., do.
Clarke, S. R. (Chentu)
Thompson, D.B., do.
Dorward, A. C. (Hunan.)
Parker, G. (Kansuh.)
Parker, Mrs., do.
Wilson, Miss, (Hanchung.)
Jones, Miss H. (Kansuh.)
Easton, G. F. (Hanchung.)
Easton, Mrs., do.
King, Geo., do.
Hunt, H. W. (Kansuh.)
Hunt, Mrs. do.
Sambrook, A. W. (Fancheng.)
Coulthard, J. J. (Wuchang.)
Dick, H. (Honan.)
Stevenson, O. (Yunnan.)
Butland, Miss (Chentu.)
Dowman, Miss do.
Strond, Miss do.
Edwards, Dr. E. H. (Ch'king.)

CHURCH OF ST. JOHN THE EVANGELIST.
In charge of Wesleyan and London Mission Societies.
Ramsay, H. F.,
Hon. Sec. & Tres.

館醫英授敎
Chiao-su-ying-shoo-kwan.

FOSTER, Rev. ARNOLD, B.A.

會敦倫 *Lun-tun-hway.*

LONDON MISSIONARY SOCIETY.
John, Rev. Griffith
Bonsey, Rev. A.
Gillison, Rev. Thomas, M.D.
Owen, Rev. William (Wuchang)
Bryson, Rev. T. (Wuchang) (absent.)

翰約計 *Chi-yoh-han.*

NATIONAL BIBLE SOCIETY OF SCOTLAND.
Archibald, John

堂主天 *Tien-choo-tang.*

ROMAN CATHOLIC MISSION.
Vandagna, Rev. Angelo
Poell, Rev. Martin
Lera, Rev. Diego (Wuchang.)
Carlassare, Rev. E. do.
Hofman, Rev. J.
Umile, Dr. Volta (Wuchang.)

堂嬰育 *Yü-in-tang.*

ROMAN CATHOLIC ORPHANAGE.
Mother Paula Viemara, Superior,
Sister Carolina Tarchini.
" Rosa Piccinelli.
" Rachele Paloari.
" Giovanna Biancardi.
" Teresa Archinti.
" Giuseppina Galli.
" Santa Mosini.
" Florinda Gandini.
" Giuditta Bornasconi.
" Natalina Pietra.
" Erminia Nardon.
" Maria Bonza
" Regina Galbiati

堂音福 *Fuh-yin-tang.*

WESLEYAN METHODIST MISSIONARY SOCIETY.
Scarborough, Rev. W.
Nightingale, Rev. A. W.
Nightingale, Mrs.
Mitchill, C. W.
Hill, Rev. D. (Wuchang.)
Brewer, Rev. Jno. W. do.
Brewer, Mrs. do.
Bramfitt, Rev. Thos. (Wusueh.)
Bramfitt, Mrs. do.
North, Rev. T. E. do.
North, Mrs. do.
Watson, Rev. D. H. do.
Watson, Mrs. do.
Bell, Rev. Joseph (Tehngan.)

洋保正 *Chan-po-yang.*

MUNICIPAL COUNCIL.
Woodward, R.H.S., Chairman
Braden, R. E.
Molchanoff, J. M.
Sharp, W. F., Secy.
Olsen, A., Manager, Local Post Office.

洋保巡英大
Ta-ying-sun-po-yang.

MUNICIPAL POLICE.
Olsen, A., Sergeant.
27 Chinese Constables.

如麗 *Lee-su.*

ORIENTAL BANK CORPORATION
Jardein & Co., Agents.

順寶 *Po-shun.*

P. & O. S. N. Co.
Evans, Pugh & Co.

昌阜 *Fow-cheong.*

PIATKOFF, MOLCHANOFF & Co.
Piatkoff, M. F. (absent)
Molchanoff, J. M.
Molchanoff, N. M.
Titoushkin, N. N.
Panoff, J. K.
Bazorimanoff, N. K.
Sobonnikoff, P. A.
Totchninoff, S. A.
Martsinkevics, P. P.
Richards, J.
Koosnetzoff, W. M. (K'kiang)
Spashiloff, S. J. (Foochow.)
Chirkoff, S. A. do.
Moskaleff, A. P. do.
Cheredoff, P. N. do.
Belogolovy, A. A., Tientsin Agent.

順恒 *Hung-shun.*

PONOMAREFF, P. A., & Co.
Litvinoff, S. W.
Cumming, N. A.
Parshakoff, P. S.
Robertson, jr., H.
Molontloff, J. E. (Tientsin)
Nikiforoff, M. G. do.
Agents — Russian "Volunteer Fleet Society."

PRICE, ALEXANDER,
Bill and Bullion Broker.

平太 *Ta-ping.*

RAMSAY, HUGH F.
Agent—Universal Marine Insurance Co., Limited.
Agra Bank, Limited.
Royal Insurance Co. (Fire)
Steamers of Geo. McBain.
Straits Insurance Co.

威化阿 *Ho-hwa-way.*

RODEWALD & Co.

昌桓 *Hang-chang.*

RODIONOFF, A. L. & Co.
Sharkoonoff, L. P.
Lobedeff, J. R.
Lobedeff, N. R.
Gordon, C. W.
Lobedeff, W.

昌旗 *Ke-chang.*

RUSSELL & Co.
Agents—Yangtsze Insurance Association.
Comptoir d'Escompte de Paris.

昌昇 *Sing-chang.*

SCHOFIELD & Co.,
Commission Agents.
Schofield, H.

SHARP, W. F.,
Bill, Bullion and General Broker, &c.

和普 *Poo-ho.*

SHARP, W. F.

豐順 *Shoon-foong.*

TOKMAKOFF, SHEVELEFF & Co.
Tokmakoff, J. F. (Moscow.)
Molotkoff, O. J.
Startseff, A. D. (Tientsin.)
Plesnevich, L. A.
Molotkoff, N. J.
Marsh, S.
Karelina, V. M.
Shoolingin, N. P. (Foochow)
Melnikoff, J. M. "

記華 *Wha-kee.*

TURNER & Co.
Agents Northern Assurance Co.; National Bank of India, Limited.

記泮 *Pan-kee.*

WOODWARD, R. H. S.,
Commission Merchant.

ICHANG HONG LIST,

1884.

Consulates.

大英領事署 *Ta-ying-ling-shih-shu.*

GREAT BRITAIN—
Gardner, C. T., Consul.

大美國衙門 *Ta-me-kwoh-ya-men.*

UNITED STATES—
Shepard, General Isaac F., Consul for Ichang, Hankow, Kiukiang (Resident at Hankow.)

Customs.

宜昌關 *Ich'ang Kuan.*

Morgan, F. A., *Acting Commissioner.*
Henry, A., *4th Assistant, B. (Medical Officer.)*
Au Kai-ting, *Chinese Clerk.*
Le Breton, L., *Assistant Examiner.*
Grainger, S. J., *3rd Class Tidewaiter.*

LITTLE, ARCHIBALD J., Merchant.

Missionaries.

CHURCH OF SCOTLAND MISSION.
Dowsley, Rev. Andrew, B.A.
Dowsley, Mrs.
Cockburn, Rev. George, M.A.
Cockburn, Mrs.
Wood, Peter
Wood, Mrs.

WOODWARD, R. H. S., Commission Merchant.

KIUKIANG HONG LIST,

1884.

怡和 *E-wo.*

ANDERSON, ROBT., & Co.
Anderson, Robt. (absent)
Anderson, J. H. „
Tritton, E. W. „
Grant, P. McGregor (S'hai.)
Allen, A. E.
Agents for Jardine, Matheson & Co.; the Peninsular and Oriental Steam Navigation Co.; Canton Insurance Office, Ld.; Union Insur. Society of Canton, Ld., Hongkong Fire Ins. Co., Ld., the China Fire Ins. Co., Ld., the Chinese Insur. Co., Ld.; the Marine Insur. Co., Ld.; the Yangtze Insurance Association; Ch. Mer. Bk. of India, London and China; Indo-China S. N. Co.

天裕 *Teen-yu.*

CAMPBELL, ALEX.
Campbell, Alex.
Agent for the North-China Insurance Company, Ld.
Hongkong and Shanghai Banking Corporation.
Sun Fire Office.
Str. *Saud.*
Str. *W. Corres de Viles.*

九江招商局 *Kiu-kiang-ch'o-song-chol.*

CHINA MERCHANTS' S. N. Co.
Shen Tsoo king, Manager.
Tong Fai kum, Shipping Clerk

太古躉船 *Ta Lou-tan-chuen*

CHINA NAVIGATION Co.
Hulk *Sultan,*
Kolod, J., in charge.

Consulates.

大澳領事衙門 *Ta ao Ling shih Ya-mên.*

AUSTRO-HUNGARY
Jamieson, George, Consul.

大丹領事衙門 *Ta-tan Ling-shih Ya-mên.*

DENMARK.
Jamieson, George, Consul.

大法領事 *Ta-fa ling-sze.*

FRANCE.
Imbault Huart, Act. Consul (Hankow)

大英領事衙門 *Ta-ying Ling-shih Ya-mên.*

GREAT BRITAIN.
Jamieson George, Consul.
Rowe, Charles, Constable.

大和蘭國公館 *Da ou lan kuang kuan*

NETHERLANDS.
Allen, A. E., Act. Vice Consul

大美領事衙門 *Ta-mei Ling-shih Ya mên.*

UNITED STATES.
Shepard, General Isaac F., Consul for Ichang, Hankow and Kiukiang (resident at Hankow.)

九江新關 *Kiukiang Sin-kwan.*

Customs.

Simpson, C. Lenox, Commissioner.
Morehouse, W. Noyes, 1st Assistant.
Philips, G. J. A., 3rd do.
Maclean, A. H. H., 4th do.
Günther, J. C. H., Tide-Surveyor and Harbour Master.
Land, J. M., Assistant Tide-Surveyor.
Hamlyn, J. G., Examiner.
Bono, C. V., Asst. do.
Mullins, D., do. do.
Meyer, C. A., Tidewaiter.
Johnsen, A., do.
Braun, R., do.
Nelson, H., do.
Harris, J. E., do.
Smith, S., do.
Hewett, W. J., do.

德興 *Teh-hsing.*

DRYSDALE, RINGER & Co.
Pullen, H.,
Agents for China Navigation Company, Limited;
China Traders' Insurance Company, Limited;
North British and Mercantile Insurance Company;
British and Foreign Marine Insurance Company.

九江招商局躉船 *Kiu-kiang-ch'o-song chol-tun-cun.*

Hulk "CANOPUS."
Wong Mui-she, Hulk-keeper.

天裕躉船 *Teen-yu tan chuen.*

HULK "HIRONEMUS."
Leu Sei kiap, Hulk-keeper.

怡和躉船 *E wo tan-chuen*

HULK "ORISSA."
Alsing, August Hildebrand, In charge.

怡和 *E-wo.*

JARDINE, MATHESON & Co.
Allen, A. E., Agent.

Missionaries, Churches, &c.

福音堂 *Fuh-yin-t'ang.*

AMERICAN METHODIST EPISCOPAL MISSION.
Hykes, Rev. Jno. R.
Kupfer, Rev. C. F.
Hykes, Mrs. R. S.
Kupfer, Mrs. L. E.

會地內 *Nay-ti-hway.*

CHINA INLAND MISSION.
(Ta-ku-tan.)
Cardwell, J. E.
Cardwell, Mrs. J. E.

堂主天 *Tien-tchou-tang.*

Kiang-si Sept.
(North Kiang-si.)

FRENCH MISSIONARIES.
Bishop Bray, Apost. Vicar.
Anot, Rev. Père
Sassi, Rev. Père
Portes, Rev. Père
Dauverchain, Rev. Père
Lefebvre, Rev. Père
Vic, Rev. Père
Ciceri, Rev. Père
Chasle, Rev. Père
Tamet, Rev. Père
Remy, J. P.

Kiang-si Mérid.
(South Kiang-si.)
Bishop Rouger, Apost. Vicar.
Hosent, Rev. Père
Fusco, Rev. Père
Pérès, Rev. Père
Lagarde, Rev. Père

SISTERS OF THE CHARITY.
Sister Foubert, Sup.
" Théron.
" Ducci.
" Ryan.
" Tchen.

坊子孝 學飛女 *Nü-i-hsiao Hsiao-tsü-fang.*

WOMAN'S FOREIGN MISSIONARY SOCIETY OF THE M.E. CHURCH.
Howe, Miss Gertrude (in U.S.)

昌阜 *Fow-chang.*

MOLOTKANOFF & Co.
Koosnetzoff, B. M., Manager.

MUNICIPAL COUNCIL—
Hykes, J. R., Chairman.
Allen, A. E., Hon. Secy. & Trea.

昌阜 *Fow-cheong.*

PIATKOFF, MOLOTKANOFF & Co.
Koosnetzoff, B. M.

豐順 *Shun-foong.*

TOKMAKOFF, SHEVELEFF & Co.
Kisseleff, M. G., Manager.

行順義 *E-shun.*

UNDERWOOD, GEORGE R., M.D., Physician and Surgeon.

NEWCHWANG HONG LIST,

1884.

昌旗 *Chee-chang.*

BANDINEL & Co.
Bandinel, J. J. F.
Agents for Imperial Fire Insurance;
Deutscher Lloyd;
Mitsu Bishi Mail S. S. Co.;
China Shipowners Association.

來遠 *Yuen Lae.*

BUSH, BROS.
Bush, Henry E.
Cooper, Fred. P., Assistant.
Bush, H. A., do.
Prosch, G. do.
Agents for Canton Insur. Office;
North-China Insurance Co.;
China and Japan Marine Insurance Company;
Lancashire Insurance Co.;
China Traders' Insurance Co.;
Lloyds'—London;
Hongkong Fire Insce. Office;
Scottish Imperial Insurance Co. (Life);
Chinese Insurance Company, Limited;
Underwriting and Agency Association;
Germanic Lloyds;
Yangtsze Insurance Association;
Union Insurance Society of Canton, Limited;
London Assurance Association, Limited (Fire.)

CHINA NAVIGATION COMPANY (LIMITED)
Bush, Brothers, Agents.

行洋來克
Ker-li-yang-hong.

CLYATT & Co., Store-keepers, Commission Agents, Auctioneers and Coal Merchants.
Clyatt, W. B. (absent.)

Consulates.

AUSTRO-HUNGARY.
Allen, Herbert J., Consul.

DENMARK—
Allen, Herbert J., Vice-Consul.

FRANCE—
Allen, Herbert J., Vice-Consul.

門衙事領國德大
Ta-tê-kuo ling-shih yamên.

GERMAN EMPIRE.
Allen, Herbert J., Vice-Consul.

門衙事領國英大
Ta-Ying-kuo ling-shih ya-mên.

GREAT BRITAIN—
Allen, Herbert J., Consul.
Farmer, Charles, Constable.

門衙事領國本日大
Ta Jih-pên-kuo Ling-shih Yamên.

JAPAN—
Bandinel, J. J. F., Consular Agent.

門衙事領國和大
Ta Ho-kuo Ling-shih Ya-mên.

NETHERLANDS—
Bandinel, J. J. F., Consul.

門衙事領國威瑞大
Ta Jui-wei-kuo Ling-shih Ya-mên.

SWEDEN & NORWAY—
Allen, H. J., Acting-Consul.

門衙事領國美大
Ta Mei-kuo Ling-shih Ya-mên.

UNITED STATES—
Bandinel, J. J. F., Vice-Consul.

Customs.

Moorhead, R. B., Commissioner.
Unwin, F. S., Assistant.
McOsborne, W., do.
Morrison, J., M.D., Medical Officer.
Brenan, E. V., Tide-Surveyor and Harbour Master.
Loft, L., Boat Officer.
Sayle, W. J., Examiner.
Edgar, J., Assistant Examiner.
Burns, J., Tidewaiter, 1st class.
Whitlock, G., do. 2nd class.
Hondro, C.K.R., do. 3rd class.
Jules, H. J., do. 3rd class.

LIGHTSHIP "NEWCHWANG."
Orfeur, W. W., Act. Captain.
Paulsen, P. N., 1st Mate.
Deits, J., 2nd Mate, (in charge of tender.)
Hammeran, J. H., acting 2nd Mate.

林瑞 *Sui-lin.*

DAVIES, T. & Co., Ship-Chandlers.
Davies, T.

DEUTSCHE DAMPFSCHIFFS RHEDEREI ZU HAMBURG.
(Kingsin Line.)
Bush, Brothers, Agents.

HECKENDORFF, J. J., Surveyor for Lloyds Agents, Germanic Lloyds, and Local Insurance Offices.

INDO-CHINA STEAM NAVIGATION COMPANY (LIMITED.)
Bush, Brothers, Agents.

JARDINE, MATHESON & Co., Merchants.
Bush, Brothers, Agents.

KEMPF, H.,
Ship's Compradore and Proprietor of "The Union Inn."

Missionaries.

Hunter, J., M.D.
Ross, Rev. John.
Macintyre, Rev. John.
Carson, Rev. James.
Webster, Rev. J.
Christie, Dr. Dugald
Webster, Mrs.
Christie, Mrs.
Ross, Mrs.
Carson, Mrs.
Macintyre, Mrs.

ROMAN CATHOLIC MISSION.
Duball, C., Evêque of Hollina, Apost. Vicar Mandchourie.
Emonet, N. M., Apost. Mis.
Ten Sisters of Providence.

MORRISON, W., M.B. & C.M., Edinr. Univ.

𨵾港寫字房
Lin-can-hsei-tze-ton.

PILOTS—
Pilot Office, on the Bund,
F. A. Schultze & Co., Agents.
McThorn, H.
Blachford, B. F.
Richards, O. C.
Fredrickson, A.
Tandberg, L. J.
Smith, A. L. E.
Jorgensen, J. (absent)
Banker, W. S.
Place, J. E.
Jürgensen, A.

Carlos, B.

吟利洋行
Hu-li-yang-hang.

SCHULTZE, F. A., & Co.,
Shipchandlers and General Storekeepers, Auctioneers, Ship Brokers, Commission Agents and Oil Refiners.
Houckendorff, J. J.
Elberg, J.

UNION INN, THE
Kempf, H., Proprietor.

瓦先生英國領事衙門
Wa-hsien-shêng Ying-kuo-ling-shih-ya-men.

WATSON, J., M.D., Edin. Un., L.R.C.S.E.

NINGPO HONG LIST,

1884.

COMMERCIAL UNION ASSURANCE CO. OF LONDON.
Life Department.
Davidson & Co., Agents.

Consulates.

AUSTRO-HUNGARY—
Cooper, W. M., Consul.

DENMARK—
Cooper, W. M., Vice-Consul.

大德領事衙門
Dah-ta ling-z-ngô-meng.

GERMANY—
Meyer, H. B., V.-Consul (abt.)
Hartmann, Julius, Acting Vice-Consul.

大英公館
Ta-ying Kung-kuan.

GREAT BRITAIN—
Cooper, W. M., Consul.
Wilkinson, Will. Henry, Assistant.
Tomlinson, Walter L., Constable.

BRITISH POSTAL AGENCY.
Wilkinson, Will. Henry, Packet Agent.

大荷蘭領事衙門
Who-lang-ling-z-ngô-meng.

NETHERLANDS—
Hartmann, J., Acting-Consul.

大瑞威瑙威領事衙門
Sa-weh-nau-wey-ling-z-ngô-meng

SWEDEN AND NORWAY—
Hartmann, J., Acting-Vice-Consul.

大美公館
Da-meh Kung-kuan.

UNITED STATES—
Stevens, Edwin, Consul.
Yang Ho Hang, Interpreter
Chang Per Chên, Writer.

浙海關 *Ché-hai-kwan.*

Customs.

Kleinwächter, F., Commissioner
Grimani, E. H., 2nd Assistant.
Innocent, J. W., 3rd do.
Lay, W. G., 4th do.
Henderson, W. A., Medical Officer.
Klieve, A., Tide Surveyor and Harbour Master.
Clarke, G., Assistant Tide Surveyor (Chinhai.)
Burke, J. W., Examiner.
Kingsley, T. H., 3rd class Tidewaiter.
Haughton, F., 2nd do. do.
Mondini, P., 3rd do. do.
Allsborn, F. J., 3rd do. do.
Wright, J., 3rd do. do.
Truby, J. T., Prob. do.

廣源 *Quong-yuen.*

DAVIDSON & Co.
Davidson, Wm. (absent)
Davidson, R. M.
Davidson, P.
Davidson, G.

Agents for Canton Insur. Office;
China Fire Insurance Co.;
Indo-China Steam Navigation Company, Limited;
North-China Insurance Co.;
Hongkong Fire Insurance Co.;
Hongkong & Shanghai Banking Corporation, (Limited);
China Navigation Co. (Ld.);
Lloyds'.

美益洋行 *Me-ih.*

HARTMANN, J., Merchant.
Agent for the
Hanseatic Fire Insurance Co. of Hamburg;
Yangtsze Insurance Association;
Chinese Insurance Co., Ld.;
Messrs. Siemssen & Co.'s line of steamers.

寧順 *Ning-shing.*

McCASLIN & Co.,
Straw Goods and Commission Merchants.
McCaslin, U.

Missionaries, Churches, &c.

大美浸禮公會
Da Me Tsing-li Kong-wo.

AMERICAN BAPTIST MISSION.
Lord, Rev. E. C., D.D.
Jenkins, Rev. H. (Shaou-hying)
Jenkins, Mrs. (absent.)
Barchet, S. P., M.D.
Barchet, Mrs.
Goddard, Rev. J. R. (absent.)
Goddard, Mrs. do.
Mason, Rev. G. L.
Mason, Mrs.
Lightfoot, Miss [illegible]. B.
Inveen, Miss Emma.
Adams, Rev. J. S. (Kin-hwa)
Adams, Mrs. do.

大美國長老公會
Da Me Koh Trâng Lao Kong W[illegible].

AMERICAN PRESBYTERIAN MISSION.
(U.S.M.P.C.)
Butler, Rev. John and Mrs.
McKee, Rev. W. J. and Mrs.
Stubbert, J. E., M.D. (absent)
Warner, Miss S. A.
Judson, Rev. J. H. and Mrs., (Hangchow.)
Mills, Rev. F. V. and Mrs., (Hangchow.)

Ningpo.
Peking.
Tientsin
Wencho
Wuhu.
Corea.
Who's Who.

縣化奉 *Fung-hwa Hsien.*

CHINA INLAND MISSION.
(Chehkiang.)
Williamson, Jas.
Williamson, Mrs.
Rudland, W. D.
Rudland, Mrs.
Jackson, J. A.
Jackson, Mrs.
Randle, H.
Randle, Mrs.
Whiller, A.
Whiller, Mrs.
Murray, Miss
Boyd, Miss Fanny
Carpenter, Miss S.
Carpenter, Miss M.

會教英大
Da-ying-chiao-hui.
(CHEKEANG.)
CHURCH MISSIONARY SOCIETY.
Ningpo.
Bates, Rev. James
Hoare, Rev. J. C., M.A.
Shann, Rev. R., B.A. (ab.)
Groves, Rev. W. L., B.A. (ab.)
Russell, Mrs.
Laurence, Miss
Bates, Mrs. J.
Hoare, Mrs. J. C.
Shann, Mrs. R.
Groves, Mrs. W. L. (ab.)
Society for Female Education in the East.
Smith, Miss
Hang-chow.
Moule, Right Rev. G. E., D.D.
Elwin, Rev. A.
Lodgwick, Rev. J. H. (abt.)
Horsburgh, Rev. J. H., M.A.
Main, Dr. Duncan
Moule, Mrs. G. E.
Elwin, Mrs. A.
Horsburgh, Mrs. J. H.
Main, Mrs. Duncan
Moule, Miss M.
Moule, Miss J.
Elwin, Miss Rosie
Elwin, Miss Edith
Shaou-hing.
Valentine, Rev. J. D.
Fuller, Rev. A. R.
Valentine, Mrs. J. D.
Fuller, Mrs. A. R.

院病濟 *Tsy-ping-yuen.*
HOSPITAL SAINT JOSEPH.
Sr. Albertine Menric, Sup.
Sr. Vincent Lacôte.
Sr. Jeanne Ridez.
Sr. Marie Perrin.
Sr. Madeleine Batint.

Dans la Province du Tché-kiang.
江浙
Les Sœurs de la Charité de St. Vincent de Paul.
MAISON DE JESUS-ENFANT.
堂慈仁 *Jen-tse-t'ang.*
Ning-po.
府波甯 *Ning-po-fu.*
Sr. Louise Solomiac, Supr.
Sr. Stéphanie Looy.
Sr. Elisabeth Lethimonnier.
Sr. Françoise Giovanelli.
Sr. Germaine Danverchain
Sr. Joseph Cayrol.
Sr. Vincent Guillon.
Sr. Stéphanie Muhlinghaus.
Sr. Marie Inbert.
Sr. Augustine Perreaud.

州杭 *Hang-chow.*
MAISON SAINT VINCENT.
Dans la Province du Tché-Kiang.
Hang-tcheou.
Sr. Adèle Faure, Sup.
Sr. Gabrielle Perboyre.
Sr. Angélique Lucan.
Sr. Augustine Lazarowicz.
Sr. Marie Dupare.
Sr. Madeleine Rouvière.
Sr. Vincent Ricaud.

METHODIST FREE CHURCH MISSION (ENGLISH.)
Galpin, Rev. Frederick
Swallow, Rev. Robert
Galpin, Mrs.
Swallow, Mrs.

MISSION CATHOLIQUE DU TCHE-KIANG.
堂主天波甯
Ning-Po-Tien-Tchou-T'ang.
Mgr. E. F. Geierry, Vic. Ap.
M. J. Rizzi.
M. A. R. Guillot.
M. J. B. Bret.
M. J. Urgé.
M. D. V. Procacci.
M. P. M. Reynaud.
M. L. Perras.
M. A. Heckmann.
M. U. L. Iberruthy.

海定山舟
Chu-san Ting-hay.
SISTERS OF CHARITY.
堂嬰憐 *Lien-jug-t'ang.*
Sr. Françoise Archenault.
Sr. Louise Roddier.
Sr. Joseph Houlès.
Sr. Joseph Reayer.
Sr. Philomène Gilbert.

NINGPO PILOT CO.
Peterson, P. M., Pilot Boat *Teazer.*
Smith, J., Pilot Boat *Orphan.*

房捕巡 *Tshung-bu-woong.*
POLICE STATION.
Watson, J. C., Magistrate and Controller of Police.
Willis, John, Sergeant.
1 Interpreter.
2 Native Corporals.
8 Native Constables.

生利 *Lee-sung.*
SASSOON, D., SONS & CO.
Benjamin, S. S., Agent.
Kelly, E. S.
Isaac, I.
Agents for the Union Insurance Society of Canton.

遜沙新 *Sing-so-sing.*
SASSOON, E. D., & CO.
David, A. J., Agent.
Nissim, M.

順華 *Wha-shing.*
WADMAN & CO.
Wadman, E.
Agents for the
Imperial Fire Insurance;
China Traders' Insurance Co., Limited.

PEKING HONG LIST,

1884.

Legations.

Austro-Hungary.

Hoffer von Hoffenfels, Chevalier Max, *Minister Resident in China, Japan and Siam (on leave.)*

Belgium.

Noidans-Calf, Le Comte de, *Minister Resident.*
Michel, Charles, *Student Interpreter.*

France.

Patenôtre, J., *Envoy Extraordinary and Minister Plenipotentiary.*
Semallé, Vicomte de, *2nd Secretary.*
Frandin, Hse., 1st *Interpreter.*
Collin de Plancy, Victor, *Interpreter-Chancelier.*
Vissière, A., 2nd *Interpreter.*
Haltoe, T., 3rd *Interpreter* (absent.)
Mirabel, Dr., *Physician.*
Allois, Rév. P., *Chaplain.*

館公差欽國德大
Ta Tê-kuo ch'in-ch'ai kung-kuan.

German Empire.

M. von Brandt, *Envoy Extraordinary and Minister Plenipotentiary*
Von Tattenbach, Count, *Chargé d'Affaires.* [absent.
Arendt, C., 1st *Chinese Interpreter.*
Dr. Lenz, Rethaus, Dr. Merz, Heinsdorf, *Student Interpreters.*
Pampel, *Clerk.*
Kierulf, *Constable.*

Great Britain.

Parkes, Sir Harry S., K.C.B., G.C.M.G., *Envoy Extraordinary and Minister Plenipotentiary and Chief Superintendent of British Trade in China.*
———, *Secretary of Legation.*
Maude, C. T., *2nd Secretary.*
Baber, E. C., *Chinese Secretary* (absent.)
Hillier, Walter C., *Acting Chinese Secretary.*
Everard, C. W., *Acting Assistant Chinese Secretary.*
Pirkis, A. E., *Accountant.*
Bushell, S. W., M.D., *Physician.*
Brereton, W., *Chaplain.*
Scott, James, *2nd Assistant.*
Coulthard, J. B., *2nd Assistant.*
Fittock, G. V., *Acting 2nd Assistant.*
Escort:—Constables, R. D. Herring, J. Wilkie, W. Bruce, F. Poucett.

Italy.

De Luca, Ferd., *Minister Resident* (Shanghai).

館使公國本日大
Ta Jih-pên-kuoh kung-shih-kuan.

Japan.

Enomotto, Vice-Admiral Takeaki, *Envoy Extraordinary and Minister Plenipotentiary* (absent.)
Yoshida, Djiro, *Secretary of Legation.*
Fokushima, Captain Yasumasa, *Military Attaché.*
Watanabé, Yoitchiro, *Attaché.*
Nakashima, Takéshi, *Attaché.*
Goh, Kéita, *Attaché and Interpreter.*
Tei, Nagakuni, *Student Interpreter* (Tientsin.)
Goh, Daigoro, *Student Interpreter.*

署公差欽國和大
Ta Ho-kuo-chin-ch'ai-kung-se.

Netherlands.

Ferguson, J. H., *Minister Resident.*
Rhein, J., *Secretary-Interpreter.*

Russia.

Popoff, S. K., *Envoy Extraordinary & Minister Plenipotentiary.*
Ladijensky, N., *1st Secretary of Legation.*
Von Wrangel, Baron N., *2nd Secretary of Legation.*
Popoff, P., *1st Interpreter.*
Protaisieff, J., *2nd Interpreter.*
Schishmareff, M., *Student.*
Schoolsky, N., *Student.*
Bretschneider, E., M.D., *Physician* (absent.)
Gomboeff, N., *Telegraphic Agent and Postmaster.*
Fritsche, H., *Director of the Meteorological Observatory.*
Schuevour, Colonel N., *Military Attaché.*

Spain.

Rodriguez y Muñoz, Tiburcio, *Minister Plenipotentiary* (absent.)
Uribarri, Ramiro Gil de, *1st Secretary of Legation.*
Agar, Luis de, *3rd Secretary of Legation* (absent.)
Marzal, Juan de Liciopolis, *Interpreter.*

United States of America.

Young, John Russell, *Envoy Extraordinary and Minister Plenipotentiary.*
Holcombe, Chester, *Secretary of Legation and Chinese Interpreter.*
Bergholz, Leo. A., *Private Secretary.*

—o—

Inspectorate-General of Imperial Maritime Customs.

署公司務稅總 *Tsung-shui-wu-ssŭ-kung-shu.*

Hart, Sir Robert, *Inspector-General.*
McKean, E., *Chief Secretary.*
Hippisley, A. E., *Chinese Secretary.*
Smith, J., *Audit Secretary.*
Drew, E. B., *Statistical Secretary.**
Campbell, J. Duncan, *Non-Resident Secretary.*†
———, *Marine Secretary.*
Brazier, J. R., *Acting Assistant Secretary* (absent)
Happer, A. P., *Acting Assistant Chinese Secretary.*
———, *Assistant Audit Secretary.*
Hirth, F., *Assistant Statistical Secretary.**
Liot, E., *Private Secretary.*
Hillier, H. M., *First Assistant, B.*†
Schierzer, F. A., *Third Assistant, B.*
Lyall, H., *Fourth Assistant, A.*
Moorhead, T. D., *Fourth Assistant, B*† (on prob.)
Tanner, P., } *Studying Chinese.*
Rosthorn, A. E. von, }
Bowring, C. T., }
Bland, J. O. P., }
Edkins, Rev. Dr. Joseph, *Translator.*
Van Aalst, J. A., *Postal Clerk.*
Child, Thos., *Gas Engineer.*
Meara, C. B., *Fitter.*
Dudgeon, J., M.D., *Medical Officer.*
Dalberg, F. W. E., *Clerk.**
Palamountain, B., *Printing Office Manager.**
Bright, Wm., *Proof Reader.**
Morlees, A. G., *Proof Reader.**

———

College of Peking.

館文同 *Tung-wen-kuan.*

Martin, Rev. W. A. P., LL.D., *President.*
Billequin, A., *Professor of Natural History and Chemistry.*
Vapereau, C., *do. French.*
Dudgeon, John, M.D., C.M., *Professor of Anatomy and Physiology.*
Pander, E., *Professor of Russian and German.*
Oliver, C. H., *Professor of English.*
Russell, S. M., *Professor of Astronomy and Physics.*
Native Professors of Chinese (three.)
Chinese Proctors (four.)

—o—

Missionaries.

American.

American Board of Commissioners for Foreign Missions.

Blodget, Rev. H., D.D.
Ament, Rev. W. S.
Noble, W. C., *Supt. of the Press, Treasurer.*
Porter, Miss Mary H., at P'ang-chia-chuang.
Chapin, Miss J. E.
Haven, Miss Ada
Stanley, Rev. C. A., at Tientsin.
Perkins, Rev. H. P., do.
Porter, Rev H. D., M.D., at P'ang-chia-chuang.
Smith, Rev A. H., do.
Chapin, Rev. F. M., at Kalgan.

* Resides at Shanghai. † Resides in London.

Chapin, Rev. L. D., at T'ungchow, *Secretary.*
Sheffield, Rev. D. Z., do.
Goodrich, Rev. Chauncey, do.
Andrews, Miss Mary E., do.
Evans, Miss J. E., do.
Holbrook, Miss M. A., M.D., do.
Williams, Rev. Mark, at Kalgan.
Sprague, Rev. W. P., do.
Diament, Miss N., do.
Roberts, Rev. J. H., do.
Garretson, Miss Elsie M., do.
Pierson, Rev. Isaac, at Pao-ting-fu.
Peck, A. P., M.D., do.

———

Methodist Episcopal Mission.

Lowry, Rev. H. H., and family.
Pyke, J. H., and family (absent.)
Gamewell, Frank D.
Davis, George R., and family.
Cushman, Miss C. M.
Sears, Miss A. B.
Hobart, Rev. W. T.

———

Presbyterian Mission.

Wherry, Rev. J.
Wherry, Mrs. S. E.
McCoy, Rev. D. C.
McCoy, Mrs. A. P.
Whiting, Rev. J. L.
Whiting, Mrs. J. L.
Atterbury, B. C., M.D.
Barr, Miss M. E.
Strong, Miss F. M.

———

British.

London Missionary Society.

Dudgeon, John, M.D., C.M., (family absent.)
Owen, Rev. G. S., and family.
Gilmour, Rev. J., M.A., and family.
Meech, Rev. S. Evans, and family.
Rees, Rev. W. H., and family.

———

Society for the Propagation of the Gospel.

Brereton, Rev. W., and wife.

———

National Bible Society of Scotland and Blind Institute.

Murray, W. H.

———

French.

Mission Catholique de Peking.

Congregation de la Mission.

Delaplace, Mgr. L. G., *Evêque, Vicaire Apostolique.*
MM. Favier, A.; Del-masure, J. B.; Humblot, A.; Sarthou, J. D.; Garrigues, J.; Wijnhoven, P.; Fioritti, J. B.; Provost, A.; Chevrier, L.; Jean, G.; Delebarre, S.; Salette, J.; Allois, J.; MacVeigh, J.; Maës, T.; Dumonteil, B.; Tonzy, J.; Guyon, F.

———

仁慈堂 *Jen-tse-tang.*

Maison de l'Immaculée Conception.

Sœur de Jaurias, Rev. Mother *Superioress.*
Sr. des Roys, Sr. Vernny, Sr. Laracine, Sr. Doyen, Sr. Decurtyl, Sr. Maillard, Sr. Galindo, Sr. Parada, Sr. Bernadôs, Sr. Ducheix, Sr. Werner; Sr. Gilhedde; six Sœurs Chinoises.

———

南堂 *Nan-tang.*

Hôpital St. Vincent de Paul.

Sœur Leclercq, *Superioress.*
" Joséphine.
" Julie.
" Vincent.
" Marie.
Two Chinese Sisters.

———

Russian.

Greek Church Mission.

Nicolas, Rev.
Alexis, Rev.

—o—

Hotel de Peking, (Messrs. L. Vrard & Co.)
Tallieu, Leopold, *Manager.*
Pierre, —, *Clerk.*

———

昌先生 *Chang-sien-sung.*

Jeanneraud, Charles, *Agent for Curios, Speciality of Peking Enamels.*

———

Kierulff, F., *Commission Agent, &c.*
Kierulff, P.

———

Moore, Charles F.

TIENTSIN HONG LIST,

1884.

ASTOR HOUSE HOTEL.
Ritter, G., Proprietor.

—

通 阜 *Fow-tung.*

DELOGOLOVY, A. A.
Bologolovy, A. A.
Popoff, F. A.

—

新 飛 龍 *Hsin Fei Lung.*

DLOW, H., & Co.,
General Storekeepers, Wine and Spirit Merchants.
Dlow, H.
Knox, H.

—

利 益 *I-li.*

DOODILLE W. J.
Doodille, W. J.
Velesatoff, J. M.

—

局務礦平開

Kai-ping-gang-wu-chok.

CHINESE ENGINEERING AND MINING Co.
Tong King-sing, Managing Director.

—

Kinder, C. W., A.M.I.C.E., Chief-Engineer.

—

Stevens, James, Mining Engineer.
Petersen, F. B., Mining Student.
Chen Tung-kwei, do.
Purcell, John, Overman.
Wardell, Wm., do.
Naylor, John., do.
Purcell, Stephen, Sub-Overman
Williams, C., do.

—

Wood, Isaac, Foreman Mechanic.
Jarvis, M., Locomotive Driver.
Wileman, W., Engine Winder.
Goulding, J. W., do.
Yuen Yu-sau, do.
Bulmer, Wm., Boiler-maker.
Michell, S., Sinker.

—

Kwong King-yong, Store-keeper.
Kwong Yung-kwong, Telegraph Student.
Liang Poo-chow, Book-keeper.
Kwong Hoin-chow, Machinist.

—

Butlles, E. K., Chemist and Electrician.

—

Brown, R. M., Secretary.

—

Principal Works at Tong Colliery, Kaiping, Chihli.

Address for Foreigners, care of H.B.M.'s or U.S. Consulate, Tientsin.

林 高 *Kao-lin.*

COLLINS, G. W., & Co.
Storekeepers, Ship-Chandlers, Wine and Spirit Merchants and Commission Agents.
Collins, G. W.
Anderson, W. C. C. (London)
Dickinson, W. W.
Wilson, J.
Dickinson, J. M.
Agents for Messrs. Cockburn & Co., Leith and London;
Sole Agents for Priestman Bro. Hull, Patent Steam Dredgers for all ports North of Shanghai;
Agents for London and Lancashire Fire Insurance.

—

Consulates.

官事領國奧大

Ta Aou-kuo ling-shih kwan.

AUSTRO-HUNGARY.
Davenport, A., Actg. Consul.

—

BELGIUM.
Forbes, William, Consul.

—

門衙事領國法大

Ta Fa-kuo ling-shih Yamên.

FRANCE.
Frandin, Hte. Acting Consul.
Gall, J., Constable.

—

署事領國德大

Ta Teh-kuo ling-shih shu.

GERMAN EMPIRE—
Pelldram, A., Consul.
Feindel, Ch., Interpreter.
Milcek, J., Constable.

—

官事領國英大

Ta Ying-kuo ling-shih kwan.

GREAT BRITAIN.
Davenport, A., Consul.
Holland, W., Interpreter.
Yeomans, H., Constable.

—

官事領國蘭和大

Ta Ho-lan-kuo Ling-shi-kuan.

NETHERLANDS.
Davenport, A., Actg. Consul.

—

PORTUGAL.
Hatch, J. J., Consul.

事領津天國俄大
署官

Ta-ngoo-kuo tien-tsin-ling-shih kuan-wei.

RUSSIA—
Waeber, C., Consul.

—

SWEDEN & NORWAY—
Frandin, Hte., Acting Vice-Consul.

—

署事領國美大

Ta Mei-kuo ling-shih-shu.

UNITED STATES—
Zook, Jas. C., Consul (abt.)
Pitcher, L. W., Vice-Consul.
Mackay, R. H., Acting Interpreter.
———, Marshal.

—

遠 信 *Sin-yuen.*

CORDES, A., & Co.,
Cordes, August C. (Hamburg.)
Reinders, B.
Bahow, P.
Agents for the Yangtsze Insurance Association;
German Lloyds';
Scottish Imperial Insurance Co.;
Hamburg Magdeburg Fire Insurance Co. of Hamburg;
Fire Insurance Company of 1877 in Hamburg.

—

Customs.

關 海 津 *Ching Hai-kuan.*

Hobson, H. E., Commissioner.
Hobson, R. M., Assistant.
Morse, H. B., do.
Smith, F. J., do.
Davies, C. W., do.
Brosche, H., do.
Poletti, P., Clerk.
Menzies, A. B., do.
Tronnock, R. J., Harbour Master and Tide-Surveyor.
Castro, G. B. A., Examiner.
Ghika, N. D., do.
Ottaway, E. P., Assist. do.
Ecclestone, J., do. do.
Lynburg, C. P C., do. do.
Ward, W. S., Tidewaiter.
Keeble, G., do.
Schweiger, H. do.
Clemmow, J. L. do.
Prichard, H. L. L., do.

TAKU.

Stevenson, W. F., Assistant Tide-Surveyor.
French, W., Tidewaiter.
Meyer, H., do.

LIGHT-VESSEL "TAKU."

Sloane, James, Captain.
Frandsen, H. A., Mate.
Knight, W., Lightkeeper.

—

昌 滙 *Way-chang.*

McDONALD, J., & Co., General Merchants and Commission Agents.
McDonald, J.

行 記 仁 *Jên-chi-hong.*

FORBES, WILLIAM,
Merchant & Commission Agent.
Graham, W. J., Assistant.
Agencies—
Imperial Fire Insurance Co.;
North British and Mercantile Insurance Co.;
China Traders' Marine Insurance Co.;
Lloyd's Agent;
Mitsu Bishi Mail Steam-Ship Co.;
China Navigation Co.;
The Marine Insurance Co.

—

FRAZER, JNO., L.R.C.P., L.M., M.R.C.S.I.

—

和 昌 大 *Ta-chang-ho.*

GLOBE HOTEL.
Taylor, —., Manager.
Takkai, K.

—

GRABE, OTTO, & Co., Merchants.
Grabe, Otto
Hagge, H.

—

昌 啟 *Chi-chong.*

HARTMANN, J., & Co.,
Storekeepers, Bakers and Navy Contractors.
Hartmann, J.

—

順 寶 *Pau-sung.*

HATCH, FORBES & Co.
Hatch, John J.
Forbes, W. H.
Forbes, Geo. H.
Agents for
National Marine Insurance Association for China and Japan, Limited;
London and Liverpool and Globe Fire Insurance Co.

—

隆 廣 *Quang-loong.*

HENDERSON, JAMES

—

茂 增 *Tsun-mow.*

HIRSBRUNNER, JAMES,
General Merchant and Commission Agent.
Brunner, Ch. A.

—

局總造製

Chih-tsao-tsung-chü.

IMPERIAL ARSENAL
Stewart, J., Supt. Engr.

—

INDEPENDENT ORDER OF GOOD TEMPLARS.
Tientsin Lodge No. 2, China.
Myres, C., V.D.G W C.T.
Candlin, Rev. G. T., Lodge Deputy.

—

和 怡 *E-wo.*

JARDINE, MATHESON & Co.
Cousins, Ed., Agent.
Agents Indo-China S. N. Co.;
P. & O. S. N. Co.;
Glen-Line Steamers;
Canton Insurance Office;
Hongkong Fire Insurance Co., Limited.

—

MACKENZIE, DR.

—

MEDICAL PRACTITIONERS.
Frazer, John.
Irwin, Andrew.

昌世 *Shih-chang.*

MEYER, E., & Co.
Meyer, E. (Hamburg.)
Fischer, G.
Wolter, C.
Hullanf, H.
Rump, C.
General Agents for China, for Sächsische Maschinenfabrick zu Chemnitz vorm. Rich Hartmann at Chemnitz;
Hoerder Bergwerks & Hutten Verein at Hoerde;
Breslauer Action Gesellschaft für Eisenbahnwagenbau at Breslau;
Department of Civil and Mechanical Engineering:
Ernst Jacobi, Civil Engineer.
Agents for
Samarang Sea and Fire Insurance Co.;
Union Insurance Society of Canton;
Prussian National Insurance Company of Stettin;
Hanseatic Fire Insurance Co., Hamburg.

Missionaries, Churches, &c.

AMERICAN BOARD OF COMMISSIONERS FOR FOREIGN MISSIONS.
Stanley, Rev. C. A.
Stanley, Mrs. U. J. (absent.)
Perkins, Rev. Henry P.
Smith, Rev. A. H., P'ang Chia, Shantung.
Smith, Mrs. E. D., do.
Porter, Rev. Henry D., do.
Porter, Mrs. E. C., do.

GENERAL HOSPITAL—SISTERS OF CHARITY.
Sister Superior—Sister Doyen.
Five Sisters.

LONDON MISSIONARY SOCIETY.
Lees, Rev. Jonathan, and family.
King, Rev. A.

METHODIST EPISCOPAL MISSION
Pilcher, Rev. L. W.
Willits, Rev. O. W.
Howard, Miss L. A., M.D.
Yates, Miss E. U.
Akers, Miss L. E., M.D.

METHODIST MISSIONARY SOCIETY (ENGLISH).
Innocent, Rev. J. & family.
Robinson, Rev. J. & family.
Candlin, Rev. G. T. & family.
Stenhouse, D., L.R.C.P., &c., Edin., & family.
Hinds, Rev. J. & family.
Innocent, Mr. G. M.

堂主天 *Tien-chu-tang*

ROMAN CATHOLIC MISSION.
Coqset, Rev. Père A.

部工 *Kung-pu.*

MUNICIPAL COUNCIL.
Hobson, H. E., Chairman.
Bovis, F. de, Hon. Treasurer.
Cousins, H., Secretary.
Forbes, W., Member.
Startseff, A. D., do.
Williams, S. E., Superintendent of Police, &c.
Yeomans, H., Sergeant.

行洋和順豬商俄

MYERS, C.
Myres, C., Merchant.

順隆 *Lung-shun.*

NEFEDIEFF, N. A.
Ponomareff, P. A., & Co., Agents.

行洋昌豐 *Fung-chang.*

PETHICK, MACLAY & Co.
Pethick, W. N.
Maclay, R. H.
Agents for the China Fire Insurance Company, Limited, of Hongkong.
Chinese Marine Insurance Company, Limited, of Hongkong.

昌阜 *Fow-chang.*

PIATKOFF, MOLCHANOFF & Co.
Belogolovy, A. A., Agent.

順恆 *Hun-shun.*

PONOMAREFF, P. A., & Co.
Meleutieff, J. E.
Nikiforoff, M. G.

昌恆 *Hun-chang.*

RODIONOFF, A. L., & Co.
Startseff, A. D., Agent.

遜沙 *Sa-soon.*

SASSOON, D., SONS & Co.
Moses, R.
Shekury, G. J.

遜沙新 *Sing-sa-soon.*

SASSOON, E. D., & Co.
Siles, A. S., Agent.
Ellis, M. E.

SCHMIDT & Co.
Schmidt, Chas.
Schmidt, John

TAKU PILOT COMPANY.
Tulpey, A. H.
Bond, W.
Blanchard, W.
Hill, J. C.
Lembke, G.
Mitchell, O.
Watts, J.
Young, J.
Sherman, C. B.
Crowlie, H.
Hill, J. C., Secretary.

TAKU TUG AND LIGHTER CO.
Watts, J., Secretary.
Collins, G. W., Director.
Crawbie, H., do.
Dexter, A. G., do.
Kossow, C., Clerk.
Tug *Peiho*,
Crowlie, H., Captain.
Tug *Gem*,
Watts, J., Captain.
Tug *Orphan*,
———, Captain.
McMurray, J., Engineer.
Wells, E., Engineer.

TELEGRAPH COLLEGE (THE IMPERIAL CHINESE.)
Chu Tsin-jen, Director.
Poulsen, C. H. O., Teacher.
Liang Dou-yin, Asst. Teacher.

TIENTSIN DAIRY FARM.
Moore, Mrs. J. M., Manager.

TIENTSIN WATER WORKS.
Hao Loong chee, Manager.

局西器機津天
Tien-tsin-ke-ch'i-chok.

TIENTSIN WEST ARSENAL.

豐順 *Shun-fung.*

TOKMAKOFF, MOLOTKOFF & Co.
Startseff, A. D.
Dmitrieff, W. W.
Kouznetsoff, A. N.
Aslamoff, N. K.
Koorneff, N. W.
Gridnfeld, M. A.

TOKMAKOFF, SHEVELEFF & Co. (Kalgan.)
Messrs. Molchanoff and Kokorin, Agents.

利遜市
Hua-li-shi

VRARD, L., & Co.
Loup, P.
Loup, A.
Kruger, J.
Vaucher, E.

房藥大氏臣屈
Wa-son-si Tai yuet-fong.

WATSON, A. S., & Co., Hongkong Dispensary.
Family and Dispensing Chemists, Perfumers and Mineral Water Dealers, Wine, Spirit and Cigar Merchants.
Tice, R.

WILSON, JAMES, Merchant and Commission Agent.
Agent China Shipowners' Association,
Mitsu Bishi Kaisha,
Sun Fire Office,
North China Insurance Co., &c., &c.

WENCHOW HONG LIST,

1884.

Consulates.

Austro-Hungary—
Parker, E. H., in charge.

Germain Empire—
Parker, E. H., in charge of German interests.

門衙事領國英大 *Ta-ying-kwoh-ling-shih yamen.*

Great Britain—
Parker, E. H., Acting-Consul.
Compton, J., Constable.

Sweden and Norway—
Parker, E. H., in charge of the interests of the United Kingdom.

Customs.

關海甌 *Ou-hai-kwan.*

D'Arneau, Comio G., Assistant in charge.
Macgowan, D. J., M.D., Assistant and Medical Officer.
Henisch, S., Clerk.
Wong Kwai-ching, Chinese Clerk.
Cunniffy, P., Assistant Examiner.
Shamborst, G. D., Tidewaiter.
Martin, F. R., do.

Missionaries.

China Inland Mission.
Stott, Rev. G., and Mrs. Stott.
Whiller, Rev. Andrew, and Mrs. Whiller.

Methodist Free Church Mission (English.)
Soothill, Rev. W. E.

WUHU HONG LIST,

1884.

局商招 *Chau-shang-keuk.*
China Merchants' Steam Navigation Co.
Lau Kit-look, Manager.
Chao Yuk-ting, Clerk.
Hulks—*Bombay* and *Geo. Washington.*

Consulate.

門衙事領英大
Ta-Ying-kuo ling-shih ya-mên.

Great Britain—
Scott, B. C. G., Consul.
Perkins, G., Constable.

門衙事領國美大
Ta-mei-kwoh-ling-shi Ya-mên.

United States—
Smithers, E., Consul.
Bergholz, Leo., V.-Consul.
Emery, D. A., Interpreter.

Customs

(Imperial Maritime.)

關新湖蕪 *Wuhu-hsin-kuan*

Schmoloke, J. F., Assistant-in-charge.
Doane, A. S., Assistant and Medical Officer.
Whittlesey, H. C., Assistant.
Armour, J., Tide-Surveyor and Harbour Master.
Nutter, G., Boat Officer.
Pollock, W., Examiner.
Cartman, F. A., Asst. do.
Williamson, T., 1st class Tidewaiter.
Ramasse, A., 2nd do.
Swanstrom, C. A., 3rd do.
Sjolund, P. O., 3rd do.
Sung A-sow, Chinese Clerk.

泰謙 *Him-tai.*

Hemder, S.

Hulk "Spirit of the Age."
McBain, George, Proprietor.
Homber, S., Agent.

Missionaries.

堂主天 *Tien-chu-tang.*

Society of Jesus.
Seckinger, Rev. Père J., and others.

利得興 *Wu-te-lee.*

Methodist Episcopal Mission
Woodall, Rev. G. W.
Woodall, Mrs.

Sassoon, E. D. & Co.
Perry, M. E., Agent.
Moyer, A. E.

昌亨 *Hun-chang.*

Verril, Edward, Commission Agent.
Chong Chook-foo, C'pradore, do.
Chuck Kou, do.

Woodward, R. H. S., Commission Merchant.

COREA DIRECTORY.

1884.

SEOUL.

Foreign Office

Min Yong mok, President.

Kim Hung chip, Mollendorff, P. G. von, Li Tso-you, Kim Wan-shik,	Vice Presidents.

Chinese Representatives.

Chen Shu-tong, Chief Commissioner

Chen Yuen chang, Li Hsing chu,	Assistant Commissioners.

Tan Kwai-han, Secretary

Chen Wai-yuen, Cheng Chih-ting,	Assistant Secretaries.

Japanese Legation.

Takezoye, S., Minister Resident.
Kobayashi, T., Secretary of Legation, (Consul at Jenchuan).
Kinoshita, S., Attaché.
Yoshida, Y. S., French Interpreter.
Asayama, K., Corean Interpreter.
Oba, E.
Kato, G., Chinese Interpreter.
Yasuda, K., English Interpreter.
Isobayashi, Captain S., Staff Officer, Attaché Militaire
Kainoshi, H., Physician.

United States Legation.

Foote, L. H., Envoy Extraordinary and Minister Plenipotentiary.
Scudder, C. S., Secretary.

Royal Corean Customs.

Mollendorff, P. G. von., Chief.
Haas, Joseph, Commissioner.
Macbeth, J. R., Chief Assistant.
Arnous, H. G., Assistant.
Woo Chang-yen, do.

School.

Hallifax, T. E., Teacher.

FUSAN.

Fusan is situated in the province of Kin-sang and lies on the South-east coast of Corea, in Latitude 35°6′ 6″ N and Longitude 129° 3′ 2″ E.

The Japanese have a well laid out Settlement at the head of the harbour and are said to number over two thousand persons, of whom about one-half are from the island of Tsushima. The principal Japanese merchants are from Tokio, Kobe, Osaka, Nagasaki and Satsuma.

The Japanese have had a small Settlement at Fusan for a great number of years, where they have traded with Coreans; but which never became of any importance until they made a Treaty with Corea about eight years ago, when the trade rapidly increased, and last year (1883) the total value of the Exports and Imports amounted to over a million ($1,000,000) dollars.

Fusan possesses a large and capacious harbour with a sufficient depth of water to accommodate the largest vessels.

There are some eight Corean villages situated at the head of the harbour and within a few miles of the Japanese Settlement. The district city Tong Li Fu is distant about eight miles, and is the local centre of trade.

The principal Exports are.—Hides, Horns, Bones, Seaweed (Red and White), Dried Fish, Shark's Fins, Beans, Nut Galls, Oil-cake, Cotton Piece Goods, Grass Cloth, Raw Silk and sundry Medicines.

The chief Imports are.—Piece Goods, Lead, Glass, Blankets, Matches (Japanese), Paper and Sundries.

The climate is very salubrious, and the place considered extremely healthy. Sea bathing may be had in perfection.

The readings of the Thermometer for August, September and October, 1883, are as under:—

	Highest.	Lowest.
August	88°	72°
September	82°	62°
October...	75°	61°

A branch of the Foreign Customs Service was established in July 1883, and the port opened under Customs Regulations on the 3rd November, 1883.

The Mitsu Bishi Mail Steamship Company run a regular line of steamers between Kobe and Vladivostock, calling at Nagasaki, Fusan, and Yuensan; and started a regular line from Kobe to Jenchuan in 1883, calling at Nagasaki and Fusan.

A small steamer, the *Chindzi Maru*, runs from Kobe to Jenchuan, calling at Nagasaki and Fusan, once a month.

Consulate & Public Offices.

館事領本日

JAPANESE CONSULATE GENERAL.

Miyamoto, H., Acting Consul General.
Kazoei, A., Interpreter.

局議會務商本日

JAPANESE CHAMBER OF COMMERCE.

Oashi, H., President.
Yamada, S., Chairman.
Ohia, Y., Secretary.

院醫本日

JAPANESE GENERAL HOSPITAL.

Benten Street.

Koike, M., Director-in-charge.
Yatahru, T., Assist.-Surgeon.
Kokoboo, T., Accountant.

館信書本日

IMPERIAL JAPANESE POST OFFICE.

At Imperial Consulate.

Iwall, T., Postmaster.
Miieshn, K., Sorter.
Koisoh, K., „

局捕巡本日

JAPANESE POLICE STATION.

Horn Street.

Morokashi, K., Superintendent.
Ito, S., Inspector.
And 16 men.

關海鮮朝大

ROYAL MARITIME CUSTOMS.

關海

CUSTOM HOUSE.

Lovatt, W. Nelson, Commissioner.

Assistants:
Duncan, Chesney.
Reynolds, H. A.
Tong Sui Yi.
Takeslta, E.

Harbour Master:
Posthumus, O. P.

Examiner:
Hawkins, H. H.

Tidewaiters:
Civilini, J. P.
Smith, J. H.
Lewis, B. J.

局報電本日

IMPERIAL TELEGRAPH OFFICE.

(To be in working order in January 1884.)

Steamship, Schooner and Junk Companies.

MITSU BISHI MAIL STEAMSHIP COMPANY.

1, Breakwater.

Yamada, S., Agent.
Sakamoto, M., Accountant.
Enomoto, F., Interpreter.
Shimaoochi, S.

Steamers:—
Tsuruga Maru.
Chitose Maru.
Tamaura Maru.

KIODO GWAISHA COMPANY.

8, Kotobera Street.

Takasoh, K., Agent.
Oahli, Y.
Ouob, T.

Schooners:—
Hiyehdmah.
Dofook No. 1.
Dofook No. 2.
Dofook No. 3.
Dofook No. 4.

KAISHO GWAISHA COMPANY.

ASA SHIMASHI KAISHA.

11, Benten Street.

Korai, K., Agent.
Nakamorah, T., Accountant.
Ichi, K., Freight Clerk.

Steamer:—
Chindzi Maru.

Schooners.—*Discing, Kitzu, Kietzu No. 1, Kietzu No. 2, Hazu, Flokh, Hoti Maru No. 1, Hoti No. 2, Hoti No. 3, Hoti No. 4, Hoti No. 5, Suyu No. 1, Suyu No. 2, Suyu No. 3.*

KOGERO, MARTZIA (Junk Agent)

Horn Street.

Kogero, M.

Junks:—*Nadioshi, Kompert, Simiyoshi, Ibiss, Zewza, Majura, Zuhoma, Kuzoko, Fookoch, Zotokil, Sauza, Maheiyeh.*

Merchants.

HAMADA, P., & Co.

1, Horn Street.

Hamada, P.
Satow, N.
Yosudah, N.
Moorlsih, T.

HAMASAGI, G.

Horn Street.

Hamasagi, G.

HATASIMAH, H., & Co.

Kotobera Street.

Hatasiumh, H.

HIGOOD & Co.
3, Horn Street.
Higood, P.
Moritah, W.

HOLIKEW, A., & Co.
13, Horn Street.
Holikew, A.

IWATAH & Co.
5, Kitahama Street.
Iwatah, J.

KIDDAH & Co.
30, Horn Street.
Kiddah, W.
Inakurah, J.

MORITAH & Co.
18, Horn Street.
Moritah, A.

MIYADAH & Co
10, Kitahama Street.
Miyadah, K.

MIKI, S.
Kotohera Street.
Miki, S.

NIHARA & Co.
13, Horn Street.
Nihara, P.

NAKAGAWA, J., & Co.
Horn Street.
Nakagawa, J.

OKAHARRA & Co.
14, Horn Street.
Okahara, P.

OMAHRARRA, L., & Co.
Benten Street.
Omaharra, L.
Koomahiah, W.

OSIH, J., & Co.
Nish Street.
Osih, J.

ORIH, T., & Co.
Eri Street.
Orih, T.

PENGHWAH, F., & Co.
Horn Street.
Penghwah, F.

SEEMORRAH, G.
Kotohera Street.
Seemorrah, G.

SUZUKIH & Co.
Benten Street.
Suzukih, W.
Moritah, W.

SAITO & Co.,
5, Benten Street.
Saito, W
Saito, A.

SHENOSAKI & Co.
2, Horn Street.
Shenoseki, A.
Okagawa, W.

SHIRRYAMAH & Co.
6, Sil..ai Street.
Shirryamah, K.

TOMETAH, GOOJERO & Co.
Horn Street
Tometah, K.

德興
TICK HING & Co
5, Horn Street
(Chinese Merchants & General Storekeepers)
Ah Chi } Managers.
Wi Sing }

TODAH & Co.
Horn Street.
Todah, S.

WADAH & Co.
Horn Street.
Wadah, W.

YAMADA, S.
Kotohera Street.
Agent for Mitsu Bishi S. S Co; Chairman, Chamber of Commerce.

YAMAMOTO, & Co.
Eri Street.
Yamamoto, S.

Banks.

1st NATIONAL BANK.
Horn Street.
Oashi, A., Manager.
Suyikawa, W., Accountant.
Igumi, P.
Yamamoto, H.

102nd NATIONAL BANK
Horn Street.
Hatashimah, A., Manager.
Kuroyawa, P., Accountant.

KANSHEDUKIWATARESHI BANK.
Hotohera Street.
Shiryah W., Manager.
Tamurah, N., Accountant.

Hotels.

KOFUKUTAI HOTEL.
Benten Street
Maki, K., Proprietor.
Seki, K., Steward.

NISH RESTAURANT
Nish Street.
Harriyah, A., Proprietor.

Japanese Imperial Naval Depot.
Lieut. Nishi, Officer in-charge.

JENCHUAN.

ROYAL COREAN CUSTOMS.
Stripling, A. B., Commissioner
Schulze, F. W., Harbour Master.
Bekofsky, N. S., Engineer.
Laporte, E., }
Krebs, C., }
Woo Li-tang, } Assistants.
Shiku Nakabayashi, }
Chow Cheong-ling, }
Morrel, F. H., Boat Officer.
Boriul, F., Examiner.
Ladage, A., Tidewaiter.

YUENSAN.

JAPANESE CONSULATE
Loyeda, S., Consul
Oku, Y., Clerk.
Suzuki, L., Eng. Interpreter.
Yoshinaje, K
Nakamura, K

H. COREAN MAJESTY'S CUSTOMS
Wright, T W., Commissioner.
Rosenbaum, S., Assistant.
Narita, G., Asst. & Interp.
Kofoed, N. C
Laucht, H. W.
Knott, J.
Schmidt, W.

GOVERNMENT HOSPITAL
Kitajima, K., Physician.
Oishi, M., Interpreter.
Tanaka, R.

CONSULAR POLICE.
Kurotaki, K., Chief Inspector.
Twelve Constables.

CHAMBER OF COMMERCE.
Sato, T., President.
Sato, J., Clerk.

FIRST NATIONAL BANK OF JAPAN.
Sato, T., Manager.
Toine, T., Clerk.

MITSHU BISHI M. S S Co
Okumura, T., Agent.

KIODO-SHO-KAI.
Nishi, T., Manager.

RITSHIU-SHO-KAI.
Nakamura, C., Manager.

BOYEKI-SHO-KAI.
Nishiwara, T., Manager

OTSUKA KUMI.
Oki, R., Manager.

KAMEI KUMI.
Kamei, J., Manager

OGAWA-KUMI.
Kawanishi, J., Manager.

Agency of Corean Customs, Shanghai,
H. Snethlage, Agent.

WHO'S WHO.

AN ALPHABETICAL LIST OF FOREIGN RESIDENTS AT SHANGHAI, FOOCHOW, NINGPO, NORTHERN & RIVERINE PORTS; SEOUL, FUSAN, JENCHUAN, AND YUENSAN (COREA.)

1884.

[*Where the Name of the Place is omitted, Shanghai will be understood.*]

ABB—AND.

Abbey, Rev. R. E.	Am. Presbyterian Mission, Nanking
Abdoola, A.	Abdoola & Co.
Abdoolajis, Goolamally	Mahomedan Church
Abdoorah-man, Goolamally	Mahomedan Church
Abdulla Hassumboy	Talay Building
Abraham, A. E. J.	Corner of Kiangse & Kiukiang Roads
Adan, A.	John Wilson
Adam, T. B., M.B.	Drs. Rennie & Adam, Foochow
Adams, Rev. J. S.	Am. Baptist Mis., Kinhwa (Ningpo)
Adler, M.	Reiss & Co.
Adrian, I.	Boyd & Co.
Agar, Luis de	Spanish Legation, Peking (absent)
Ahmed, Carsom	Abdoola & Co.
Aitchison, W.	Jardine, Matheson & Co.
Akaba, S. N.	Okura & Co.
Alabaster, C.	H.B.M.'s Consulate, Hankow
Alexis, Rev.	Greek Church Mission, Peking
Algar, Albert	28, Kiangse Road
Allan, H. T.	Jardine, Matheson & Co.
Allan, J. M.	Kiangnan Arsenal
Allanson, Wm.	Dyce & Co.
Allcot, G.	Customs, Chinkiang
Allen, A. E.	Robt. Anderson & Co., Kiukiang
Allen, E. L. B.	H.B.M.'s Consulate, Foochow
Allen, Herbert J.	H.B.M.'s Consulate, Newchwang
Allen, H. N., M.D.	Am. Presbyterian Mission
Allen, J. W.	Mackenzie & Co.
Allen, J. H. B.	Geo. Oliver & Co.
Allen, R. B.	Geo. Oliver & Co., Foochow
Allen, Rev. Young J., D.D.	13, Quinsan Road
Allène, J.	French Police Force
Allimahomet, A.	616, Nanking Road
Allin, L.	Cornabé & Co., Chefoo
Allofs, J.	Roman Catholic Mission, Peking
Allshorn, F. J.	Customs, Ningpo
Allum, W. E.	Jardine, Matheson & Co.
Almeida, A. F. d'	Char. Bank of I. A. & China
Almeida, A. J. d'	Shanghai Waterworks' Co., Ld.
Almeida, C. M. d'	E. Millot & Co.
Almeida, E. F. d'	Shanghai Horse Bazaar
Almeida, F. A. M. d'	Geo. McBain
Almeida, I. E. d'	Melchers & Co.
Almeida, J. F. d'	9, Seward Road
Almeida, Jr., L. F. d'	9, Seward Road
Alsing, Aug. Hildebrand	Hulk "Orissa," Kiukiang
Alvares, E. M., M.D.	8, Seward Road
Ambrose, J.	Iveson & Co.
Amelunxen, E. A. von	Elliott & Co.
Ament, Rev. W. S.	Am. B. of C. for For. Missions, P'king
Amoore, H. E.	Shanghai Club (absent)
Amy, C. G.	'Shantung' Lighthouse, Chefoo
Anderson, F. T.	Customs, Lighthouse Department
Anderson, N. P.	Commd., R. Cruiser "Kwa-haing"
Anderson, R. A. J.	Pilot, care of Mustard & Co.
Anderson, Arthur	David Gilmour, Hankow Road
Anderson, F.	Holliday, Wise & Co.
Anderson, J.	'Shantung' Lighthouse, Chefoo
Anderson, J. H.	Robt. Anderson & Co. (absent)
Anderson, R. A. J.	Pilot
Anderson, Rev. D. L.	South. Meth. Mission, Nantsiang

AND—BEK.

Anderson, Robt.	Robert Anderson & Co. (absent)
Anderson, W. C. C.	G. W. Collins & Co., Tientsin (abt.)
Anderson, W. H.	Primrose & Co.
Andrew, Geo.	China Inland Mission, Yünnan
Andrews, J. W.	Customs
Angus, A. Forbes	Purdon & Co., Foochow
Annoi, J.	French Police Force
Anot, Rev. F.	French Mission, North Kiangse
Antonio, L.	Customs, Lighthouse Department
Ans, O.	Mang., Chefoo Filanda, Ltd., Chefoo
Appleton, Rev. G. H.	St. John's College
Aquino, A. M. d'	*Celestial Empire* Office
Aquino, J. C. d'	Adamson, Bell & Co.
Aquino, J. F. d'	Noronha & Sons
Aquino, Thos. d'	7, Seward Road
Arbuthnot, E. O.	Reid, Evans & Co.
Archibald, John	N. Bible Soc. of Scotland, Hankow
Arendt, C.	German Legation, Peking
Armour, J.	Customs, Wuhu
Armstrong, O.	Farnham & Co.
Arnhold, Ph.	Arnhold, Karberg & Co.
Arnous, H. G.	Customs, Seoul (Corea)
Arranger, J.	Comptoir d'Escompte de Paris
Artindale, R. H.	Iveson & Co.
Ashley, C. J.	Old Dock, Hongkew
Ashton, John	Secretary, Shanghai Club
Aslanoff, N. K.	Tokmakoff, Molotkoff & Co., Tientsin
Astill, R. W.	Shanghai Waterworks' Co.
Atkinson, John	Loong-hwa Powder Factory
Atkinson, Bronan	Thos. W. Kingsmill
Atterbury, B. C., M.D.	Am. Presbyterian Mission, Peking
Aubert, F. B.	Butterfield & Swire
Baber, E. C.	British Legation, Peking (absent)
Baessler, Joh.	Neubourg & Co.
Bagnall, B.	Am. Bible Society, Peking
Bailey, John	24, Nanking Road
Bailey, O. E.	Customs
Bain, W. B.	Pilot, care of Mustard & Co.
Baird, J.	China & Japan Trading Co.
Baker, H.	Butterfield & Swire, Foochow
Baldwin, Rev. C. C., D.D.	Am. Board Foreign Missions, F'chow
Baldwin, Rev. S. L.	Am. Meth. Ep. Mission, F'chow (abt.)
Balfour, Frederic H.	*North-China Herald* Office
Balfour, L. C.	Hongkong & Shanghai Bank
Ballard, J. A.	Russell & Co.
Ballard, T. J.	Customs
Ballauf, H.	E. Meyer & Co., Tientsin
Baller, Frederick W.	China Inland Mission, Chefoo
Bamford, Rev. A. J., B.A.	Union Church, Shantung Road
Ban, S.	Japanese Consulate
Bancal, E.	Ulysse, Pila & Co.
Bandinel, J. J. F.	Bandinel & Co., Newchwang
Banister, Rev. W.	Church Miss. Society, Foochow
Banker, W. S.	Pilot, Newchwang
Bannerman, Jas.	Shanghai Tug-Boat Association
Barchet, S. P., M.D.	Am. Baptist Mission, Ningpo
Barff, F. W.	Hongkong & S'hai Bank, Foochow
Barkham, T. W.	T. Weeks & Co.
Barnes, Alfred	Chief Constable, British Cons. Gaol
Barretto, L.	Holliday, Wise & Co.
Barrière, Ch.	Procure des Lazaristes
Barry, R.	Boyd & Co.
Bartley, A.	E. E. A. & C. Telegraph Co.
Bartolini, A.	Customs
Barton, Zeph.	Gov. Mar. Surveyor, 7, Canton Road
Bassormanoff, N. K.	Piatkoff, Molchanoff & Co., Hankow
Bastien, E.	French Police Force
Bastien, Ed.	French Municipal Council Office
Basto, J.	Drysdale, Ringer & Co., Hankow
Basuiau, R. F., S.J.	St. Joseph's Church
Bates, Rev. James	Church Missionary Society, Ningpo
Bathgate, John	Bathgate & Co., Foochow
Baumann, A.	Sieber-Waser
Baxter, A. G.	Pilot, Taku
Bean, W.	Merchant, Chinkiang
Beattie, Joseph	Ilbert & Co.
Beauchef, P., S.J.	St. Joseph's Church
Beauchamp, H. L.	Mackintosh, Dudgeon & Co.
Becke, F. G.	Customs, Hankow
Beckhoff, James	Municipal Council Surveyor's Office
Begg, Ch., M.D.	Customs, Hankow
Begley, C. W.	Foochow Ice Co., Foochow
Bekofsky, N. S.	Customs, Jenchuan (Corea)

BEL—BOW.

Belobre, Marquis Leonard de, French Consulate-General
Bellelu, E. .... Customs
Bellarey, Alexander...... Police Force
Bell, F. H. .... Adamson, Bell & Co.
Bell, Rev. Joseph .... Wesleyan Meth. Miss. Soc., Tah-ngan
Bell-Irving, J. J. .... Jardine, Matheson & Co. [(H'kow)
Belogolovy, A. A. .... Merchant, Tientsin
Benjamin, B. D.............. 17, Yangtsze Road
Benjamin, S. S. .... D. Sassoon, Sons & Co., Ningpo
Bennett, C. C. .... Mustard & Co. (absent)
Bennett, J. W. .... Mustard & Co.
Bennett, William G. .... Police Force
Berdonlot, J. .... French Police Force
Bergen, Rev. Paul D....... Am. Presb. Mission, Chinan-fu
Bergholz, Leo............... U.S. Vice-Consul, Chinkiang
Bernard, E .... Customs
Bernières, A. M............ Customs
Berthelot, C. .... French Municipal Police Station
Berthon, L................... French Post-Office
Betts, T. .... Customs (Chefoo)
Beurmann, C................ Arnhold, Karberg & Co.
Bevis, H. M. .... Hongkong and Shanghai Bank
Beyer, Ludwig .... E. Schellhass & Co. (absent)
Bidwell, H. S................ Bubbling Well Road
Bieber, Theodor........... Justus, Lembke & Co. (absent)
Biehl, J. C .... H. Sietas & Co., Chefoo
Bielfeld, Alex................ 4, Canton Road
Bielfeld, Franz .... 4, Canton Road
Bigsby, W. E. D. .... Shanghai Club
Billequin, A. .... College of Peking, Peking
Binos, J. .... French Police Force
Birck, V. .... Wolmuchs & Co.
Birt, Wm. .... Wm. Birt & Co.
Bisbee, A. M. .... Coast Inspector and Harbour Master
Bishop, J. D. .... Peking Road
Blachford, B. F............. Pilot, Newchwang
Black, D. T.................. Farnham & Co.
Blair, E. T. .... Jardine, Matheson & Co.
Bland, J. O. P. .... Inspt.-Gen. of I. M. Customs, Peking
Blanchard, W. .... Pilot, Taku
Blasky, P. .... Carlowitz & Co.
Block, J. .... H. Sietas & Co., Chefoo
Blodget, Rev. H., D.D. ... Am. B. of C. for For. Miss., Peking
Blow, H. .... H. Blow & Co., Tientsin
Bluntschli, G............... Coesn & Girand
Boad, W...................... Customs
Boad, W. .... Pilot, Taku
Böger, H...................... Kirchner & Böger (absent)
Bohnen, C. .... Dufour Brothers & Co.
Bohr, H. .... Great Northern Telegraph Co.
Bois, J. C. .... Butterfield & Swire (absent)
Bois, Edward .... White & Welch
Boll, R......................... Sayle & Co.
Bollard, J. .... 12, Nanzing Road
Bolmida, G.................. 6, Rue du Consulat
Bolton, C. J. .... Marine Supernt., C.M.S.N. Co., &c.
Bomanjee, F. .... Cawasjee, Pallanjee & Co.
Bonaboau, J. .... Secretary, French Municipal Council
Bond, C. W. .... Customs, Lighthouse Department
Bonneau, E.................. Customs
Bono, C. V................... Customs, Kiukiang
Bonsey, Rev. A............ London Missionary Society, Hankow
Boodifin, W. J. .... Merchant, Tientsin
Boone, H. W., M.D. ...... 4, Ming-hong Road
Boone, Rev. W. J.......... St. John's College
Borchardt, F. .... Shanghai Gas Co.
Borini, F...................... Customs, Jenchuan (Corea)
Börner, H. .... Siemssen & Co.
Boscat, Rev. F. .... French Mission, South Kiangsu
Boscongar.................... French Police Force
Boswell, Captain J. B.... Care of Mustard & Co.
Botelho, B. M............... Wiener & Co.
Botelho, E. .... 7A, Miller Road
Botelho, J. M............... Noronha & Sons
Botelho, J. M. B. .... Adamson, Bell & Co.
Botelho, R. .... China Traders' Insurance Company
Bottu, A....................... French Municipal Council Office
Boucher, H., S.J. .... St. Joseph's Church
Bourke, Ralph.............. Police Force
Bourlier, A................... French Police Force
Bovet, A...................... Bovet Bros. & Co. (absent)
Bowman, A. R. .... The Hall & Holtz Co. Co.
Bowman, J.................... British Consular Gaol
Bowring, C. T. .... Inspt.-Gen. of I.M. Customs, Peking

BOY—BUS.

Boyer, Edouard .... Kiangnan Arsenal
Boyd, H. .... Chartered Mercantile Bank
Boyd, J. S. .... Customs
Bradfield, J. .... Shanghai Medical Hall
Bragg, F. C. .... Lane, Crawford & Co.
Bragg, J. .... 32, Chapoo Road
Bragg, J. C.................. E. E. A. & C. Telegraph Co.
Bramann, M. .... E. Schellhass & Co.
Bramfitt, Rev. Thos. ...... Wesleyan Meth. Mission, Wusueh
Brand, David .... Brand, Brothers & Co
Brand, E...................... Pilot
Brand, Wm.................. Brand, Brothers & Co.
Brandon, E. F. .... Customs, Hankow
Brandt, M. von .... German Minister, Peking (absent)
Brandt, O. .... Shanghai Club and B. Well Road
Braun, L...................... 15, Nanking Road
Braun, R...................... Customs, Kiukiang
Bray, Monseigneur......... Bishop, French Miss., North Kiangsu
Brazier, J. R. .... Insp.-Gen. I. M. Customs, Peking
Brazier, H. W. .... Customs, Chinkiang
Bredon, R. E .... Customs, Hankow
Brenan, Byron.............. H.B.M.'s Consul, Chefoo
Brenan, E. V. .... Customs, Newchwang
Brereton, Dr. J. G. .... Chefoo
Brereton, Rev. W.......... Soc. for the Prop. of the Gospel, Peking
Bret, J. B. .... Mis. Catho. du Tche-kiang, Ningpo
Bretschneider, E., M.D.... Russian Legation, Peking (absent)
Brewer, Rev. John W.... Wesleyan Meth. Mission, Wuchang
Brianskih, N. N............ P. A. Ponomareff & Co., Foochow
Bright, Wm. .... Customs' Printing Office
Brinkworth, B. J. S. ...... Kelly & Walsh
Brinkworth, George ...... Kelly & Walsh
Britto, J. .... China & Japan Trading Co.
Brockett, G. T. .... Foochow Hotel, Foochow
Brosche, H.................. Customs, Tientsin
Broumton, James F. .... China Inland Mission, Kwei-chao
Brown, A. D. .... Shanghai Electric Co.
Brown, Ch. .... Hotel des Colonies
Brown, E...................... Sweetmeat Castle
Brown, J. L. .... Butterfield & Swire
Brown, R. M. .... Sec., Ch. Eng. & Mining Co., T'tsin
Brown, Thomas .... Kelly & Walsh
Browne, T. McC............ Hongkong & Shanghai Bank
Bruce, Wallace .... Constable, British Legation, Peking
Bruine, J. .... Astor House
Bruine, Jh. .... Hotel des Colonies
Brun, J. .... Pilot, care of Mustard & Co.
Brunat, P. .... Russell & Co., & 33, F'chow Road
Brunner, C. A. .... J. Hirsbrunner, Tientsin
Bryson, Rev. Thomas ... London Miss. Society, Wuchang (ab.)
Buchanan, C .... Super. Engineer Indo-China S.N. Co.
Buchanan, Jas. .... J. P. Bisset & Co.
Buchanan, W................ J. P. Bisset & Co.
Bucher, H. .... Chefoo Filands (Limited) Chefoo
Buchheister, J. J. .... 1, Ningpo Road
Buck, H. .... Sayle & Co.
Buckley, H. P. .... Alfred Dent & Co.
Bukow, P. .... A. Cordes & Co., Tientsin
Bull, E......................... Customs, Pagoda Anch., Foochow
Bulmer, W. .... Ch. Eng. & Mining Co., Tientsin
Burchardi, Fr. A........... Gipperich & Burchardi (absent)
Burge, F. J., M.D. .... Riverbank, 71, Broadway
Burgoyne, Geo. .... Merchant, Chefoo
Burgoyne, J. W. H. ...... Adamson, Bell & Co.
Burjorjee, D. .... 6, Siking Road
Burke, J. W. .... Customs, Ningpo
Burkill, A. R .... 3, Kiukiang Road
Burman, A.................... Dyce & Co.
Burmeister, Ed. .... Schmidt & Co. (absent)
Burmeister, Emil .... Schmidt & Co.
Burnett, J. H................ Merchant, Hankow
Burnett, Robert............. Nat. Bible Soc. of Scotland, Shensi
Burnett, W. E. .... China Inland Mission, Yang-chow
Burns, B. H. .... Oriental Bank Corporation
Burns, J. .... Customs, Newchwang
Burr, W. A. .... Pilot
Burrows, A.................. Butterfield & Swire
Burtenshaw, John .... Police Force
Bury, A. J. .... Wilkinson & Co.
Buschmann, E. .... E. Schellhass & Co. (absent)
Buse, J. .... Merchant, 15, Canton Road
Bush, H. A. .... Bush Bros., Newchwang
Bush, Henry E. .... Bush Bros., Newchwang
Bush, L. L.................... Russell & Co.

BUS—CHR.

Bushell, S. W., M.D.	British Legation, Peking
Bushendorff, A. W.	Proprietor, Beach Hotel, Chefoo
Butcher, Very Rev. C. H.	The Deanery (absent)
Butler, Arthur	Kiangnan Arsenal
Butler, G. A.	Agent, C.M.S.N. Co.
Butler, Geo..................	11, Szechuen Road
Butler, Rev. John	Am. Presbyterian Mission, Ningpo
Buttles, E. K................	Ch. Eng. & Mining Co., Tientsin
Byres, G. M.	Hongkong & Shanghai Bank
Byrne, E......................	The Hall & Holtz Co. Co.
Caldbeck, E. J.	Caldbeck, Macgregor & Co.
Callado, H.E. E.	Brazilian Minister (absent)
Callaway, J. W............	Harris, Goodwin & Co.
Camajee, H. D.	D. N. Camajee & Son (absent)
Cameron, Ewen	Hongkong & Shanghai Bank
Cameron, H.	Pilot, care of Mustard & Co.
Cameron, James	China Inland Mission, Hanchung (ab)
Campana, D.	French Police Force
Campbell, Alex.	Merchant, Kiukiang
Campbell, C.	Shanghai Waterworks' Co., Limited
Campbell, D. C.	Pilot
Campbell, H.	F'chow Hair Dressing Saloon, F'chow
Campbell, J. D.	Insp.-Gl. I.M. Customs, P'ing (L'don)
Campbell, R. M............	Agra Bank, Limited
Campbell, Rev. Wm.......	Eng. Presb. Mission, Taiwan-fu
Campbell, S.	Customs, Chefoo
Campbell, T. M............	Customs, Chefoo
Campos, A. P...............	Cozon & Giraud
Campos, F. N. P. de......	Messageries Maritimes Co.
Cance, W.....................	Shanghai Club
Candlin, Rev. G. T.	Meth. Missionary Society, Tientsin
Cane, Alex.	Butterfield & Swire
Cane, Geo....................	Boyd & Co.
Canning, Robert L.........	Police Force
Cardwell, J. E.	China Inland Mission, Kiangsi
Carion, F. F.	The Hall & Holtz Co. Co.
Carion, L. J..................	Noronha & Sons
Carl, F. A.	Customs
Carlassaro, Rev. E........	Roman Catholic Mission, Wuchang
Carles, W. R.	H.B.M. Consulate
Carlill, A. J. H.	Adamson, Bell & Co.
Carlos, B.....................	Pilot, Newchwang
Carlsen, F.	Great Northern Telegraph Co.
Carlson, W..................	Harbour Master's Office
Carnie, F.....................	Merchant, Chinkiang
Carr, R. A.	Customs
Carr, R. P.	Customs
Carrall, J. W.	Customs, Foochow
Carson, Rev. James	Irish Presb. Ch. Mission, Newchwang
Carter, J......................	Upper Yangtze Pilot, Rue du C'sulat
Carter, W. H.	Carter & Co. (absent)
Cartman, F. A.	Customs, Wuhu
Carvalho, P. M. de........	Oriental Bank
Castillo, S. P.	Recvg.-Ship "Corea"
Castro, G. H. A............	Customs, Tientsin
Catton, E. A.	E. D. Sassoon & Co., Foochow
Cave-Thomas, F.	Adamson, Bell & Co., Foochow
Cavolti, T.	16, Rue du Consulat
Chaigneau, J.	French Police Force
Chalmers, J. L.	Customs, Hankow
Chambers, H. J. J..........	John Gittings & Co., Foochow
Chapin, Rev. L. D.	Am. Board of For. Miss., Tungchow
Chapin, Rev. F. M.	Am. Board of For. Mission, Kalgan
Chapin, Rev. O. H.	Am. Presbyterian Mission, Nanking
Chapsal, J.	Agent, Mess. Mar. Co., French Bund
Charters, James	Inspector, Police Force
Chasle, Rev. F.	French Mission, North Kiangsu
Chaumont, M................	Customs
Cheerkoff, S. A.	Piatkoff, Molchanoff & Co., Foochow
Cheetham, J. F.	Turner & Co
Chenoweth, R.	2nd officer str "Kwa-hsing"
Cheredoff, P. N............	Piatkoff, Molchanoff & Co., Foochow
Cheshire, F. D.	U.S. Vice Consul-General
Chevalier, R. F., S.J. ...	Roman Cath. Mission, Tchen-kiang
Chevrier, L..................	Roman Catholic Mission, Peking
Chie, F. F.	Wong Bros. & Co., Chinkiang
Child, Thos..................	Insp.-Gen. of I.M. Customs, Peking
Ching Tu-chai..............	Director, Imperial Chinese Telegraphs
Chirkoff, S. A..............	Piatkoff, Molchanoff & Co., Foochow
Christensen, L.	Customs, Hankow
Christiansen, A.	Municipal Council Office
Christie, Dr. Dugald	Newchwang
Christiernsson, Dr. B. ...	Sweden & Norway V.-Consul-Gen.

CHU—CRO.

Chu Ta-jen	Director, I. C. Toloy College, Tientsin
Chu Yu-chee	Manager, C.M.S.N. Co.
Church, W.	Maitland & Co.
Churchill, H. W.	Hodge & Co., Foochow
Ciceri, Rev. F.	French Mission, North Kiangsu
Citti, G.	Customs
Civilini, J. P.	Customs, Fusan (Corea)
Claremont, G..............	Customs, Hankow
Clark, C. B..................	Surveyor, Municipal Council
Clark, J.	Customs
Clark, J. D.	*Shanghai Mercury* Office
Clarke, B. A.	Jardine, Matheson & Co. (absent)
Clarke, G.....................	Customs, Ningpo
Clarke, George W..........	China Inland Mission, Yunnan
Clarke, Samuel R.	China Inland Mission, Si-chuan
Clarke, William A.........	Police Force
Clarke, W. J.	Clarke, Head & Co., Chefoo
Clataud, J.	48, 50, 52, Rue Montauban
Clayson, F.	Customs
Cloinance, J. L.	Customs, Tientsin
Clément, C...................	French Consulate-General
Clifford, W. W.	The Hall & Holtz Co. Co.
Clifton, A. S. T............	North-China Insurance Co., Limited
Clifton, F.	Shanghai Waterworks' Co., Limited
Clough, B.	Upper Yangtze Pilot
Clyatt, W. D.	4, Quangse Terrace
Clynn, H.	Gibb, Livingston & Co., Foochow
Coates, J. E.	Pilot
Cochinard, F.	Comptoir d'Escompte, Foochow
Cock, A. C..................	Agra Bank
Cockburn, Rev. Geo., M.A.	Church of Scotland Mission, Ichang
Coe, F. E., D.D.S.	1, Kiukiang Road
Coffey, J......................	U.S. Consulate-General
Coffin, F. M.	Customs, Lighthouse Department
Coffin, J. A.	Hedge & Co., Foochow
Cole, Chas.	Maitland & Co.
Cole, C. J.	E. E. A. & Ch. Telegraph Co.
Colgan, Thos. H............	*Celestial Empire* Office
Collaço, J. M...............	Customs, Lighthouse Department
Collin de Plancy, Victor..	French Legation, Peking
Collins, G. W..............	G. W. Collins & Co., Tientsin
Collomb, F..................	French Police Force
Comins, C.	8, Kiukiang Road
Compton, J.	H.M.'s Consulate, Wênchow
Cook, M. H.	A316 & 316 & 317, Broadway, H'kew
Cooper, F. D.	Galton & Co., Foochow
Cooper, Fred. P.	Bush Bros., Newchwang
Cooper, H.	Shanghai & Hongkew Assd. Wharves
Cooper, John	Cunliffe & Co.
Cooper, William...........	China Inland Mission, Ganking
Cooper, W. M.	H.B.M. Consul, Ningpo
Cooverjee, Rustomjee ...	Cawasjee, Pallanjee & Co.
Copp, Alfred	American Bible Society, Chinkiang
Coqset, Père A.	Roman Catholic Mission, Tientsin
Corbach, W. von	Pilot, care of Mustard & Co.
Corbett, Rev. H.	Am. Presbyterian Mission, Chefoo
Cordeiro, P. A.	E. E. A. & Ch. Telegraph Co.
Cordes, August C.	A. Cordes & Co., Tientsin (absent)
Corfe, Rev. C. J., M.A....	Chefoo
Cornabé, W. A.	Cornabé & Co., Chefoo (absent)
Cornelli, J.	Customs
Corner, G. R.	19, Szechuen Road
Corneveaux, A.	French Police Force
Cory, J. M...................	1, Kiukiang Road
Costa, F. G..................	Fonceca & Co.
Costa, G. G.	Sieber-Waser
Costa, J. C. da	*North-China Herald* Office
Cottam, J. P.	The Hall & Holtz Co. Co.
Coulson, Chs.	Elliott & Co.
Coulthard, John J.........	China Inland Mission, Hankow
Coulthard, J. R............	H.B.M. Legation, Peking
Courbon, H.	French Police Force
Courbon, M. J.	French Police Force
Cousins, E.	Jardine, Matheson & Co., Tientsin
Couto, E. J. de	Jardine, Matheson & Co.
Coutts, George W.........	Bubbling Well Road
Cowles, Jr., J. P.	U. S. Consulate, Foochow
Cox, Edwin..................	Police Force
Cranston, D.	S. C. Farnham & Co.
Craven, T.	Hyde, Hertz & Co
Crawbie, H.	Taku Tug & Lighter Co., Tientsin
Crawford, Rev. T. P., D.D.	Am. South. Bapt. Mission, Tengchow
Crighton, R. T.	Customs, Lighthouse Department
Croal, R. W.	Capt. Receiving-ship "Ariel"

CRO—DIN.

Crocker, E. A.	Geo. Oliver & Co., Foochow
Cronnie, Chas.	3, Kiukiang Road
Cronon, A. B.	Customs
Crowlie, Capt. H.	Taku Tug & Lighter Co., Tientsin
Crutch, S. J.	Reiss & Co.
Cumine, Chas.	Cumine & Co. (absent)
Cumine, A. G. T.	Cumine & Co.
Cumming, N. A.	P. A. Ponomareff & Co., Hankow
Cunniffy, P.	Customs, Wenchow
Cunningham, T.	Customs, Lighthouse Department
Cushny, Jr., Alex.	J. P. Bisset & Co.
Czar, G.	French Police Force
Daae, I. M.	Commissioner of Customs, Chefoo
Daeth, John	Lucas & Co.
Dale, Herbert W.	Waters & Dale
Dons, W. A., M.D.	Am. Episcopal Mission, Wuchang
Dalgliesh, W. H.	Carter & Co.
Dallas, Arthur	Mun. Council Surveyor's Office
Dallas, Barnes	Bubbling Well Road
Dallas, Frank	The Hall & Holtz Co. Co.
Dalrymple, S. O.	Pilot, care of Mustard & Co.
Daly, S.	33, Szechuen Road
Dalziel, James	China Inland Mission, 2, Seward Rd.
Dampney, J.	Watson & Co., Foochow
Danenberg, J.	Drysdale, Ringer & Co.
Danforth, A. W.	Shanghai Cotton Cloth Mill Co.
Daniel, H. W.	Gibb, Livingston & Co.
Darko, G. T.	Fan Chang & Co.
Darling, D. A.	Barlow & Co.
Darnell D.	Temperance Hall
D'Arheux, Comte G.	Customs, Wenchow
Dasilva, J. P. N.	"The Farm"
Dauverchain, Rev. F.	French Mission, North Kiangsu
Dauverchain, Rev. F.	Roman Catholic Mission, Kiukiang
Davenport, A.	H.B.M. Consul, Tientsin
Davey, John	A. S. Watson & Co.
David, A. J.	E. D. Sassoon & Co., Ningpo
David, D. M.	Merchant, Chinkiang
Davidson, G.	Davidson & Co., Ningpo
Davidson, P.	Davidson & Co., Ningpo
Davidson, R. M.	Davidson & Co., Ningpo
Davidson, Wm.	Davidson & Co., Ningpo (absent)
Davies, C. W.	Customs, Tientsin
Davies, G. W.	Assistant to Inspector of Nuisances
Davies, T.	T. Davies & Co., Newchwang
Davies, W.	G. J. Morrison
Davis, Edward	Wisner & Co.
Davis, J. Kennard	North-China Insurance Co., Ld.
Davis, Rev. D. H.	St. Catharine's Bridge, West Gate
Davis, Rev. Geo. R.	Am. Meth. Episcopal Mission, Peking
Davis, Rev. J. W.	Am. Presbyterian Mission, Soochow
Dawoodbhoy, Abdoolally	A. Ebrahim & Co.
Dawson, C. P.	Customs, Chefoo
Deacon, Herbert	John Forster & Co., Foochow
Deane, A. Sharp, M.D.	Customs, Wuhu
Deck, A.	French Gas Works
Décoppe	Hotel des Colonies
De Costa, Henry J.	Police Force
Dechevrens, R. F., S.J.	Director of Zikawei Observatory
Deighton-Braysher, C.	Asst. Harbour Master
Deitz, G.	Lightship "Newchwang," N'chwang
De Laut, F. J.	Customs, Hankow
Delaplace, Mgr. L. G.	Roman Catholic Mission, Peking
Deldbarro, S.	Roman Catholic Mission, Peking
Delemasure, J. B.	Roman Catholic Mission, Peking
Delostre, J. E.	Customs
De Luca, Ferdinand	Italian Minister (absent)
Domée, A. C.	Customs, Hankow
Denman, William	Kiangnan Arsenal
Denny, O. N.	U.S. Consulate-General (absent)
Dent, Alfred	Alfred Dent & Co. (absent)
Dent, V. E. J.	Customs, Hankow
Deriner, T. M.	Adamson, Bell & Co., Foochow (abt.)
Derrick, G.	Shanghai Electric Co.
Desflèches, Right Rev. Bp.	Vic. Ap. of Szechuen
Desjacques, R. F., S.J.	St. Joseph's Church
Deville, W. N.	Licensed Pilot (Reserve)
Dick, H.	China Inland Mission, Hunan
Dick, James	S. C. Farnham & Co.
Dickinson, W. W.	G. W. Collins & Co., Tientsin
Dickinson, J. M.	G. W. Collins & Co., Tientsin
Diniz, Adelino F.	Chartered Bank of I., A. and China
Diniz, A. J.	Hongkong & Shanghai Bank

DIN—ENG.

Diniz, S. J.	Chartered Bank of I., A. and China
Dmitrovsky, P. A.	Russian Consul, Hankow
Dmitrieff, W. W.	Tokmakoff, Molotkoff & Co., Tientsin
Dobie, W.	Receiving-ship "Yuen Fah"
Dodwell, G. B.	Adamson, Bell & Co.
Donaldson, C. M.	1, Canton Road
Donaldson, C. P. M.	H.B.M. Office of Works
Donnelly, A. R.	Cornabé & Co., Chefoo
Donovan, J. P.	Customs
Dorward, Adam C.	China Inland Mission, Hunan
Douglas, R.	Saunders' Photographic Studio
Douthwaite, Arthur W.	China Inland Mission, Chefoo
Dowdall, Chas.	Myburgh & Dowdall, 21, F'chow. Rd.
Dowdall, W.M., A.R.I.B.A.	21, Foochow Road
Dowley, E. H.	Butterfield & Swire
Dowsley, Rev. A., B.A.	Ch. of Scotland Mission, Ichang
Doyle, Wm. H.	Agent China Paper Mill Co.
Drage, Z. D.	Mar. Superintd. Indo-China S.N. Co.
Drake, Samuel B.	China Inland Mission, Shansi
Drew, E. B.	Insp.-Gen. I.M. Customs, Statistical Department
Drew, Henry	Police Force
Driekusen, Peter	Police Force
Drummond, W. V.	4, Balfour Buildings, & B. Well Rd.
Dubail, C.	Vic. Apos., Rom. Cath. Miss., N'chwang
Du Bose, Rev. H. C.	Am. Presb. Mission, Soochow
Dudgeon, C. J.	3, Nanking Road
Dudgeon, J., M.D., C.M.	London Missionary Society, Peking
Duer, Yeend	Agent, Mitsu Bishi M.S.S. Co.
Duff, T. W.	Merchant, Chinkiang
Dufour, R.	French Police Force
Du Jardin, F.	Fergusson & Co., Chefoo
Dullberg, F. W. E.	Customs, Statistical Department
Dumonteil, B.	Roman Catholic Mission, Peking
Duncan, Chesney	Customs, Fu-san (Corea)
Dunn, C. A. L.	Thurburn & Dunn
Dunn, John G.	Shanghai Club
Deane, J. J.	American Clock & Brass Co.
Dunman, W.	34, Nankin Road
Duval, V.	French Municipal Council Office
Dynn, J. M.	Synagogue "Beth El."
Dyce, C. M.	Dyce & Co.
Dyer, H.	The Hall & Holtz Co. Co.
Dyer, S.	Br. & For. Bible Society, 3a, W'poo Rd.
Dziouk, M. F.	Astor House
Eason, Arthur	China Inland Mission, Sz-chuen
Easterbrook, S. T. F.	Geo. Oliver & Co.
Eastlack, R. F.	Frazar & Co.
Eastlack, W. R.	China and Japan Trading Co.
Easton, A. J.	Union Insurance Society of Canton
Easton, George F.	China Inland Mission, Shensi
Eccles, J.	"Houki" Lighthouse, Chefoo
Ecclestone, J.	Customs, Tientsin
Eckford, A. M.	Cornabé & Co., Chefoo
Eckhold, M.	Customs
Eddie, Alexander	Police Force
Edgar, J.	Customs, Newchwang
Edkins, Rev. Joseph, D.D.	London Missionary Society, Peking
Edwards, Dr. E. H.	China Inland Mission, Sz-chuen
Edwards, W. J.	Boyd & Co.
Ehlers, Aug.	6, Szechuen Road
Eitter, G.	Mun. Council, Surveyor's Office
Ekstrand, T. A.	Mitsu Bishi M.S.S. Co.
Elberg, J.	F. A. Schultze & Co., Newchwang
Ekdor, A. G.	Customs, Chefoo
Elias, E. E.	30, Kiangse Road
Elias, R. H.	R. S. Raphael
Ellert, Arnold	Schmidt & Co.
Ellerton, H. B.	Gilman & Co., Foochow
Ellis, M. E.	E. D. Sassoon & Co., Tientsin
Elliston, W. L.	China Inland Mission, Chefoo
Elwin, Rev. A.	Church Miss. Society, Hangchow
Emens, W. S.	Melchers & Lehmann
Emery, D. A.	Merchant, Chinkiang
Emonet, N. M.	Roman Catholic Mission, Newchwang
Encarnação, Albino d'	c80, Honan Road
Encarnação, C. C.	c80, Honan Road
Encarnação, Cesar d'	c80, Honan Road
Encarnação, F. X. d'	Arnhold, Karberg & Co.
Encarnação, J.	c80, Honan Road
Encarnação, L.	A. Robinson
Endicott, H. B.	Butterfield & Swire
England, C. R.	Corner of Kiangse and Nanking Rds.

ENG—FRA.

England, F. H. .... Merchant, Foochow
Enomotto, Vice-Admiral Takeaki, Japanese Minister, Peking (ab)
Esoofally, Bhaymia ...... A. Ebrahim & Co.
Estevas, F. M. .... 27, Nanking Road
Evans, A. E. M. .... Shanghai & Hongkew Wharf
Evans, H. .... H. Evans & Co., Ming-hong Rd. H'kew
Evans, J. H. .... Evans, Pugh & Co. (absent)
Evans, M. P. .... Reid, Evans & Co.
Eveleigh, J. .... Inspector, Police Force
Everall, H. .... The Hall & Holtz Co. Co.
Everard, W. C. .... British Legation, Peking
Exley, Rev. R. I. .... Meth. Free Ch. Mission, Wenchow
Ezekiel, J. S. .... D. Sassoon, Sons & Co.
Ezekiel, N. D. .... D. Sassoon, Sons & Co., Foochow
Ezra, E. M. .... E. D. Sassoon & Co.

Faber, E. P. .... Great Northern Telegraph Co.
Fabris, E. A. .... Municipal Council Office
Fabris, J. M. .... Bubbling Well Road
Fairhurst, T. .... Newman & Co., Foochow
Farmer, Charles .... H.M.'s Consulate, Newchwang
Farnham, Rev. J. M. W., D.D., Outside South Gate (absent)
Farrell, H. A. .... Customs, Chinkiang
Faurel, A. A. .... Customs, Hankow
Favier, Alph .... Roman Catholic Mission, Peking
Fawcett, T. H. .... Customs, Hankow
Fearon, C. H. .... Fearon, Low & Co.
Fearon, J. S. .... Fearon, Low & Co.
Featherstonhaugh, M. H. Geo. Oliver & Co., Foochow
Feindel, Ch. .... German Consulate, Tientsin
Felton, E. .... Customs
Fenton, Geo. B. .... Professor of Music, 1, Sunkiang Rd.
Ferguson, Hon. J. H. ... Netherlands Minister, Peking
Ferguson, John C., C.E. Nanking Rd., Sassoon's New B'dings
Ferguson, Robt. .... Morriss & Ferguson
Ferguson, Thos. T. ...... Ferguson & Co., Chefoo
Féro, A. .... French Police Force
Ferrand, R. F., S.J. ...... St. Joseph's Church
Ferreira, C. .... 1, Chapoo Road
Ferreira, L. .... Actg. Consul-General for Portugal
Ferris, F. F. .... *North-China Herald* Office
Fetherstonhaugh, J. ...... Customs, Chinkiang
Field, A. W. .... Customs, Chinkiang
Figueiredo, H. C. V. de... Fearon, Low & Co.
Findlay, John .... Major Bros.
Fiol, D. .... French Police Force
Fioritti, J. B. .... Roman Catholic Mission, Peking
Fishburne, R. B., M.D. ... Am. Presb. Mission, Hangchow
Fischer, G. .... E. Meyer & Co., Tientsin
Fisher, E. .... Bill and Bullion Broker, Hankow
Fisler, L. F. .... Fisler, L. F. & Co., 14B, Foochow Rd.
Fitch, Rev. Geo. F. ...... Am. Presbyterian Mission, Soochow
Fittock, G. V. .... H.B.M.'s Legation, Peking
Flothow, E. .... Siemssen & Co., Foochow
Fock, O. .... R. Telge, Tulay Buildings
Foncoca, A. A. .... Foncoca & Co., 13, Peking Road
Foncoca, J. B. .... Butterfield & Swire
Foncoca, V. P. .... Receiving-Ship "Wellington"
Fonseca, F. V. da .... Evans, Pugh & Co.
Foote, L. H. .... Minister for the U.S.A., Seoul (Corea)
Forbes, Geo. H. .... Hatch, Forbes & Co., Tientsin
Forbes, H. de C. .... Russell & Co. (absent)
Forbes, William .... Merchant, Tientsin
Forbes, W. H. .... Hatch, Forbes & Co., Tientsin
Ford, Colin M. .... H.B.M.'s Consulate
Ford, John .... Boyd & Co.
Ford, T. .... Butterfield & Swire
Fordham, Rev. J. S. ...... Wesleyan Meth. Mission, Wusueh
Foreshaw, Ernest .... Hyde, Hertz & Co.
Forrester, Wm. .... Forrester & Co.
Forster, John .... John Forster & Co., Foochow (abt.)
Fortamp, A. .... French Police Force
Foster, James .... Mackenzie & Co.
Foster, Rev. Arnold, B.A. Hankow
Fougerat, J. H. .... Customs, Chinkiang
Fourniol, J. .... Schönhard & Co.
Fowler, W. .... Inspector, Central Police Station
Francis, R. .... 10, Peking Road
Frandin, Hte. .... French Consulate, Tientsin
Frandon, E. .... French Consul, Foochow
Frandsen, H. A. .... Customs, Lighthouse Dept., Taku
Fraser, E. H. .... British Consulate, Foochow
Frazar, Everett .... Frazar & Co. (absent)
Frazer, J., L.R.C.P., &c... Tientsin

FRE—GOU.

Fredrickson, A. .... Pilot, Newchwang
Freeth, G. J. .... Customs, Hankow
French, W. .... Customs, Taku
Fritsche, H. .... Russian Legation, Peking
Fritz, J. .... Mustard & Co.
Fry, F. W. .... Weeks & Fry, Foochow (absent)
Fryer, H. .... P. & O. Co.
Fryer, John .... Kiangnan Arsenal
Fuhrmann, Richard ...... Justus, Lembke & Co.
Fukuhara, Y. .... Mitsui Bussan Kaisha
Fukushima, Capt. Yasumasa, Japanese Legation, Peking
Fulford, H. E. .... H.B.M.'s Consulate
Fuller, Rev. A. R. .... Church Miss. Society, Shaouhing
Fuller, W. R. .... H. Consterdine & Co., Chefoo
Fusco, Rev. F. .... French Mission, South Kiangse

Gabriel, H., Dr. jur. .... German Consulate-General
Gale, S. R. .... Shanghai Library
Galembert, P. M. G. de... Customs
Gall, J. .... Constable, French & U.S. Con., T'tsin
Galles, F. W. .... S. C. Farnham & Co.
Galles, G. .... S. C. Farnham & Co.
Galletti, N. J. B. .... Customs, Pagoda Anchorage, F'chow
Galpin, Rev. Frederick ... Meth. Free Church Mission, Ningpo
Galton, W. P. .... Galton & Co., Foochow
Gamewell, Rev. Frank D. Meth. Episcopal Mission, Peking
Gamman, Edwin .... Edwin Gamman & Co.
Gande, J. W. .... Caldbeck, Macgregor & Co.
Gardner, C. T. .... H.B.M.'s Consul, Ichang
Gardiner, Geo. E. J. .... Birley & Co., Foochow
Gardner, J. P. Wade ... Hongkong & S'ghai Bank, Foochow
Gardner, W. A. R. .... Glen Vue House, Chefoo (absent)
Garnier, Mon. V., S.J. ... Bishop of Titopolis, Vicar Apostolic of Kiang-nan
Garrett, Capt. .... Shanghai Tug-Boat Association
Garrigues, J. .... Roman Catholic Mission, Peking
Garwood, Francis .... Police Force
Gatti, C. .... Jardine, Matheson & Co.
Goering, J. G. W. .... Merchant, Chinkiang (absent)
Gebhardt, F. .... H. M. Schultz & Co.
Genin, Paul .... Hyde, Hertz & Co.
Gessoit, A. .... 60, French Bund
Getley, A. .... Pilot, care of Mustard & Co.
Ghika, N. D. .... Customs, Tientsin
Ghisi, E. .... Dufour Brothers & Co.
Gilbert, William .... John Forster & Co., Foochow
Giles, J. .... S. C. Farnham & Co.
Giles, H. A. .... H.B.M.'s Vice-Consul (absent)
Gillenders, A. .... S. C. Farnham & Co.
Gillard, F. .... Parisian Saloon
Gilley, H. H. .... E. E. A. & Ch. Telegraph Co.
Gillison, Rev. Thomas, M.B., London Miss. Society, Hankow
Gilmour, David .... Hankow Road (absent)
Gilmour, Rev. J., M.A. ... London Missionary Society, Peking
Ginart, Manuel .... Consul for Spain
Gipperich, E. .... Gipperich & Burchardi
Gipperich, G. .... Chefoo Filande (Limited), Chefoo
Giquel, Prosper .... Arsenal, Foochow (absent)
Girard, U. .... Cuzon & Giraud
Gittins, John .... John Gittins & Co., Foochow (absent)
Gittins, Jr., Thomas ...... John Gittins & Co., Foochow
Giudicelli, T. .... French Municipal Council Office
Glass, Duncan .... Mngr., S. & H. & J.'s Ass. Wharves
Glover, G. B. .... Commissioner of Customs
Go, S. .... Japanese Consulate
Goddard, Rev. J. R. ...... American Baptist Mission, N'po (ab.)
Godwin, A. A. .... Customs
Goetz, A. .... 25, Kiangse Road
Goh, Daigoro .... Japanese Legation, Peking
Goh, Kdita .... Japanese Legation, Peking
Golding, T. B. .... 5, North Soochow Road
Gomboeff, N. .... Russian Legation, Peking
Goodfellow, W. .... Shanghai Gas Co.
Goodrich, Rev. Chauncey. Am. Board for For. Miss., T'ungchow
Goodwin, Oliver .... Harris, Goodwin & Co.
Goolamully Mahomed Ajum, Mahomedan Church
Gordon, C. W. .... A. L. Rodinoff & Co., Hankow
Gordon, H. L. .... C. & J. Trading Co.
Gordon, William Grant... Gordon Brothers, Hankow
Gore-Booth, E. H. .... The Club
Gore-Booth, R. H. .... The Club
Gough, Rev. F. F., M.A. ... Church Missionary Society, Ningpo
Gouilloud, L. .... Russell & Co.
Gould, J. .... Municipal Council Office

GOU—HAR.

Goulding, J. W.	Ch. Eng. & Mining Co., Tientsin
Goussory, J., S.J.	Roman Cath. Mission, Tchou-kiang
Gove, Frank	Wheelock & Co.
Gowing, Lionel Francis	*North-China Herald* Office
Grabe, Otto	Otto Grabe & Co., Tientsin
Graesel, Arthur (Kalgan)	Care of G. W. Collins & Co., T'tsin
Graham, Wm.	Hunter, W. L., Foochow
Graham, W. J.	William Forbes, Tientsin
Grainger, S. J.	Customs, Ichang
Gram, C. C.	Customs
Grandguillaume, A.	L. Vrard & Co.
Grandon, Capt.	Shanghai Tug-Boat Association
Grant, C. Lyall	Adamson, Bell & Co. (absent)
Grant, L. M. F.	Gilman & Co., Foochow
Grant, P. McGregor	Robt. Anderson & Co.
Grant, P. V.	Boyd & Co.
Gratton, Fredk. M.	1, Kinkiang Road
Graves, Rev. F. R.	Am. Episcopal Mission, Wuchang
Gray, A. T.	Wheelock & Co.
Grayston, B. R.	The Hall & Holtz Co. Co.
Greathead, Astle	*North-China Herald* Office
Greaves, A. R.	Turner & Co., Foochow
Green, A. G.	Shanghai Medical Hall
Green, F. J.	Russell & Co.
Green, S. A.	Great Northern Telegraph Co.
Greenwood, Rev. M.	Church of England Mission, Peking
Greig, M. W.	Russell & Co., Foochow
Grosard, Louis	Pharmacie de l'Union
Grimani, E. H.	Customs, Ningpo
Grimmer, James	Temperance Hall
Grönner, A.	Corner of N'king & S'chuen Rd. (ab.)
Grose, Frank	W. Hewett & Co.
Grosclaude, E.	Szechuen
Groves, Rev. W. L., B.A.	Church Missionary Society, N'po (ab.)
Groves, L. J.	The Hall & Holtz Co. Co.
Growloff, Nicholas	Police Force
Grünfeld, M. A.	Tokmakoff, Molotkoff & Co., T'tsin
Gubbay, Reuben A.	Corner of Kiangse & Kinkiang Roads
Gubbay, Y. A.	E. D. Sassoon & Co.
Guierry, Mgr. E.F., V.Ap.	Mission Cath. du Tche-kiang, N'po
Guieu, C.	Guieu Frères
Guieu, L.	Guieu Frères
Guillen, R. F., S.J.	Church of Sacred Heart of Jesus
Guillot, A. R.	Mission Cath. du Tche-kiang, N'po
Gulick, Rev. L. H.	Agt., Am. Bib. Soc., 18, PekingRd.
Günther, J. H. C.	Customs, Kiukiang
Gurney, James	The Hall & Holtz Co. Co.
Gutierres, D. M.	Hongkong & Shanghai Bank
Gutierres, L. M.	Mackintosh, Dudgeon & Co.
Guyot, F.	Roman Catholic Mission, Peking
Haas, Joseph	Commissioner of Customs, Seoul
Habibbhoy Ahmedbhoy	French Bund
Habibbhoy, R.	French Concession
Hagen, C.	Crasemann & Hagen, Chefoo
Hagge, H.	Otto, Grabe & Co., Tientsin
Haggitt, J. R.	Oriental Bank
Hague, F.	Corner of Szechuen & Hankow Roads
Haitce, J.	French Legation, Peking
Halcomb, Rev. N. W.	Am. Baptist Mission, Chefoo
Hall, Dr. J. Ward	36, Nanking Road
Hall, H. E.	Rue de Peres
Hall, James	Butterfield & Swire
Hall, Nathaniel	Police Force
Hallifax, T. E.	Customs, Seoul (Corea)
Halton, Jr., E.	Gibb, Livingston & Co.
Hamilton, Henry	Police Force
Hamlin, W. P.	Shanghai & Hongkew Wharf
Hamlyn, J. G.	Customs, Kiukiang
Hammerann, J. H.	Lightship "Newchwang," N'chwang
Hammond, J. L.	Morris & Co.
Handro, C. E. R.	Customs, Newchwang
Hanisch, S.	Customs, Wenchow
Hannen, C.	Commissioner of Customs, Foochow
Hansen, Adolph	H. Sietas & Co., Chefoo
Hansen, H. A.	H. Sietas & Co., Chefoo
Hansen, J.	Great Northern Telegraph Co.
Happer, A. P.	Inspt.-Gen. of I.M. Customs, Peking
Happer, Rev. A. P., D.D.	18, Peking Road
Harling, J. W.	Turnbull, Howie & Co.
Hardy, Roderick	Police Force
Hardoon, E. A.	5, Hankow Road
Harling, G.	E. Schellhass & Co.
Harman, G.	Foochow

HAR—HOF.

Harmor, William	Police Force
Harris, A. H.	Customs, Hankow
Harris, J. E.	Customs, Kiukiang
Harris, T.	P. & O. Co.
Harris, W. F.	S. Moutrie
Harris, Wilmer	Wm. Birt & Co.
Hart, G. M.	Municipal Council Office
Hart, J. H.	Commissioner of Customs (absent)
Hart, J. W.	Engineer-in-ch. Sh. Waterwork's Co.
Hart, Sir Robert	Inspector-General, Customs, Peking
Hart, Rev. V. C.	Am. Meth. Episcopal Miss., Nanking
Hartmann, H. U.	Customs, Lighthouse Department
Hartmann, J.	Hartmann & Co., Tientsin
Hartmann, J.	Merchant, Ningpo and Tientsin
Harton, Jr., W. H.	Gilman & Co., Foochow
Hartwell, Charles S.	U.S. Consulate, Foochow
Hartwell, Rev. C.	Am. Board Foreign Missions, F'chow
Harvie J. Alex.	28, Kiangse Road
Harvie, W. M.	28, Kiangse Road
Harwood, H. G.	R. E. Wainewright
Hasobe, N.	Mitsui Bussan Kaisha
Haskell, F. E.	China & Japan Trading Co.
Haskell, F. H.	China & Japan Trading Co.
Hatch, John J.	Hatch, Forbes & Co., Tientsin
Haughton, F.	Customs, Ningpo
Haupt, H.	Melchers & Co.
Hawes, J. A.	Evans, Pugh & Co.
Hawkins, H. H.	Customs, Fusan (Corea)
Hay, C. W.	Boyd & Co.
Hay, D.	Wheelock & Co.
Hayden, G. W.	Customs, Lighthouse Department
Hayes, Rev. J. N.	Am. Presbyterian Mission, Nanking
Hayes, Rev. W. M.	Am. Presbyterian Mission, Tungchow
Hayward, W.	The Hall & Holtz Co. Co.
Head, R. L.	Clarke, Head & Co., Chefoo
Hearn, H. R.	Alfred Dent & Co.
Heckmann, A.	Mission Cath. du Tche-kiang, Ningpo
Hegrat, F. J.	Customs
Hember, S.	Merchant, &c., Wuhu
Henderson, W. A., M.D.	Customs, Ningpo
Henderson, E., M.D.	5, Hongkong Road
Henderson, D. M.	Engineer-in chief, Customs
Henderson, James	Merchant, Tientsin
Henningsen, J.	Great Northern Telegraph Co.
Henry, A.	Medical Officer, Customs, Ichang
Herring, R. Dawson	Constable, British Legation, Peking
Hertz, Henry	Hyde, Hertz & Co.
Hesse, E.	Smith & Co., Chefoo
Heuckendorff, J. J.	F. A. Schultze & Co., Newchwang
Heude, R. P., S.J.	Sikawei Museum
Hewett, E. A.	P. & O. Co.'s Office
Hewett, W. H.	Lane, Crawford & Co.
Hewett, W. J.	Customs, Kiukiang
Hey, E.	2, The Bund
Hickens, F. D.	Sayle & Co.
Hickey, P. S.	Upper Yangtsze Pilot
Hiosalu, G.	Japanese Consul, Chefoo
Hildesley, W. S.	Chefoo
Hill, Charles E.	9, Hotel des Colonies
Hill, Rev. David	Wesleyan Meth. Mission, Wuchang
Hill, J. C.	Pilot, Taku
Hills, J. C.	Customs Lighthouse, Department
Hillier, E. G.	Hongkong & Shanghai Bank
Hillier, H. M.	Insp.-Gen. I. M. Customs, (London)
Hillier, W. C.	British Legation, Peking
Hincelot, F.	Comptoir d'Escompte de Paris
Hinds, Rev. J.	Meth. Missionary Society, Tientsin
Hippisley, A. E.	Inspt.-Gen. of I.M. Customs, Peking
Hirsbrunner, James	7, Seking Road
Hirsbrunner, John	Hirsbrunner & Co.
Hitch, F. D.	Russell & Co.
Hirth, F.	Customs, Statistical Department
Hjonsbery, E. H.	Pilot
Hoar, J. H.	Pilot, c/o Mustard & Co.
Hoare, Rev. J. C., M.A.	Church Miss. Society, Ningpo
Hobart, Rev. W. T.	Am. Meth. Episcopal Miss., Peking
Hobson, H. E.	Customs, Tientsin
Hobson, R. M.	Customs, Tientsin
Hodge, James	Hirsbrunner & Co.
Hofler von Hoffenfels, Max.	Austro-Hungary Minister Resident in China, Japan and Siam (on leave)
Hoflich, A.	A. Grimmer & Co.
Hoflich, Joseph	15, Nanking Road

HOF—JAM.

Hofman, Rev. J. .... Roman Catholic Mission, Hankow
Högemann, A. H .... S. C. Farnham & Co.
Hogg, E. Jenner .... 10, Peking Road
Holcombe, Chester .... Secretary, U.S. Legation, Peking
Holdinghausen, F. .... Alex. Bielfeld
Holwill, E. T. .... Customs
Holland, C. J. .... Secretary, Masonic Club
Holland, W. .... H.B.M. Consulate, Tientsin
Holliday, Chas. J. .... Holliday, Wise & Co.
Holm, Adolf .... Carlowitz & Co.
Holmes, G. N. .... Boyd & Co.
Holt, Rev. W. S. .... Am. Presb. Miss. Press, 18, P'king Rd.
Hope, E. R. .... Sayle & Co.
Hopkins, F. .... Customs
Hopkins, G. G. .... Broker, Foochow Road
Hopkins, W. B. .... Co-Operative Cargo Boat Co.
Hore, T. .... H.B.M. Supreme Court
Hörning, J. .... Customs, Chefoo
Horsburgh, Rev. J. H., M.A. Church Miss. Society, Hangchow
Hu Sun-chee .... Secretary, China Merchants' Marine and Fire Insurance Co.
Hosie, Alex. .... Szechuen (on special service)
Hough, T. F. .... Jardine, Matheson & Co.
Hough, R. .... Customs
Houllegate, P. .... French Police Force
Houston, Rev. M. H. ... Am. Presbyterian Mission, H'chow
How, A. J. .... 1, Hongkong Road
How, G. T. .... Hongkong & Shanghai Bank
Howard, Geo. .... Inspector, Police Force
Howard, W. C. .... Customs
Howell, J. .... Inspector, River Police
Howes, A. .... Boyd & Co.
Howes, J. .... Municipal Inspector of Nuisances
Howie, Wm. .... Turnbull, Howie & Co.
Hübbe, P. G. .... Siemssen & Co.
Huchting, F. .... Rodewald & Co.
Huestis, B. N. .... 3, Quinsan Road
Huey, B. E. .... Superintendent, Sailors' Home
Hugues, C. .... French Police Force
Hughes, P. J. .... H.B.M.'s Consul, The Bund
Hühn, G. R. .... W. L. Hunter, Foochow
Humblot, A. .... Roman Catholic Mission, Peking
Hunnex, Rev. W. J. .... Am. Baptist (Southern) Miss. Chink'g
Hunt, Henry W. .... China Inland Mission, Kansuh
Hunt, W. E. .... 40, Kiangse Road
Hunter, A. C. .... Russell & Co.
Hunter, H. E. R. .... Hongkong and Shanghai Bank
Hunter, Rev. S. A. D., M.D. Am. Presb. Mission, Chinan-fu
Hunter, J., M.D. .... Irish Presb. Ch. Mission, N'chwang
Hunter, J. M. .... Customs, Pagoda Anch., Foochow
Hunter, Rev. S. A., M.D. Am. Presb. Mission, Tsinan-fu
Hutchings, C. H. .... 12, Peking Road
Hyde, W. W. .... Hyde, Hertz & Co. (absent)
Hykes, Rev. J. R. .... Am. Meth. Episcopal Miss., K'kiang

Iharruthy, B. L. .... Mission Cath. du Tche-kiang, Ningpo
Iburg, C. .... Iveson & Co.
Iburg, I. C. H. .... 10, North Soochow Road
Iffland, A. .... Customs
Ignatio, T. .... 710, Seward Road
Ilbert, A. .... Ilbert & Co. (absent)
Imbault-Huart, Camille .. French Consul, Hankow
Inayama, K. .... Japanese Post-Office
Inchbald, C. C. .... Comptoir d'Escompte de Paris
Inglis, R. .... Jardine, Matheson & Co., Hankow
Innocent, G. M. .... Meth. Missionary Society, Tientsin
Innocent, J. W. .... Customs, Ningpo
Innocent, Rev. J. .... Methodist Missionary Soc., Tientsin
Inverarity, A. J. M. .... Chartered Bank of I. A. & Ch.
Irons, F. .... Crasemann & Hagen, Chefoo
Irwin, Andrew, M.D. .... Tientsin
Isaac, I. .... D. Sassoon, Sons & Co., Ningpo
Isaac, R. Michael .... David Sassoon, Sons & Co.
Ishida, N. .... Mitsui Bussan Kaisha
Ismer, C. .... H. Muller & Co.
Iveson, Egbert .... Iveson & Co. (absent)
Iwaii, T. .... Japanese Postmaster, Fusan (Corea)

Jackson, David .... Hongkong and Shanghai Bank
Jackson, Josiah A. .... China Inland Mission, Chehkiang
Jackson, W. S. .... Russell & Co.
Jacobi, Ernst .... Civil Engineer, Meyer & Co., Tientsin
Jairazbhoy Peerbhoy .... Taley Building
James, W. .... H. Evans & Co.

JAM—KIN.

Jamieson, Geo. .... H.B.M.'s Consul, Kiukiang
Jamieson, R. A., M.A., M.B. 1A, Kiukiang Road
Jamieson, W. B. .... Jamieson & Co.
Jansen, D. C. .... Astor House
Jansen, J. E. .... 28, Nanking Road
Jantzen, Carl .... Melchers & Co.
Jardin, F. du .... Fergusson & Co., Chefoo
Jarno, P. .... French Police Force
Jarvis, M. .... Chinese Eng. & Mining Co., T'tsin.
Jean, G. .... Roman Catholic Mission, Peking
Jeanrenaud, Charles .... Peking
Jeffrey, T. .... Sayle & Co.
Jego, L. M. .... French Police Force
Jenkins, M. A. .... U. S. Consulate, Hankow
Jenkins, Rev. H. .... Am. Baptist Mission, Shaou-hying
Jennings, T. C. .... Harbour Master, Chefoo
Jensen, C. J. .... Great Northern Telegraph Co.
Jensen, J. L. .... Iveson & Co.
Jerdein, F. .... Jerdein & Co., Hankow
Jerdein, M. S. .... Merchant, Chinkiang
Jezewski, J. von .... Customs, Nantai (Foochow)
Joergens, R. .... Carlowitz & Co.
John, Rev. Griffith .... London Miss. Society, Hankow
Johansen, A. .... Customs, Kiukiang
Johnsford, A. .... Municipal Council Office
Johnsford, W. .... S. C. Farnham & Co.
Johnson, Capt. .... Shanghai Tug-Boat Association
Johnson, F. .... Pilot, Pagoda Anchorage, Foochow
Johnson, H. .... Customs, Lighthouse Department
Johnson, Rev. J. S. .... Am. Presb. Mission, Hangchow
Johnston, D. M. .... S. C. Farnham & Co.
Johnston, James .... Boyd & Co.
Johnston, James, M.D. ... 2, Shantung Road
Joly, H. B. .... British Consulate, Hankow
Jouveur, P., S.J. .... St. Joseph's Church
Jones, A. E. .... Local Postmaster
Jones, Douglas .... Union Insurance Society of Canton
Jones, Henry .... Police Force
Jones, James .... China & Japan Trading Co.
Jones, Malcolm .... H.B.M. Supreme Court
Jones, Rev. A. G. .... Eng. Baptist Mission, Ching-chow-fu
Jones, Theo. F. .... Hedge & Co., Foochow
Jordan, M. .... Assistant to Inspector of Nuisances
Jorge, H. .... Comptoir d'Escompte de Paris
Jürgensen, A. .... Pilot, Newchwang
Jürgensen, J. .... Pilot, Newchwang (absent)
Joseph, H. H. .... P. & O. Co.'s Office
Joseph, J. .... 5, Nankin Road
Joseph, S. S. .... E. D. Sassoon & Co.
Judd, C. H. .... China Inland Mission
Judd, Walter .... E. E. A. & C. Telegraph Co.
Judah, R. S. .... D. Sassoon, Sons & Co.
Judson, Rev. J. H. .... Am. Presb. Mission, Hangchow
Jules, B. J. .... Customs, Newchwang
Jürgens, H. .... 13, Szechuen Road
Jürgensen, J. .... Pilot
Javet, Leo (absent) .... James Hirsbrunner, Agent

Kahler, W. F. .... Customs (11, Dumbarton Terrace)
Köhler, W. F. .... Custom
Kahler, W. R. .... *North-China Herald* Office
Kalb, M. .... Reiss & Co.
Karuline, V. M. .... Tokmakoff, Sheveloff & Co., Hankow
Keeble, G. .... Customs, Tientsin
Keeke, F. C. .... Ollia, D.D., & Co., Foochow
Kesling, Frederick .... Police Force
Kelly, E. S. .... D. Sassoon, Sons & Co., Ningpo
Kelly, K. S. .... Kelly Brothers
Kelly, M. S. .... Kelly Brothers
Kempf, H. .... Newchwang
Keng Yam, L. .... Manager, Fung-hing Hong
Kennedy, R. .... Jardine, Matheson & Co.
Kennelly, T. F. .... 2, Tiendong Road
Kenney, E. H. .... Jardine, Matheson & Co.
Kerr, C. D. .... Fearon, Low & Co.
Kerr, J. A. .... Customs
Keswick, J. J. .... Jardine, Matheson & Co.
Khan, S. C. .... Cawasjee, Pallanjee & Co.
Kierulff, P. .... Commission Agent, Peking
Kierulf, — .... Constable, German Legation, Peking
Killeen, C. .... Customs
Kinder, C. W., A.M.I.C.E. Ch. Engin. & Mining Co., Tientsin
King, C. .... Jardine, Matheson & Co., Foochow
King, George .... China Inland Mission, Shensi

KIN—LAV.

King, C. H. .... Brand Bros. & Co.
King, Paul H. .... Customs (Hotel des Colonies)
King, Rev. A. .... London Missionary Soc., Tientsin
Kingsley, T. H. .... Customs, Ningpo
Kingsmill, T. W. .... 24, Nanking Road
Kinnear, H. R. .... Gibb, Livingston & Co.
Kirchhoff, H. I. H. .... Ping Chuan Mining Co., Tientsin
Kirchner, A. .... Kirchner & Böger
Kiseleff, M. G. .... Tokmakoff, Sheveleff & Co., Kiukiang
Kito, W. .... Engineer, Mun. Council Fire Dept.
Kitts, Rev. J. T. .... English Baptist Mission, Chefoo
Klampermeyer, F. .... Hongkew Hair-Dressing Saloon
Klein, A. .... Customs, Lighthouse Department
Klein, W. .... Gipperich & Burchardi
Kleinwächter, F. .... Commissioner of Customs, Ningpo
Kliene, A. .... Customs, Ningpo
Kluth, O. .... Inspector, Police Force
Knights, Capt. A. E. .... Str. "Kiang-yu," 31, Szechuen Road
Knight, W. .... White Chapel Road, Chefoo
Knight, W. .... Customs' Lightship, Taku
Kock, Chs. .... Elliott & Co.
Knoepfler, J. L. .... Customs, Chinkiang
Knox, J. .... Customs, Yuensan (Corea)
Knott, R. .... Pilot
Knowles, John S. .... S. C. Farnham & Co.
Knox, H. .... Blow & Co., Tientsin
Knop, Ernest G. .... James Hirsbrunner
Kobayashi, T. .... Japanese Consul, Jenchuan (Corea)
Kock, M. .... German Consulate-General
Kofod, F. A. A. .... Pilot, care of Mustard & Co.
Kofod, J. .... Hulk "Sultan," Kiukiang
Kofod, V. .... Great Northern Telegraph Co.
Kofoed, N. C. .... Customs, Yuensan (Corea)
Kohler, C. B. .... D. D. Gilin & Co., Foochow
Kölling, W. .... German Consulate-General
Korseff, N. W. .... Tokmakoff, Molotkoff & Co., Tientsin
Kosnutzoff, R. M. .... Pianoff, Molchanoff & Co., Kiukiang
Kopp, G. .... Customs, Chinkiang
Korff, A. .... Melchers & Co.
Körner, F. .... E. Schellhass & Co.
Kossow, C. .... Taku Tug & Lighter Co., Tientsin
Kotaro, S. .... Toilet Club
Koumetsoff, A. N. .... Tokmakoff, Molotkoff & Co., Tientsin
Krogh, Lieut. C. H. .... Gt. Northern Telegraph Co., Foochow
Kraul, W. H. .... Harbour Master's Office
Krauss, A. .... Carlowitz & Co.
Krauss, A. A. .... Mackintosh, Dudgeon & Co.
Krebs, O. .... Customs, Jenchuan (Corea)
Kreitner, Lieut. Gustav C. Act. Consul for Austro-Hungary
Krohn, Werner .... Schönfeld & Co., Foochow
Krüger, J. .... L. Vrard & Co., Tientsin
Kupfer, Rev. C. F. .... Am. Meth. Episcopal Mis., Kiukiang
Kwong Ki-chiu .... Shanghai Taotai's Yamên

Labussiere, E. .... Messageries Maritimes Co.
Lachelard, — .... French Police Force
Ladage, A. .... Customs, Jenchuan (Corea)
Ladijensky, N. .... Russian Legation, Peking
Laet, F. J. de .... Customs, Hankow
Laganlo, Rev. F. .... French Mission, South Kiangsu
Lagerheim, O. de .... V.-Consul for Sweden & Norway
Laidler, T. W. .... Customs
Laidrich, A. .... L. Vrard & Co.
Lajont, G. .... Cozon & Giraud
Lalcaca, E. P. .... 4, Kiangse Road
Lambuth, W. R., M.D. ... 42, Kiangse Road
Lambuth, Rev. J. W. ... 42, Kiangse Road
Laming, R. S.J. .... St. Joseph's Church
Lamond, Wm. .... Carter & Co.
Land, J. M. .... Customs, Kiukiang
Landale, Rev. R. J., M.A. China Inland Mission, Tai-yuen-fu
Lang, William .... Butterfield & Swire
Lanning, Geo. .... 10, Upper Yuen-ming-yuen Road
Lant, T. .... Customs, Hankow
Laporte, E. .... Customs, Jenchuan (Corea)
Latham, Capt. .... Shanghai Tug-boat Association
Latham, T. .... 4, Balfour Buildings
Latty, E. H. .... Sayle & Co.
Lauh, J. L. Geo. .... Hongkong Dispensary, Hankow
Lauchi, H. W. .... Customs, Yuensan (Corea)
Laughlin, Rev. J. H. .... Am. Presbyterian Mis., Wei-hien
Launay, A. .... French Police Force
Laurent, F. .... French Police Force
Lavers, E. H. .... Lavers & Co.

LAV—LUH.

Lavers, P. F. .... Cornabé & Co., Chefoo
Law, D. R. .... Adamson, Bell & Co.
Law, R. .... Shanghai and Hongkew Wharf
Law, W. C. .... Receiving ship "Corea"
Lawrence, Samuel .... Police Force
Lay, W. G. .... Customs, Ningpo
Leach, A. J. .... 4, Balfour Buildings
Leach, A. W. .... Customs
Leaman, Rev. C. .... Nanking, care of Am. Presb. Mission
Lebedeff, J. R. .... A. L. Rodionoff & Co., Hankow
Lebedeff, N. R. .... A. L. Rodionoff & Co., Hankow
Lebedeff, W. .... A. L. Rodionoff & Co., Hankow
Le Breton, L. .... Customs, Ichang
Le Cornec, L., S.J. .... St. Joseph's Church
Ledgwick, Rev. J. H. .... Church Missionary Soc., Hangchow
Lees, Rev. Jonathan .... London Missionary Society, Tientsin
Lefebvre, Rev. F. .... French Mission, North Kiangsu
Leffmann, J. H. .... 25, Foochow Road
Legaspy, J. .... 42, Yang-king-pang, Fr. Con.
Legg, W. H. .... H. Consterdine & Co., Chefoo
Lehrberger, J. S. .... Customs, Hankow
Leich, Thomas .... Police Force
Leith, A. .... Hongkong & S'ghai Bank, Hankow
Lemaire, G. .... French Consul-General
Lemmerhaud, F. W. .... Agra Bank
Lembke, O. .... Pilot, Taku
Lent, R. J. .... Customs
Lent, R. L. .... Boyd & Co.
Lenz, Dr. P. .... German Legation, Peking
Leon, Rev. D. .... Roman Catholic Mission, Wuchang
Lester, H. .... Architect, 1, The Bund
Letchford, R. H. .... Evans, Pugh & Co.
Levy, S. E. .... D. Sassoon, Sons & Co., Foochow
Lewes, William Frederick 5, Nanking Road
Lewis, A. .... Customs
Lewis, B. J. .... Customs, Fusan (Corea)
Lewis, George .... Foochow Road
Lewis, Rev. S. .... Am. Meth. Ep. Mission, Chinkiang
Leyburn, Frank .... Odell & Leyburn, Foochow
Leyenberger, Rev. J. A. ... Am. Presbyterian Mission, Chefoo
Lhuigre, J. .... Customs
Liang Boo, T. .... Fung Hing Hong
Liddell, A. .... Boyd & Co.
Liddell, C. O. .... Wm. Birt & Co.
Liedecke, L. .... Customs, Hankow
Lieder, P. .... R. Telge
Lim Ho-Cheow .... Manager, Lim Ho-Cheow & Co.
Limby, H. J. .... Lavers & Co.
Lind, Adam .... P. & O. Co., 24, The Bund
Lindsay, Geo. .... Mybergh & Dowdall
Lindsay, G. A. .... P. Maclean & Co.
Liot, E. .... Insp.-Gen. I.M. Customs, Peking
Little, Arch. J. .... 8, Kiukiang Road
Little, I. S., M.D., B.A., F.R.C.S., 10, Kiukiang Road
Little, Robt. W. .... 14, Yuen-ming-yuen Road
Little, W. B. .... Carter & Co.
Litvinoff, S. W. .... P. A. Ponomareff & Co., Hankow
Livingston, J. .... Customs, Pagoda Anchorage, F'chow
Llewellyn, J. .... Primrose & Co.
Lloyd, Rev. L. .... Church Missionary Society, F'chow
Loam, W. H. .... Customs
Lobel-Mahy, R. de .... French Consulate-General
Locke, Rev. A. H. .... Am. Episcopal Mission, Wuchang
Loehr, Rev. G. R. .... South. Meth. B. of For. Miss. U.S.A.
Loft, L. .... Customs, Newchwang
Longden, Rev. W. C. .... Meth. Episcopal Mission, Chinkiang
Lord, E. C., D.D. .... Am. Baptist Mission, Ningpo
Lorentzen, J. C. .... Customs
Louail, J., S.J. .... St. Joseph's Church
Loup, A. .... L. Vrard & Co., Tientsin
Loup, P. .... L. Vrard & Co., Tientsin
Lovatt, W. N. .... Commr. of Customs, Fusan (Corea)
Low, E. G. .... Fearon, Low & Co.
Lowder, E. G. .... Customs, Foochow
Lowe, R. .... Pagoda Anchorage, Foochow
Lowry, Rev. H. H. .... Am. Meth. Ep. Mission, Peking
Loyeda, S. .... Japanese Consul, Yuensan (Corea)
Lubeck, H. C. .... Russell & Co.
Lubeck, L. A. .... Russell & Co.
Lucini, O. .... 112, Boone Road
Lucas, Clement .... Lucas & Co.
Luce, C. W. .... Customs
Lücke, G. .... Melchers & Co.
Lührsen, J., Dr. jur. .... German Consul-General

LUI—MAR.

Lui, John	Roman Catholic Church, Chefoo
Luther, C. A.	Harris, Goodwin & Co.
Luther, C. F.	Sergeant, River Police
Lux, L. J. A. da	Customs, Lighthouse Department
Lyell, T.	Marine Surveyor, Chefoo
Lynborg, C. P. C.	Customs, Tientsin
Macbeth, J. R.	Customs, Seoul (Corea)
MacCallum, A.	Boyd & Co.
Macdonald, T. J.	Reid, Evans & Co.
MacDougal, Dr. A.M.(ab)	Care of Hirsbrunner & Co.
Macfarlane, W.	*Shanghai Mercury* Office
Macgowan, D. J., M.D.	Customs, Wênchow
MacGregor, A. P.	Turnbull, Howie & Co.
Macgregor, R.	Jardine, Matheson & Co.
Macgregor, J.	Caldbeck, Macgregor & Co.
Macgregor, John	Hirsbrunner & Co.
Machado, F. G.	British Post-Office
Machado, J. M. E.	Ilbert & Co.
MacInnes, Alex.	Kiukiang
Macintyre, Rev. John	U. Presb. Ch. of Scot. M., N'chwang
Mack, A.	Inspector, Police Force
Mackay, R. H.	U. S. Consulate, Tientsin
Mackenzie, Dr.	Tientsin
Mackenzie, Jas	Boyd & Co.
Mackenzie, John	Kiangnan Arsenal
Mackenzie, M.	Customs, Chinkiang
Mackenzie, Robert	Mackenzie & Co.
Mackintosh, L.	Mackintosh, Dudgeon & Co. (absent)
Maclay, R. H.	Pethick, Maclay & Co., Tientsin
Maclean, Geo. F.	Merchant, Chefoo
Maclean, Peter	1, Foochow Road
Maclean, A. H. H.	Customs, Kiukiang
Maclean, J. L.	1, The Bund
Maclellan, J. W.	*North-China Herald* Office
Macleod, Neil, M.D.	9, Kiangse Road
Macmurray, J.	Char. Bank of I., A. & China
Macomber, W. H.	Care of Adamson, Bell & Co.
Mactavish, J. W.	Mactavish & Lehmann
MacVeigh, J.	Rom. Catholic Mission, Peking
Maertens, A. H.	25, Szechuen Road
Maës, J.	Rom. Catholic Mission, Peking
Magnan, B.	4, Nanking Road
Maher, D.	*Shanghai Mercury* Office
Maher, F.	*Shanghai Mercury* Office
Maher, J. M.	Russell & Co.
Mahomed Rahimtoolla	Talay Buildings (absent)
Main, Dr. Duncan	Church Miss. Society, Hangchow
Maitland, Frank	Maitland & Co.
Maitland, H.	Jardine, Matheson & Co.
Maitland, John	Maitland, J., & Co.
Maitland, J. A.	Maitland & Co. (absent)
Maitland, W.	Shanghai Paper MillCo.
Major, Ernest	Major Bros.
Major, Frederick	Major Bros.
Malherbe, R. de	Bovet, Brothers & Co.
Malcampo, Joaquim	Malcampo & Co. (absent)
Man, D.	City Bowling Saloon
Mandl, H.	R. Telge
Mann, F.	Manager, Kiangsu Acid Works
Mansfield, J. J.	S. Moutrie, 28, Kiangse Road
Mansfield, R. W.	H.M.'s Vice-Consul, Pag. Anchorage
Manzanares, S.	Rec.-ship *Cadiz*, Chinkiang
Marçal, G. F.	Lane, Crawford & Co.
Markwick, R.	Customs
Markwick, jr., R.	21, Whangpoo Road
Marmando, P.	Rue Montauban
Marsh, S.	Tokmakoff, Sheveleff & Co., Hankow
Marshall, A. C.	Char. Bank of India, A. & C., F'chow
Marshall, D.	Customs, Chefoo
Marshall, F. Julian	H.B.M. Office of Works
Marshall, F. L.	J. M. Cory
Marshall, Thos.	Rue Montauban
Martel, A.	Customs
Martin, D.	Licensed Pilot (Reserve)
Martin, F. R.	Customs, Wenchow
Martin, G.	Butterfield & Swire, Foochow
Martin, Rev. J.	Church Missionary Society, Foochow
Martin, Rev. W. A. P., LL.D.	College of Peking, Peking
Martinet, Rev. J. B.	Procure des Mission Etrangeres
Martins, J. A. Rodrigues	Consul-General for Brazil
Martins, José	Brazilian Consulate-General
Martins, R. F.	*Celestial Empire* Office
Martsinkovicz, P. P.	Piatkoff, Molchanoff & Co., Hankow

MAR—MIT.

Marzal, Juan de Licópolis	Spanish Legation, Peking
Mason, A.	Customs
Mason, J.	Sayle & Co.
Mason, Rev. G. L.	Am. Baptist Mission, Ningpo
Mason, William J.	Police Force
Mateer, Rev. C. W., D.D.	Am. Presb. Mission, Tungchow
Mateer, Rev. R. M.	Am. Presb. Mission, Wei-hien
Mathieson, A.	S. C. Farnham & Co.
Matthews, G. A.	Dyce & Co.
Matsumoto, O.	Japanese Consulate
Maude, C. T.	H.B.M. Legation, Peking
Mawbey, Rev. Dr. W. G.	London Miss. Society, Hankow
May, F. N.	Customs
May, Herbert J.	6, Quinsan Road
May, John H.	Customs (6, Quinsan Road)
McBain, George	Merchant, French Bund
McCappin, A.	Upper Yangtsze Pilot
McCarthy, J.	Inspector, Police Force
McCaslin, C.	McCaslin & Co., Ningpo
McCaslin, Capt. C.	Shanghai Tug-boat Association
McCaslin, R. J.	Pilot, care of Mustard & Co.
McCoy, Rev. D. C.	Am. Presbyterian Mission, Peking
McCulloch, Rev. J. T.	Am. South. Bapt. Mission, Chefoo
McDonald, Alexander	Police Force
McDonald, J.	Merchant, Tientsin
McEwen, J. T.	Jardine, Matheson & Co.
McFarlane, E. P.	Am. Meth. Episcopal Mis., Yangchow
McGrath, J. J.	Customs, Chinkiang
McInnes, H. A.	Customs, Chinkiang
McKay, A.	Pilot, Pagoda Anchorage, Foochow
McKay, A.	River Police
McKean, E.	Inspt.-Gen. of I.M. Customs, Peking
McKechnie, A.	3rd officer str. "Kwa-hsing"
McKee, Rev. W. J.	Am. Presbyterian Mission, Ningpo
McKeige, F.	C. & J. Trading Co.
McKie, James	Jardine, Matheson & Co.
McLean, James	Police Force
McLeod, Alex.	Gibb, Livingston & Co.
McMurray, J.	Engineer, Tug "Gem," Taku
McQuire, F.	Customs, Chinkiang
McThorn, H.	Pilot, Newchwang
Meadows, James	China Inland Mission, Chehkiang
Mears, C. D.	Insp. Gen. of I. M. Customs, Peking
Medard, L.	Arsenal, Foochow
Meech, Rev. S. E.	London Missionary Society, Peking
Meier, H. H.	Great Northern Telegraph Co.
Meldrum, A.	Pilot, care of Mustard & Co.
Meldrum, E. D.	Hongkew Medical Hall
Melantioff, J. E.	Ponomareff & Co., Tientsin
Melnikoff, J. M.	Tokmakoff, Sheveleff & Co., Foochow
Melvin, A.	Shanghai Paper Mill Co.
Mendes, A. N.	Turner & Co., Foochow
Mendes, J.	Great Northern Telegraph Co.
Menzies, A. B.	Customs, Tientsin
Merrilees, A. G.	Customs, Printing Department
Merrill, H. F.	Customs
Merritt, Ch.	Municipal Storekeeper
Merz, Dr. C.	German Legation, Peking
Mesny, J.	Customs, Hankow
Mesquita, F.	A. Grünner & Co.
Meuguiot, Ph.	Procure des Lazaristes
Meuser, O.	Adamson, Bell & Co.
Meyer, C. A.	Customs, Kiukiang
Meyer, E.	E. Meyer & Co., Tientsin (absent)
Meyer, A. E.	E. D. Sassoon & Co., Wuhu
Meyer, H.	Customs, Taku
Meyerink, Wm.	W. Meyerink & Co.
Michael, J. R.	David Sassoon, Sons & Co.
Michaelsen, St. C.	Melchers & Co.
Michel, Charles	Belgium Legation, Peking
Middleton, Orborne	Manager, Old Ningpo Wharf
Mielenhausen, J. W.	Wilck & Mielenhausen
Mileck, J.	German Consulate, Tientsin
Milhe, E.	Customs
Miller, J. I.	White & Miller
Millot, E.	Millot & Co. (absent)
Mills, Henry	Police Force
Mills, Rev. C. R., D.D.	Am. Presb. Mission, Tungchow
Mills, Rev. F. V.	Am. Presbyterian Mission, Hangchow
Mingledorff, Rev. O. G.	South Meth. B. of F. Missions, U.S.A.
Ming Yong-mok	President, Foreign Office, Seoul
Mirabel, Dr.	French Legation, Peking.
Mitchell, G.	Pilot, Taku
Mitchell, J. F.	Ship-builder, Pootung

MIT—NAS.

Mitchell, S.	Ch. Eng. & Mining Co., Tientsin
Mitchell, T.	River Police
Mitchell, W. J.	Pilot, Pagoda Anchorage, Foochow
Mitchil, C. W.	Wesleyan Meth. Miss. Soc., Hankow
Miyamoto, H.	Japanese Consul, Fusan (Corea)
Molaby, George	Yangtsze Pilot, Temperance Hall
Moffat, J.	Hongkong and Shanghai Bank
Molchanoff, J. M.	Piatkoff, Molchanoff & Co., Hankow
Molchanoff, N. M.	Piatkoff, Molchanoff & Co., Hankow
Möllendorff, P. G. von	Chief, Corean Customs, Seoul
Moller, Chrystopher	Nils Möller
Möller, Nils	Fogg's Buildings, The Bund
Moller, Joh. F.	Siemssen & Co.
Molloy, E.	Customs, Chinkiang
Molotkoff, N. J.	Tokmakoff, Sheveleff & Co., Hankow
Molotkoff, O. J.	Tokmakoff, Sheveleff & Co., Hankow
Momonoi, Y.	Mitsui Bussan Kaisha
Moncrieff, A. L. M.	16, Szechuen Road
Mondini, P.	Customs, Ningpo
Monteiro, J. X.	10, Seward Road
Moore, Bernard	Shanghai & Hongkew Wharf
Moore, C. F.	Photographer, Peking
Moore, Charles G.	China Inland Mission (absent)
Moore, Louis	11, Canton Road
Moorhead, R. B.	Customs, Newchwang
Moorhead, T.	Customs, Hankow
Moorhead, T. D.	Insp.-Gen. of I.M.C., Peking (London)
Moorehead, J. M.	Customs, Hankow
Moses, J.	E. D. Sassoon & Co.
Mordhorst, O.	Gipperich & Burchardi
Morehouse, W. Noyes	Customs, Kiukiang
Morgan, F. A.	Customs, Ichang
Morgan, J.	Customs, Hankow
Morgan, G.	Sayle & Co.
Mori, Tsudta	*North China Herald* Office
Moritz, A.	Schmidt & Co.
Morris, B. J.	B. J. Morris & Co., Foochow
Morris, John	Kelly & Walsh
Morris, John	Morris & Co.
Morriss, Henry	Morriss & Fergusson
Morrison, G. J.	1, Kiukiang Road
Morrison, J., M.D.	Customs, Newchwang
Morrison, George	Police Force
Morrison, W., M.D.	Newchwang
Morse, Capt. A. H.	Care of Mustard & Co.
Mörsel, F. H.	Customs, Jenchuan (Corea)
Morse, H. B.	Customs, Tientsin
Mortimore, R. H.	H.B.M. Consulate
Moses, E. J.	2, Ningpo Road
Moses, M. J.	30, Kiangse Road
Moses, M. M.	David Sassoon, Sons & Co.
Moses, R.	David Sassoon, Sons & Co., Tientsin
Moskaloff, A. P.	Piatkoff, Molchanoff & Co., Foochow
Motchiyeski, S., M.D.	21, North Soochow Road
Mottet, L.	Siemssen & Co.
Moule, Ven. A. E., B.D.	18, Kiangse Road
Moule, Right Rev. G. E., D.D.	Church Missionary Society, H'chow
Moutrie, Sydenham	28, Kiangse Road
Mowat, R. A.	Asst. Judge, H.M.'s Supreme Court
Moxham, W. E.	13, Boone Road
Muirhead, Rev. Wm.	London Mission, 3, Shantung Road
Muhlenstoth, H.	Great Northern Telegraph Co.
Müller, B. J.	Pilot
Müller, C. E.	Broker, care of Club Concordia
Muller, G. F.	Customs, Foochow
Mullins, D.	Customs, Kiukiang
Mur, J. M.	Russell & Co.
Murasé, T.	Japanese Consulate
Murray, D.	Br. & For. Bible Society
Murray, G. S.	Chartered Mercantile Bank
Murray, G. T.	Customs, Chefoo
Murray, Rev. John	Am. Presb. Mission, Tsinan-fu
Murray, W. H.	National Bible Society, Peking
Mustard, R. W.	Mustard & Co.
Myburgh, Alexander	Myburgh & Dowdall, 21, F'chow Rd.
Myers, H. S.	Crasemann & Hagen, Chefoo
Myres, Chas.	Merchant, Tientsin
Nachtrieb, A.	Schönhard & Co.
Nachtrieb, G.	Schönhard & Co. (absent)
Neal, Chas. H.	Forcester & Co.
Nakashima, Takeshi	Japanese Legation, Peking
Narita, G.	Customs, Yuensan (Corea)
Nash, Rev. O. B.	Church Miss. Society, Hangchow

NAT—OVE.

Nathan, S. A.	E. D. Sassoon & Co.
Naudin, F.	Kirchner & Böger
Navarro, A.	*Shanghai Mercury* Office
Naylor, John	Chinese Engin. & M. Co., Tientsin
Naxer, R.	Customs, Hankow
Neal, Rev. Jas. B., M.D.	Am. Presbyterian Miss., Tungchow
Neilson, J. R.	Sayle & Co.
Nelson, H.	Customs, Kiukiang
Nelson, M.	Pilot, care of Mustard & Co.
Nembrini Gonzaga, Marquis C. de, Italian Consulate	
Nenendi, A.	French Police Force
Nesbitt, D.	Butterfield & Swire
Nesbitt, J. E.	Foochow Dock Yard, Foochow
Neuburg, A.	Neubourg & Co.
Nevius, Rev. J. L., D.D.	Am. Presbyterian Mission, Chefoo
Newman, E. S.	Chefoo Family Hotel, Chefoo
Newman, Walter	Newman & Co., Foochow (absent)
Newton, W.	Kiangnan Arsenal
Nichol, F. E.	Holliday, Wise & Co.
Nicholson, J. C.	Hongkong & Shanghai Bank, H'kow
Nickels, M. C.	41, Rue Montauban
Nicol, A. J.	Hongkong & Shanghai Bank
Nicolas, Rev.	Greek Church Mission, Peking
Nicoll, Geo.	China Inland Mission, Sz-chuen
Nielsen, F.	Great Northern Telegraph Co.
Nightingale, Rev. A. W.	Wesleyan Meth. Mission, Hankow
Nightingale, J. H.	Chefoo
Nikiforoff, M. G.	P. A. Ponomareff & Co., Tientsin
Ninomiya, K.	Okura & Co.
Nissim, M.	E. D. Sassoon & Co., Ningpo
Noble, W. C.	Am. B. of C. for For. Missions, Peking
Nocentini, Lodovico	Acting Consul for Italy
Noel, G. W.	Maitland & Co.
Noel, W. W.	China Traders' Insurance Co.
Noidans-Calf, Le Comte de, Belgium Minister, Peking	
Nölting, J.	Telge, Nölting & Co.
Noronha, A. J.	Butterfield & Swire
Noronha, J.	12, Canton Road
Noronha, L.	Noronha & Sons (absent)
North, Rev. T. E.	Wesleyan Meth. Miss. Soty., Wusuch
Northey, H. A.	Gallon & Co., Foochow
Novion, A.	Commissioner of Customs, Chinkiang
Nully, Raoul de	Customs
Nunes, A.	Robt. Anderson & Co., Kiukiang
Nunes, G.	12, Canton Road
Nunes, I. S.	*North-China Herald* Office
Nunes, J. C. S.	C. & J. Trading Co.
Nutter, G.	Customs, Wuhu
Nygaard, P.	Great Northern Telegraph Co.
Oberg, G.	Nils Möller
Odell, John	Odell & Leyburn, Foochow (absent)
Oelkers, H.	Nils Moller
Oeltze, C.	Pilot, Pagoda Anchorage, Foochow
Oestmann, C.	Crasemann & Hagen, Chefoo
Ohlinger, Rev. F.	Am. Meth. Ep. Mission, Foochow
Okumura, T.	Agent, M.B.M.S.S. Co. Y'san, Corea
Okura, K.	Japanese Consulate
Olive, P.	Toilet Club
Oliveira, A. M. d'	Spanish Consulate
Oliveira, F. M. d'	Portuguese Consulate
Oliveira, F. S.	*North-China Herald* Office
Oliver, C. H.	College of Peking, Peking
Oliver, Geo.	Geo. Oliver & Co., Foochow (abt.)
Ollerdessen, H.	Morris & Co.
Olsen, A.	Customs, Chefoo
Olsen, A.	Police Force, Hankow
Olsson, A.	British & Foreign Bible Society
Ommundsen, A.	Police Force
O'Neil, John	U. S. Consulate-General
Ooi, Y.	Mitsui Bussan Kaisha
Ord, J. Wallace	Boyd & Co.
Orfeur, W. W.	Lightship "Newchwang," N'chwang
Orion, J.	French Post-Office
O'Rourke, D.	The Hall & Holtz Co. Co.
Orsoni, A.	French Police Force
Osborn, E.	Customs, Lighthouse Department
Osborne, H.	Customs
Osborne, Jas. H.	Mackenzie & Co.
Osborne, W. McC.	Customs, Newchwang
Oswald, R. R.	S. C. Farnham & Co.
Ottaway, E. F.	Customs, Tientsin
Ottomeier, P. A. W.	Siemssen & Co.
Overbeck, Chas.	Overbeck & Co.

OVE—PIE.

Overbeck, H. .... Overbeck & Co. (absent)
Owen, Rev. G. S. .... London Mission, Peking
Owen, Rev. Wm. .... London Miss. Society, Hankow (ab.)
Oxenham, E. L. .... H.B.M.'s Consul, Chinkiang
Ozorio, E. C. .... Gibb, Livingston & Co.
Ozorio, F. A. .... Foochow Seamen's Hospital, Foochow

Painter, Rev. G. W. ...... Am. Presb. Mission, Hangchow (ab.)
Palamountain, B. .... Mang. Customs' Printing Office
Palin, W. G. .... The Hall & Holtz Co. Co.
Pampel, — .... German Legation, Peking
Pander, E. .... College of Peking, Peking
Panoff, J. K. .... Piatkoff, Molchanoff & Co., Hankow
Pappa, W. .... H. Evans & Co.
Pardon, Walter .... North-China Insurance Co., Ld.
Pariset, J. C. .... French Police Force
Parisot, A. .... Parisian Saloon
Park, W. H., M.D. .... Southern Meth. Mission, Soochow
Parker, E. H. .... H.B.M.'s Consulate, Wenchow
Parker, Geo. .... China Inland Mission, Kansuh
Parker, J. H. P. .... Receiving-ship *Wellington*
Parker, Rev. A. P. ...... Southern Meth. Mission, Soochow
Parkes, Sir Harry S., K.C.B., G.C.M.G., Br. Minister Plent., Peking
Parkhill, S. .... Harbour Master, Foochow
Parrott, Albert G. .... China Inland Mission, Yangchow
Parshakoff, P. S. .... P. A. Ponomareff & Co., Hankow
Passos, M. D. .... *Celestial Empire* Office
Patenôtre, J. .... French Minister, Peking
Paterson, J. W. Q. .... Harbour Master's Office
Paterson, W. .... Jardine, Matheson & Co.
Paulsen, P. N. .... Lightship "Newchwang," N'chwang
Pavletich, N. .... French Police Force
Pearse, Edward .... China Inland Mission, Shensi
Pearson, J. T. .... Customs
Peck, A. P., M.D. .... Am. B. of C. for F. Mission, Paoting-fu
Pelldram, A. .... German Consul, Tientsin
Pemberton, T. .... Wheelock & Co.
Penfold, C. E. .... Superint., Central Police Station
Penzig, A. F. C. .... Customs, Lighthouse Department
Percebois, D. .... Customs
Percival, R. H. .... Reiss & Co.
Percival, W. S. .... H.B.M. Supreme Court
Pereira, A. .... *Shanghai Mercury* Office
Pereira, A. M. .... British Post Office
Pereira, B. .... Russell & Co., Foochow
Pereira, E. F. .... Maitland & Co.
Pereira, F. .... 25, North Soochow Road
Pereira, H. A. .... *Shên-pao* Office
Pereira, J. F. .... Caldbeck, Macgregor & Co.
Pereira, J. G. .... W. Meyerink & Co.
Pereira, J. L. .... Oriental Bank
Pereira, J. P. .... Gittins, J., & Co., Foochow
Pereira, T. S. .... Noronha & Sons
Pérès, Rev. F. .... French Mission, South Kiangse
Perkins, G. .... Constable, H.M.'s Consulate, Wuhu
Perkins, H. Mason, D.D.S. 1, Kiukiang Road
Perkins, Rev. Henry P... Am. B. of C. for F. Missions, Tientsin
Perras, L. .... Mission Cath. du Tche-kiang, Ningpo
Perrott, E. S. .... Reid, Evans & Co.
Perry, J. S. .... E. D. Sassoon & Co., Foochow
Perry, M. E. .... E. D. Sassoon & Co., Wuhu
Pery, M. S. .... E. D. Sassoon & Co.
Pestonjee, R. .... Corner of Kiangse & Tientsin Rds.
Pestonjee, A. R. .... Corner of Kiangse & Tientsin, Rds.
Peters, F. .... Assistant to Inspector of Nuisances
Petersen, F. B. .... Ch. Engineering & Mining Co., T'tsin
Petersen, N. .... Great Northern Telegraph Co.
Petersen, P. M. .... Pilot, Ningpo
Peterson, J. .... Club Concordia
Peterson, P. M. .... Upper Yangtsze Pilot
Pethick, W. N. .... Pethick, Maclay & Co., Tientsin
Pfaff, L. .... H. Müller & Co.
Pfaff, Rud. .... L. Vrard & Co.
Philips, G. J. A. .... Customs, Kiukiang
Phillips, J. .... Exchange Broker, Foochow
Phipps, A. L. .... Phipps, Phipps & Co., F'chow (abt)
Phipps, H. G. .... Phipps, Phipps & Co., Foochow
Phipps, W. T. .... Corner of Kiangse & Kiukiang Roads
Piatkoff, M. F. .... Piatkoff, Molchanoff & Co., H'kow (ab.)
Pichon, G. .... French Police Force
Pichon, L., D.M.P. .... Gallo & Pichon, Corner of Peking and Kiangse Roads
Pierre, ... Hotel de Peking, Peking
Pierson, Rev. Isaac .... Am. B. of C. for F. Mission, Pao-ting-fu

PIG—RAN.

Pigott, Thomas W. .... China Inland Mission, Shansi
Pike, John .... Pilot, care of Mustard & Co.
Pila, Louis .... Ulysse Pila & Co.
Pila, Ulysse .... Ulysse Pila & Co. (absent)
Pilcher, Rev. L. W. ...... Meth. Episcopal Mission, Tientsin
Pim, Tobias .... Bathgate & Co., Foochow
Pinckvoss, J. H. .... Lucas & Co.
Piper, G. S. .... Adamson, Bell & Co.
Pirkis, A. E. .... Accountant, British Legation, Peking
Pittar, R. F., S.J. .... St. Joseph's Church
Place, J. E. .... Pilot, Newchwang
Placé, F. L. .... Comptoir d'Escompte de Paris
Placé, J. L. .... Turner & Co.
Placé, T. .... 8, Tiendong Road
Platt, A. R., M.D. .... General Practitioner, Chefoo
Plesucvich, L. A. .... Tokmakoff, Sheveleff & Co., Hankow
Plumb, Rev. N. J. .... Am. Meth. Ep. Mission, Foochow
Plumbley, Richard .... Police Force
Pinto, W. H. .... Mackenzie & Co.
Poell, Rev. Martin .... Roman Catholic Mission, Hankow
Poignand, W. .... Sh. & Hongkew Associated Wharves
Poitevin, L. .... 27, Nanking Road
Poletti, P. .... Customs, Tientsin
Poll, J. D. .... Customs
Polita, G. .... Toilet Club
Pollard, T. .... Jardine, Matheson & Co., Foochow
Pollitt, J. S. .... Barlow & Co.
Pollock, W. .... Customs, Wuhu
Pond, J. A. .... Municipal Council Office
Pontes, jr., Manuel da Silva, Vice-Consul for Brazil
Popoff, N. A. .... Russian Consul, Foochow
Popoff, P. .... Russian Legation, Peking
Popoff, P. A. .... Beloyolovy, A. A., Tientsin
Popoff, S. E. .... Russian Minister, Peking
Popp, B. .... Upper Yangtsze Pilot
Portaria, V. P. M. de...... *Shanghai Mercury* Office
Porte, B. .... Messageries Maritimes Co.
Porter, Rev. H. D., M.D... Am. B. of C. for For. Miss., P'ang-chia-chuang
Portes, Rev. F. .... French Mission, North Kiangse
Portier, E. .... French Municipal Council Office
Prassatt, F. .... Constable, British Legation, Peking
Posthumus, O. P. .... Customs, Fusan (Corea)
Postlethwaite, J. W. ...... Galton & Co., Foochow
Prentice, A. .... Sayle & Co.
Prentice, John .... Boyd & Co.
Price, Alexander .... Bill and Bullion Broker, Hankow
Price, B. J. .... H. Consterdine & Co., Chefoo
Price, H. J. .... North-China Insurance Co., Limited
Prichard, H. L. L. .... Customs, Tientsin
Primrose, W. M. .... Primrose & Co.
Procacci, D. V. .... Miss. Cath. du Tche-kiang, Ningpo
Prosch, G. .... Bush, Bros., Newchwang
Protasieff, J. .... Russian Legation, Peking
Protheroe, Thos. .... China Inland Mission, Ganking
Provost, A. .... Rom. Catholic Mission, Peking
Pruen, W. L. .... China Inland Mission, Chefoo
Pruitt, Rev. C. W. .... Am. Baptist Mission, Chefoo
Pugh, W. .... Evans, Pugh & Co. (absent)
Pullen, H. .... Drysdale, Ringer & Co., Kiukiang
Purcell, J. .... Chinese Eng. & Mining Co., T'tsin.
Purcell, Stephen .... Chinese Eng. & Mining Co., T'tsin.
Purcell, G. H. .... W. Birt & Co.
Purcell, P. H. .... Customs
Purdon, jr., James .... Maitland & Co.
Purdon, J. G. .... Maitland & Co.
Purse, Edward .... Police Force
Pye, Charles .... Odell & Leyburn, Foochow
Pyke, J. H. .... Am Meth. Ep. Mission, Peking (ab)
Pym, E. T. .... Customs, Chefoo

Quick, Jno. C. .... The Hall & Holtz Co. Co.

Rae, T. F. .... Caldbeck, Macgregor & Co.
Rae, William .... Police Force
Rago, A. de .... Union Insurance Society of Canton
Rahamim, A. J. .... D. Sassoon, Sons & Co.
Ramasse, A. .... Customs, Wuhu
Ramsay, A. C. .... Wennmohs & Co.
Ramsay, Hugh F. .... Merchant, Hankow
Ramsay, John .... Police Force
Ramsey, Thos. C. .... Old Ningpo Wharf
Randle, Horace .... China Inland Mission, Chehkiang
Rangel, I. M. .... Alex. Bielfeld
Rangel, S. J. .... Hongkong & Shanghai Bank

RAP—ROM.

Raphael, R. S.	8, Kiukiang Road
Rasmussen, C.	Great Northern Telegraph Co.
Rasmussen, P. W.	Customs, Lighthouse Department
Rathsam,	German Legation, Peking
Raynaud, F.	Hotel des Colonies
Raynor, E.	Customs, Lighthouse Department
Rawlinson, C. J.	The Hall & Holtz Co. Co.
Rawsthorne, F. W.	Boyd & Co.
Read, Thomas	Constable, British Consulate, F'chow
Reding, J. E.	China Traders' Insurance Co.
Redounet, J.	Stewart, Shanghai Club
Reeks, A. J.	Customs
Rees, Claude A.	D. Gilmour
Rees, Rev. W. H.	London Miss. Society, Peking
Reeves, Geo.	Customs, Chefoo
Reiders, E.	A. Cordes, & Co., Tientsin
Reid, Frank	1, The Bund
Reid, Joseph	Police Force
Reid, Rev. C. F.	Southern Meth. Mission, Soochow
Reid, Rev. G.	Am. Presbyterian Mission, Chefoo
Reinsdorf,	German Legation, Peking
Reilly, F. E.	Central Hotel
Remedios, A. F. dos	Jenkein & Co., Hankow
Remedios, S. D. dos	The Hall & Holtz Co. Co.
Remy, Rev. F.	French Mission, North Kiangsu
Rendall, M.	China Inland Mission, Shansi
Rennie, Dr. T.	Rennie & Adam, Nantai (Foochow)
Rennie, Kt., Sir Richard T.	Chief Justice H.B.M.'s Sup. Court
Revest, J. B.	French Police Force
Rex, A. B.	Iveson & Co.
Rey P.	Russell & Co.'s Silk Filature
Reynaud, P. M.	Mission Cath. du Tche-kiang, Ningpo
Reynell, A. E.	Jardine, Matheson & Co.
Reynell, S.	Canton Road
Reynolds, H. A.	Customs, Fusan (Corea)
Rhein, G.	43, Rue Montauban
Rhein, J.	Netherlands Legation, Peking
Riach, John	Boyd & Co.
Ricco, E.	French Municipal Council Office
Rice, E. W.	2, The Bund
Richards, G. C.	Pilot, Newchwang
Richards, T.	Piatkoff, Molchanoff & Co., Hankow
Riley, J. H.	China Inland Mission, Sz-chuan
Riley, W.	China Inland Mission, Chentu
Ringer, J. M.	Drysdale, Ringer & Co.
Ritchie, H. A.	P. & O. Co.'s Office
Ritter, G.	Astor House Hotel, Tientsin
Riva, A.	Russell & Co.'s Silk Filature
Rivero, E. T.	H.B.M. Consulate
Rivington, Chas.	*Shanghai Mercury* Office
Rizzi, J.	Mission Cath. du Tche-kiang, N'po
Robarts, C.	Rec.-ship "Corea"
Roberts, A.	Boyd & Co.
Roberts, E. A.	Customs
Roberts, G.	Customs, Chefoo
Roberts, J.	Customs
Roberts, Rev. J. H.	Am. Board of C. for For. Mis., Kalgan
Roberts, John P.	Marine Surveyor, Club Chambers.
Roberts, Capt. J.	Shanghai Tugboat Association
Roberts, W.	Assistant to Inspector of Nuisances
Robertson, A.	S. C. Farnham & Co.
Robertson, A. L.	Drysdale, Ringer & Co., Foochow
Robertson, H. J.	Architect & Builder, Foochow
Robertson, Jr., H. J.	P. A. Ponomareff & Co., Hankow
Robertson, Wm.	Boyd & Co.
Robilliard, W. S.	Chartered Mercantile Bank
Robins, M.	Shanghai Exchange Office
Robinson, Alfred	1, Yuen-ming-yuen Road
Robinson, Ed.	2, Yuen-ming-yuen Buildings
Robinson, J.	Upper Yangtsze Pilot
Robinson, Rev. J.	Methodist Mission, Tientsin
Robinson, W. J.	Butterfield & Swire
Rochs, A. C. A.	E. E. A. & Ch. Telegraph Co.
Rocher, E.	Customs
Rocher, L.	Customs, Hankow
Rodewald, J. F.	Rodewald & Co.
Rodrigues, J.	Customs, Lighthouse Department
Rodrigues, P. V.	Melchers & Co.
Rodriguez y Muñoz, T.	Spanish Minister, Peking (absent)
Rogerson, J. M.	Shanghai Gas Company
Rogister, A. C. H.	Customs, Chinkiang
Rohde, M.	W. Meyerink & Co.
Romanet, E.	French Municipal Council Office

ROM—SCH.

Romer, A.	Local Post Office
Rosenbaum, J.	Corner of Foochow & Szechuen Roads
Rosenbaum, S.	Customs, Yuensan (Corea)
Rosenstreich, M.	Shanghai Exchange Office
Ross, A.	Holliday, Wise & Co.
Ross, Rev. John	U. Presb. C. of S'land Mis., N'chwang
Ross, J.	Customs
Rosthorn, A. E. von	Inspt.-Gen. of I.M. Customs, Peking
Rouger, Monsgr. Adr.	Bishop, French Miss., South Kiangsu
Roustan, Laurent	Jardine, Matheson & Co.
Rowe, Ch.	British Consulate, Kiukiang
Rowland, E. J. O.	R. E. Wainewright.
Rowland, T. J.	Rec.-ship "Wellington,"
Royall, Rev. W. W.	South. Meth. B. of For. Mis., U.S.A.
Roza, D. da	Jardine, Matheson & Co., Foochow
Roza, P. de	Mustard & Co.
Rozario, Alf. D. do	Holliday, Wise & Co.
Rozario, Arnaldo A. do	Great Northern Telegraph Co.
Rozario, Art. A. do	*Celestial Empire* Office
Rozario, Aug. X. do	*Celestial Empire* Office
Rozario, D. do	Rozario & Co., Foochow
Rozario, F. H. do	Mackenzie & Co.
Rozario, F. do	Schönhard & Co.
Rozario, F. P. do	*Celestial Empire* Office
Rozario, J. E. do	Chartered Mercantile Bank
Rozario, J. F. do	North-China Insurance Co., Limited
Rozario, L. do	*Shanghai Mercury* Office
Rudland, William D.	China Inland Mission, Chehkiang
Rudolph, Chas.	Sieber-Waser
Ruegg, E.	Shanghai Club
Ruff, Th.	Carlowitz & Co.
Rump, C.	E. Meyer & Co., Tientsin
Russell, D. A.	French Concession
Russell, S. M.	College of Peking, Peking
Rustomjee, C.	Cawasjee, Pallanjee & Co.
Ruttonjee, B.	Hongkong and Shanghai Bank
Sá, A. F. do	Jardine, Matheson & Co.
Sá, Lino J.	Jardine, Matheson & Co.
Sachau, G.	Arnhold, Karberg & Co.
Salette, J.	Rom. Catholic Mission, Peking
Salter, A. E.	Merchant, Chinkiang
Sambrook, A. W.	China Inland Mission, Honan
Samson, J.	Reid, Evans & Co.
Sanches, C. A.	*North-China Herald* Office
Sanderson, J. L. P.	Birley & Co., Foochow
Sangster, T.	Harbour Master's Department
Sarthou, J. B.	Rom. Catholic Mission, Peking
Sassi, Rev. F.	French Mission, North Kiangsu
Sassoon, E. E.	E. D. Sassoon & Co.
Saunders, Capt. J. C.	Marine Surveyor, Pag. An., F'chow
Saunders, W.	Photographic Studio, 3, W'poo Road
Sayers, C. W.	1168, Broadway
Sayle, T. H.	Sayle & Co.
Sayle, W. J.	Customs, Newchwang
Sayres, Rev. W. S.	St. John's College
Scagliotti, A.	Customs, Chinkiang
Scarborough, Rev. W.	Wesleyan Meth. Mission Soc., H'kow
Schang, F. Césaire	Roman Catholic Church, Chefoo
Schaumlöffel, H.	Customs
Scheppelmann, C.	Shanghai Gas Co.
Schereschewsky, Rt. Rev. S. I. J.,	St. John's College, Jessfield (ab.)
Scherzer, F. A.	Inspt.-Gen. of I.M. Customs, Peking
Scherzer, Fernand	French Consulate, Hankow (absent)
Schiller, E. G.	M. H. Cook
Schismaroff, M.	Russian Legation, Peking
Schlichting, H.	23, Szechuen Road
Schlör, A. A.	Customs, Lighthouse Department
Schmidt, A.	Customs, Pagoda Anch., Foochow
Schmidt, Chas.	Schmidt & Co., Tientsin
Schmidt, John	Schmidt & Co., Tientsin
Schmidt, J. Meinhard	33, Rue du Consulat
Schmidt, P.	Municipal Council Office
Schmidt, W.	Customs, Yuensan (Corea)
Schneour, Colonel N.	Russian Legation, Peking
Schoenke, F.	Photographer, Foochow
Schönfeld, F.	Schönfeld & Co., Foochow
Schönicke, J. F.	Customs, Wuhu
Schoolsky, N.	Russian Legation, Peking
Schroeder, A.	Pharmacie de l'Union
Schrners, A.	Dufour Brothers & Co.
Schofield, R.	Schofield & Co., Hankow
Schojinns, C. J.	'Chefoo' Lighthouse, Chefoo
Schuffenhauer, O.	2, Yangtsze Road

SCH–SKO.

Schultz, H. M.	H. M. Schultz & Co.
Schulze, F. W.	Customs, Jenchuan (Corea)
Schultze, V.	Customs
Schwoig, B.	E. Schellhass & Co.
Schweiger, H.	Customs, Tientsin
Scott, B. C. G.	H.B.M.'s Consul, Wuhu
Scott, James	H.B.M.'s Legation Peking
Scott, J. H.	Butterfield & Swire
Scott, J. L.	Turnbull, Howie & Co.
Scott, J. W.	Elliott & Co. (absent)
Scott, R.	Boyd & Co.
Scott, Rt. Rev. C. P., D.D.	Peking
Scudder, C. S.	United States Legation, Seoul
Seaman, J. F.	Wisner & Co.
Seckinger, Rev. Père J.	Society of Jesus, Wuhu
Sock Loug, L.	Manager, Fung Hing Hong
Sedgwick, Rev. J. H.	Church Missionary Soc., Shauhing
Segerdal, J. N.	Customs, Pagoda Anch., Foochow
Seior, J. F. J.	Customs, Pagoda Anchorage, F'chow
Seip, F.	E. Schellhass & Co.
Seisson, A.	Hotel des Colonies
Seitz, C. L.	Customs, Hankow
Selamou, A.	Abdoola & Co.
Semallé, Vte. de	French Legation, Peking
Semonsen, E. F.	Pilot, Pagoda Anchorage, Foochow
Senna, C. M.	Adamson, Bell & Co.
Senna, E. F.	Agra Bank
Senna, Jr., J. de	Reuter's Telegraph Co. Office
Senna, Joaquim de	12, Quinsan Road
Senna, R. M.	*North-China Herald* Office
Senna, V.	Mackintosh, Dudgeon & Co.
Sentanco, W. V.	White & Welch's, 16, Canton Road
Sormys, Hubert	Belgium Consul-General
Seth, A. P.	Cornabé & Co., Chefoo
Severin, A. B.	Shanghai & Hongkew Assd. Wharves
Sewjee, P. T.	Shanghai Horse Bazaar
Shann, Rev. R., B.A.	Church Missionary Soc., Ningpo (ab)
Sharuhorst, G. D.	Customs, Wenchow
Sharp, C. S.	Gibb, Livingston & Co.
Sharp, John	Wheelock & Co.
Sharp, W. F.	Bill, Bullion & Gen. Broker, H'kow
Shaw, Rev. C.	Church Missionary Society Foochow
Shaw, R. W.	Chief engineer str. "Kua-Hsing"
Shaw, Capt. S. L.	Pagoda Anchorage, Foochow
Shaw, Rev. W. H.	Am. B. of C. for For. Miss., Paoting-fu
Sheffield, Rev. D. Z.	Am. B. of C. for For. Miss., T'chow
Shekury, G. J.	D. Sassoon, Sons & Co., Tientsin
Sheng Hung-chuen	Director Gen., Imp. Chi. Telegraphs
Shepard, Isaac F.	U. S. Consulate, Hankow
Sheppard, H.	Gibb, Livingston & Co.
Sherkoonoff, L. P.	A. L. Rodionoff & Co., Foochow
Sherman, C. B.	Pilot, Taku
Shewan, A.	Turner & Co.
Shinagawa, E.	Japanese Consulate-General
Shinagawa, H.	Boyd & Co.
Shoolingin, P. N.	Tokmakoff, Sheveloff & Co., F'chow
Short, W. H.	The Hall & Holtz Co. Co.
Shufeldt, Geo. A.	U.S. Consulate-General
Sidford, H. Æ.	D. Com. of Customs, 45, Kiangse Rd.
Siegfried, C. W.	Overbeck & Co.
Siemssen, Alfred	Siemssen & Co.
Siemssen, G.	Siemssen & Co., Foochow
Sigalas, C.	French Police Force
Silas, A. S.	E. D. Sassoon & Co., Tientsin
Silas, D. H.	Carter Road
Sillem, Hermann	L. Vrard & Co.
Silva, A. M. da	C. & J. Trading Co.
Silva, Elias da	Geo. McBain
Silva, E. da	W. Hewett & Co.
Silva, F. da	*Celestial Empire* Office.
Silva, J. P. da	Alfred Dent & Co.
Silva, P. da	Russell & Co.
Silverlock, Jr., J.	Silverlock & Co., Foochow
Simoens, J. dos R.	Comptoir d'Escompte de Paris
Simoens, N.	Russell & Co.
Simpson, C. Lenox	Commissioner of Customs, Kiukiang
Simpson, James	S. C. Farnham & Co.
Sinclair, Chas. A.	British Consulate, Foochow
Sinnott, P. W.	Customs
Sites, Rev. Nathan	Am. Meth. Ep. Mission, Foochow
Sjöblund, P. O.	Customs, Wuhu
Skeggs, C. J.	C. J. Skeggs & Co.
Skinner, George L.	Municipal Council Office
Skottowe, E. B.	Chartered Bank of India, A. & Ch.

SLA–STE.

Slade, G.	Gilman & Co., Foochow
Slevogt, Max	Merchant, 23, Szechuen Road
Sloan, R. J., M.D.	47, Kiangse Road
Sloane, J.	Customs' Lightship, Taku
Smardeley, N.	Customs, Lighthouse Department
Smidt, C.	37, Nanking Road
Smith, A.	Pilot (absent)
Smith, A. G.	Geo. Smith & Son
Smith, A. L. R.	Pilot, Newchwang
Smith, C.	Municipal Council Office
Smith, C. D.	Phipps, Phipps & Co., Foochow
Smith, E. B.	Customs
Smith, E. J.	Customs
Smith, F. A.	Turnbull, Howie & Co.
Smith, F. J.	Customs, Tientsin
Smith, Geo.	Geo. Smith & Son
Smith, G. W.	Customs
Smith, H.	Butterfield & Swire
Smith, H. R.	Butterfield & Swire, Foochow
Smith, J.	H. Consterdine & Co., Chefoo
Smith, J.	Insp. Gen. of I. M. Customs, Peking
Smith, James	S. C. Farnham & Co.
Smith, J.	Pilot, Ningpo
Smith, J. D.	Customs, Nantai (Foochow)
Smith, J. H.	Customs, Fusan (Corea)
Smith, J. R. M.	Hongkong & Shanghai Bank
Smith, John T.	Kelly & Walsh
Smith, H. R., M.D.	Am. Presb. Mission, Tengchow (ab.)
Smith, Rev. A. H.	Am. B. For. Miss., P'ang-chia-chuang
Smith, Rev. J. N. B.	Outside the South Gate
Smith, Rev. F. R., M.A.	The Deanery
Smith, Robert L.	Police Force
Smith, S.	Customs, Kiukiang
Smith, T. G.	HB.M.'s Supreme Court
Smithers, E.	U.S. Consulate, Chinkiang
Smyth, Rev. C. B.	Am. Meth. Epis., Mission, Foochow
Smyth, William	Police Force
Snethlage, H.	6, Foochow Road
Snowden, A.	Pilot, care of Mustard & Co.
Soares, E. E.	Hongkong and Shanghai Bank
Sobennikoff, P. A.	Piatkoff, Molchanoff & Co., Hankow
Sohne, T.	French Bund
Solomon, R. J.	Solomon Bros.
Solomon, S. J.	Solomon Bros.
Solomonoff, A. A.	Ponomareff & Co., Foochow
Song, T. W.	Fung Hing Hong
Sonne, C.	Great Northern Telegraph Co.
Sonnenblick, J.	722, Broadway, Hongkew
Soojaw, C. Y.	R. S. Raphael
Soonnar, Mawjee	29, Ta-lay Buildings
Soothill, Rev. W. E.	Meth. Free Church Mission, Wenchow
Sopher, J. A.	David Sassoon, Sons & Co.
Sopher, M. A.	David Sassoon, Sons & Co.
Sorabjee, J. G.	42, Yang-king-pang
Sorensen, H. B.	Outside the West Gate
Sorley, Peter	Police Force
Southey, T. S.	Harbour Master's Office
Souza, Alfredo M. de	Brazilian Consulate
Souza, B. de	Hongkong and Shanghai Bank
Souza, D. M. de	The Farm
Souza, Jr., B. D. de	John Forster & Co., Foochow
Souza, H. B. de	Adamson, Bell & Co., Foochow
Souza, J. Thos.	Hongkong and Shanghai Bank
Souza, M. de	The Hall & Holtz Co. Co.
Souza, M.	Co-Operative Cargo-Boat Co. Office
Souza, M. G. de	Frazar & Co.
Souza, S. A. de	Holliday, Wise & Co.
Souza, V. B. de	Reiss & Co.
Sowerby, Rev. H.	Am. Episcopal Mission, Hankow
Soyeshima, G.	Mitsui Bussan Kaisha
Speed, George	Police Force
Speshiloff, S. J.	Piatkoff, Molchanoff & Co., F'chow
Sprague, Rev. W. P.	Am. B. of C. for For. Missions, Kalgan
Squire, R. N.	Chinese Glass Works Co.
Stanford, G. A.	Lane, Crawford & Co.
Stanford, J. W.	Lane, Crawford & Co.
Stanley, Rev. C. A.	Am. B. for Foreign Missions, Tientsin
Starkey, B.	Merchant, Chinkiang
Starkey, R. D.	North China Insurance Co., Limited
Startseff, A. D.	Tokmakoff, Molotkoff & Co., Tientsin
Stathopolo, M.	295, Broadway
St. Croix G. C. de	Hongkong & Shanghai Bank
St. Croix, C. W. de	Customs, Foochow
Steglich, Oscar	Great Northern Telegraph Co.

STE—TET.

Stonhouse, D., L.R.C.P., &c. Meth. Missionary Society, Tientsin
Stepharius, C. .... J. J. Buchheister
Stephens, T. .... Constable, British Consulate, H'kow
Steven, Fredk. A. .... China Inland Mission, Yünnan
Stevens, Edwin .... U. S. Consul, Ningpo
Stevens, James .... Chinese Eng. & Mining Co., Tientsin
Stevenson, John W. ...... China Inland Mission, (absent)
Stevenson, O. .... China Inland Mission, Yunnan
Stevenson, W. F. .... Customs, Taku
Stewart, Alexander ...... Adamson, Bell & Co., Foochow
Stewart, Chas................. The Hall & Holtz Co. Co.
Stewart, J. Alex............ The Hall & Holtz Co. Co.
Stewart, J. .... Imperial Arsenal, Tientsin
Stewart, Rev. R. W., M.A. Church Missionary Society, Foochow
Stickler, F. M. .... J. Llewellyn & Co.
Stiles, J. W. .... 24, Nanking Road
Stimpson, Rev. M. L. ... Am. B. of C. for F. Missions, Tungchow
Stokes, Frank .... Wilkinson & Co.
Stokes, R........................ Customs, Chinkiang
Stone, E.......................... Russell & Co.
Stone, Edwin .... Hongkew Hotel
Stone, S. C...................... Kiangnan Arsenal
Stonehold, Hy................. Rec.-ship "Wellington"
Stonehouse, Rev. Joseph. London Mission, 3, Shantung Road
Storey, Thomas .... Police Force
Stott, George .... China Inland Mission, Chehkiang
Strachan, B. .... North-China Dispensary, Broadway
Strout, F. F. .... Purdon & Co., Foochow
Streich, K. .... German Consulate-General
Stripling, A. B. .... Commr. of Customs, Jenchuan (Corea)
Strong, J. P. .... Customs
Stuart, Rev. J. L. .... Am. Presb. Mission, Hangchow
Stubbert, J. E., M.D....... Am. Presbyterian Miss., Ningpo (ab)
Stuckey, Charles............ Police Force
Sturman, John .... China Inland Mission, Yang-chow
Styan, F. W..................... R. Anderson & Co.
Such, F. W. .... W. Hewett & Co.
Such, H. J....................... W. Hewett & Co.
Suenson, E...................... Capt. str. "Store Nordiske"
Suidler, L. .... Arnhold, Karberg & Co.
Sullivan, Jno. A............. Share Broker, 4, Peking Road
Sunsmith, J. H. J........... Customs, Chinkiang
Sutherland, Hugh .... John Forster & Co., Foochow
Suvoong, V. P., M.D....... Kiangnan Arsenal
Swallow, Rev. Robert ... Meth. Free Church Mission, Ningpo
Swanstrom, C. A. .... Customs, Wuhu
Sydenstricker, Rev. A. ... Am. Presb. Mission, Hangchow
Sylva, Henry .... Mitsu Bishi Mail S. S. Co.
Symons, H. .... Shanghai Horse Bazaar

Taft, Rev. Marcus L...... Meth. Episcopal Mission, Chinkiang
Tahkai, K........................ Globe Hotel, Tientsin
Takezoye, S.................... Japanese Minister, Seoul (Corea)
Talbot, T. F. .... Iveson & Co.
Taillou, Leopold .... Hotel du Peking, Peking
Talpey, A. H. .... Pilot, Taku
Taniel, Rev. F. .... French Mission, North Kiangsu
Tandberg, L. J. .... Pilot, Newchwang
Tanner, P. .... Inspt. Gen. of I.M. Customs, Peking
Tata, O. B. .... Tata & Co.
Tata, Kakaus M............. Tata & Co.
Taumeyer, Ernest .... Taumeyer & Co.
Tavares, A. J. .... *Shanghai Mercury* Office
Tavares, L. A. .... Jardine, Matheson & Co.
Tavares, P. J.................. *North-China Herald* Office
Taylor, C. H. .... Arsenal, Foochow
Taylor, F. E. .... Customs
Taylor, H. Howard ...... Oriental Bank Corporation
Taylor, H. Hudson ...... China Inland Mission, Chefoo
Taylor, Jas. A................ The Club
Taylor, J. T. .... Pilot
Taylor, J. Hudson .... Director, Ch. Inland Miss. (England)
Taylor, J. L., M.D. .... Am. Episcopal Mission, Foochow
Taylor, Sydney .... Police Force
Taylor, W. K.................. Customs, Pagoda Anchorage, Foochow
Taylor, —. .... Globe Hotel, Tientsin
Tei, Nagakuni .... Japanese Consulate, Tientsin
Teichert, C. W. P........... Customs
Teillol, A. .... E. Millot & Co.
Telge, R. .... Talay Buildings, French Bund
Tem, Pietro .... Italian Consulate
Templet, J., S.J.............. St. Joseph's Church
Tennant, H. P. .... Gibb, Livingston & Co., Foochow
Tetchatnoff, S. A. .... Piatkoff, Molchanoff & Co., Hankow

THE—VEI.

Theege, A........................ Customs, Lighthouse Department
Theisson, A.................... Customs
Thimm, E. A. .... Fergusson & Co., Chefoo
Thirkell, J. C................. *Celestial Empire* Office
Thistle, J. M. .... Shanghai Gas Co.
Thomas, J. .... Pilot
Thomas, W. E. .... Shanghai Tug-boat Association
Thompson, A. F. .... Wilkinson & Co.
Thompson, C. .... Upper Yangtze Pilot
Thompson, David .... China Inland Mission, Si-chuan
Thomson, Dr. B............. China Inland Mission, (Inland)
Thomson, Rev. E. H. ... St. John's College
Thorburn, J. D. .... Russell & Co.
Thorburn, R. F. .... Secretary Municipal Council
Thorne, Cornelius .... 1, Hankow Road
Thurburn, A. .... Thurburn & Dunn
Thyen, Joh..................... Melchers & Co.
Tier, R.......................... Hongkong Dispensary, Tientsin
Tiefenbacher, M. .... W. Meyerink (absent)
Tilley, J. W. .... Hunter, W. L., Foochow
Timm, C. F. .... Overbeck & Co.
Tinun, Julius .... Great Northern Telegraph Co.
Titoushkin, N. N. .... Piatkoff, Molchanoff & Co., Hankow
Tobe, John .... Shanghai Toilet Club
Toeg, R. E. .... Bill & Bullion Broker, 14, Szechuen Rd.
Tokmakoff, J. F. (ab)...... Tokmakoff, Sheveleff & Co., Hankow
Tolliday, T..................... Customs
Tomalin, Edwd. .... China Inland Mission, Ganking
Tomlin, E. .... Butterfield & Swire
Tomlinson, Rev. W. S.... Wesleyan Meth. M. So., Wuchang (ab)
Tomlinson, W. L. .... British Consulate, Ningpo
Tong King-sing .... Gen. Manager C.M.S.N. Co.
Tong Mow-chee .... Gen. Manager C.M.S.N. Co.
Tonkin, C. .... Customs
Tonzi, J. .... Roman Catholic Mission, Peking
Torakichi, M. .... Shanghai Toilet Club
Tottie, W. H. .... Iveson & Co.
Toucho, J. D. D. de la ... Customs, Foochow
Tournier, J. A. .... French Police Force
Tratman, J. N................. H.B.M.'s Consulate
Trannack, R. J. .... Customs, Tientsin
Trogillus, E. C. .... Customs
Trench, Frank................ China Inland Mission, Si-chüen
Tritton, E. W. .... Robt. Anderson & Co. (absent)
Troch, Max. .... Justus, Lembke & Co.
Trodd, A. B. .... Shanghai Gas Co.
Trollict, E. .... French Police Force
Truby, J. T. .... Customs, Ningpo
Trueman, T. E. .... T. Weeks & Co.
Tudleau, C. .... French Police Force
Turnbull, W. A.............. Turnbull, Howie & Co. (absent)
Turner, J. J. .... China Inland Mission, Chinkiang
Tweedie, W. L. .... Agra Bank
Twigg, P. O'B. E............ Mactavish & Lehmann
Twigg, P. H .... 32, Szechuen Road
Tardy, R. F., S.J. .... St. Joseph's Church
Tzo Tsao-fai .... Manager, S'hai Paper Mill Co.

Umile, Br. Vetta .... Roman Catholic Mission, Wuchang
Underwood, G. R., M.D.... Physician and Surgeon, Kiukiang
Underwood, Dr. J. J....... Pagoda Anchorage, Foochow
Unwin, F. S. .... Customs, Newchwang
Ure, C. W. .... J. P. Bisset & Co.
Uren, C. J. .... E. E. A. & Ch. Telegraph Co.
Urgé, J.......................... Mission Cath. du Tche-kiang, Ningpo
Uribarri, Ramiro Gil de... Spanish Legation, Peking
Urnao, B. .... French Police Force
Urquhart, John .... Mackenzie & Co.
Uyeno, S........................ Japanese Consulate, Chefoo

Valantine, B. A.............. Shanghai Horse Bazaar
Vale, T. Harold .... Agent, Am. Clock & Brass Co.
Valentine, J. .... Cumine & Co.
Valentine, Rev. J. D. ... Church Miss. Society, Shaouhing
Van Aalst, J. A.............. Inspt.-Gen. of I. M. Customs, Peking
Van der Stegen, L.......... Customs
Van der Tak, T. N. ...... 14, Makalee Terrace, Kiangse Road
Van Dosselaere, J., S.J.... St. Joseph's Church
Van Ess, W. A. .... British Consulate, Chefoo
Vapereau, Chas. .... College of Peking, Peking
Vaucher, E. .... L. Vrard & Co., Tientsin
Vaudagna, Rev. Angelo... Roman Catholic Mission, Hankow
Vaughan, J. .... Pilot
Veitch, Andrew .... Hongkong and Shanghai Bank

VEI—WHE.

Veitch, G. T. .... Jardine, Matheson & Co.
Vels, M. .... 9, Miller Road
Verril, Edward .... Merchant, Wuhu
Vic, Rev. F. .... French Mission, North Kiangso
Videau, U. .... Hotel des Colonies
Vieira, U. A. .... Receiving-ship "Yuen Fah"
Villanueva, Father Augustin, Spanish Mission, Hankow
Villanova, C. .... Harbour Master's Department
Villard, E. .... Union Frères
Vinay, H. .... Care of Comptoir d'Escompte de Paris
Vincent, J. R. .... Soc. for the Propagation of Gospel,
Vissière, A. .... French Legation, Peking., [Chefoo
Vita, Arthur .... Professor of Music, 6, Whangpoo Road.
Vizonsinovich, M. .... River Police
Voelkel, S. .... Pharmacie de l'Union
Volosatoff, J. M. .... W. J. Boodilin, Tientsin
Von Brandt, M. .... German Minister, Peking (absent)
Von Kehrberg, P. .... Customs, Hankow
Von Rosthorn, A. E. .... Inspt. Gen. of I. M. Customs, Peking
Von Tattenbach, Count ... German Legation, Peking
Von Wrangle, Baron ...... Russian Legation, Peking
Vouillemont, E. G. .... Comptoir d'Escompte de Paris

Wade, H. T. .... 12, Szechuen Road
Wade, John J. .... R.S. "Corea"
Wadleigh, E. C. .... Wadleigh & Emory, Chinkiang (abt.)
Wadman, E. .... Wadman & Co., Ningpo
Wadman, H. E. .... Customs
Waeber, C. .... Russian Consul, Tientsin
Wainewright, R. E. ...... 3, Balfour Buildings
Wake, J. P. .... Fergusson & Co., Chefoo
Walker, Rev. J. E. ...... Am. Board Foreign Missions, F'chow
Walker, Rev. W. F. ...... Am. Meth. Episcopal Miss., Tientsin
Walker, Rev. W. S. ...... Southern Baptist Con., U.S.A., S'chow
Walker, S. .... Ilbert & Co.
Walkinshaw, A. W. ...... Turner & Co., Foochow
Wallace, T. .... Mackenzie & Co.
Wallace, T. .... Shanghai Waterworks' Co.
Waller, H. J. .... Customs, Nantai (Foochow)
Waller, L. E. .... 9, Nanking Road
Walter, J. F. .... 'Chefoo' Lighthouse, Chefoo
Walter, William .... Evans, Pugh & Co., Hankow
Walter, W. B. .... Customs, Nantai, Foochow
Warburg, C. G. .... Marine Surveyor, N. C. Ins. Co., Ld.
Ward, E. .... Jardine, Matheson & Co.
Ward, W. C. .... Ireson & Co.
Ward, W. S. .... Customs, Tientsin
Wardell, Wm. .... Ch. Engineering & Mining Co., T'sin
Ware, J. .... Am. Bible Society, 18, Peking Road
Washbrook, W. A. .... Customs, Chinkiang
Wasserfall, A. .... Siemssen & Co.
Watanabé, Yoitchiro ...... Japanese Legation, Peking
Waters, T. J. .... Waters & Dale
Waters, W. .... Cheap Jack & Co.
Watkins, G. A. .... J. Llewellyn & Co.
Watson, J., M.D. .... Newchwang
Watson, J. .... Hankow Dairy, Hankow
Watson, Rev. D. H. ...... Wesleyan Meth. Miss. Soc., Wusueh
Watson, Major J. C. ...... Magistrate & Cont. of Police, Ningpo
Watson, W. .... P. Maclean & Co.
Watts, Capt. J. .... Taku Tug & Lighter Co., Tientsin
Weatherstone, T. .... China Navigation Co.'s Hulk, Hankow
Webb, E. G. C. .... Maitland & Co.,
Webster, A. .... S. C. Farnham & Co.
Webster, L. .... E. E. A. & Ch. Telegraph Co.
Webster, Sydney H. ...... Adamson, Bell & Co.
Webster, Rev. J. .... Missionary, Newchwang
Weed, James A. .... Asst. Inspector of Markets
Weeks, C. D. .... Weeks & Fry, Foochow
Weir, Thomas .... Supt. Engineer C. M. S. N. Co.
Welch, Joseph .... White & Welch
Weld, Daniel .... 2, The Bund (absent)
Wells, E. .... Engineer tug "Peiho," Taku
Wells, James .... Police Force
Wemmolts, E. .... 28, Nanking Road
West, John .... Kelly & Walsh
Westall, A. C. .... Carter & Co.
Westwater, Rev. Alex. ... U. Presb. Ch. of Scot. Miss., Chefoo
Westwater, A. McDonald, L.R.C.S. do. do.
Wetmore, W. S. .... Frazar & Co.
Wheeler, G. H. .... Russell & Co.
Wheeler, Rev. L. N., D.D. Am. Meth. Episcopal Miss., Szechuan
Wheeley, Edward .... Alfred Dent & Co. (absent)
Wheelock, T. R. .... Talay's Buildings & Bub. Well Road

WHE—XAV.

Wheen, E. .... Sayle & Co.
Wherry, Rev. J. .... Am. Presbyterian Mission, Peking
Whiller, Andrew .... China Inland Mission, Chehkiang
White, Augustus .... White & Miller
White, R. Godfrey .... Medical Officer of Customs, C'kiang
White, Wm. .... White & Welch
Whitfield, W. .... W. Birt & Co.
Whiting, Rev. J. L. ...... Am. Presbyterian Mission, Peking
Whitlock, G. .... Customs, Newchwang
Whitney, H. T., M.D. ...... Am. Board Foreign Missions, F'chow
Whittlesey, H. C. .... Customs, Wuhu
Wigton, Capt. R. H. ...... Str. "Fei-yuen"
Wijnhoven, F. .... Roman Catholic Mission, Peking
Wilck, C. .... Wilck & Miclenhausen
Wilcox, Rev. M. C. ...... Am. Meth. Episcopal Miss., F'chow
Wilcox, Rev. Myron C. ... Meth. Episcopal Mission, Foochow
Wileman, W. .... Chinese Eng. & Mining Co., Tientsin
Wilkin, James .... Constable, British Legation, Peking
Wilkins, E. .... A. S. Watson & Co.
Wilkinson, H. S. .... Crown Advocate, H.B.M. Sup. Court
Wilkinson, Will. Henry ... H.B.M.'s Consulate, Ningpo
Williams, C. .... Chinese Eng. & Mining Co., Tientsin
Williams, J. O. .... German & Scandinavian Sailors' Home
Williams, F. T. .... Shanghai Club
Williams, R. .... Pilot
Williams, Rev. Mark ... Am. B. of C. for For. Missions, Kalgan
Williams, Owen .... Belle Vue
Williams, W. H. .... Customs, Chinkiang
Williamson, Jas. .... China Inland Mission, Chehkiang
Williamson, T. .... Customs, Wuhu
Williamson, J. W. L. ...... Holliday, Wise & Co.
Williamson, Rev. A., LL.D. U. Presb. Ch. of Scot. Miss., Chefoo
Willis, J. .... Police Station, Ningpo
Willits, O. W. .... Am. Meth. Epis. Mission, Tientsin
Wills, Rev. W. A. .... Am. Bible Society, 18, Peking Road
Wilson, A. .... Inspector, Police Force (absent)
Wilson, Ed. G. .... Corner of Nankin and Kiangse Rds.
Wilson, J. .... Collins & Co., Tientsin
Wilson, J. H. .... Pharmacie de l'Union
Wilson, James .... Merchant, Tientsin
Wilson, Jno. .... Boyd & Co,
Wilson, John .... 9, Szechuen Road
Wilson, John .... The Hall & Holtz Co-operative Co.
Wilson, Robt. .... Hongkong & Shanghai Bank (abt.)
Wilson, Thomas M. ...... Police Force
Wilson, W. .... Customs
Wilson, John .... Natl. Bible Soc. of Scotland, S'chuen
Wilson, William, M.B., C.M. China Inland Mission, Shensi
Wingate, J. C. A. .... U.S. Consul, Foochow
Wingrove, G. R. .... Brand Brothers & Co. (absent)
Winn, H. H., D.D.S. ...... 2, The Bund
Wintle, V. D'O. .... Russell & Co.
Wirry, William .... Police Force
Wiss, D. .... "Shantung" Lighthouse, Chefoo
Wisner, J. H. .... Wisner & Co.
Wolfe, Rev. J. R. .... Church Missionary Society, Foochow
Wolff, Marcus .... 37, Kiangse Road
Wolter, C. .... E. Meyer & Co., Tientsin
Wong, C. T. .... C. T. Wong & Co.
Wong Yu-yü .... Manager, Wong Bros. & Co., C'kiang
Wong, K. Y. .... Fung Ging Hong
Wood, A. G. .... Gibb, Livingston & Co.
Wood, Isaac .... Ch. Engineering & Mining Co., T'sin
Wood, Marcus .... China Inland Mission, Ganking
Wood, Peter .... Church of Scotland Mission, Ichang
Wood, T. .... Drysdale, Ringer & Co., Hankow
Woodall, Rev. G. W. ...... Meth. Episcopal Mission, Wuhu
Woodbridge, Rev. S. J. ... Am. Presb. Mission, Chinkiang
Woodin, Rev. S. F. ...... Am. Board Foreign Missions, F'chow
Woodley, M. .... Adamson, Bell & Co., Foochow
Woodward, R. H. S. ...... Merchant, Hankow
Wooyeda, Y. .... Mitsui Bussan Kaisha
Wooyeno, T. .... Japanese Postal Agency
Worley, Rev. James H. ... Am. Meth. Episcopal Miss., Nankin
Worley, Rev. Thomas H. .. do. do. Chinkiang
Wortmann, R. .... Tannmeyer & Co.
Wright, J. .... Customs, Ningpo
Wright, T. W. .... Com. of Customs, Yuensan, Corea
Wrightson, C. W. .... Reid, Evans & Co.

Xavier, Carlos A. .... Kelly & Walsh
Xavier, F. P. .... *Shanghai Mercury* Office
Xavier, J. .... Comptoir d'Escompte de Paris
Xavier, J. P. .... Comptoir d'Escompte de Paris

XAV—ZWA.

Xavior, L. A. .... Receiving-ship "Ariel"

Yamada, S. .... Agent, M B M S S. Co., Fusan, Corea
Yates, Rev M. T. . .. .. Rue du Consulat
Yun, Geo. Jopu .... Shanghai Gas Company
Youmans, H .... Constable, Br Consulate, Tientsin
York, G. E .... T Weeks & Co.
York, W. C.................... Shanghai & Hongkew Wharf
York, S. P ... . Fung Hing Hong.
Yorke, R. S .... Customs, Chefoo
Yoshida, Djiro .... Japanese Legation, Peking
Youd, F. M. .... Adamson, Bell & Co. (absent)
Young, J..................... Pilot, Taku
Young, John Russell...... U S Minister Plenipotentiary, P'ing
Young, J. M. ...., ... Rodewald & Co.
Young, S........................ Customs, Nantai (Foochow)
Yvanovich, A................ Jardine, Matheson & Co
Yzolphe, G. B. .... 42, Rue Montauban

Zacharias, V., M.D .... 34, Szechuen Road
Zedelius, M.D., U. .... 11, Kiangse Road
Zi, Joseph .... French Consulate, Foochow
Zack, Jas. C. .... U.S. Consul, Tientsin (absent)
Zwarg, R. .... Central Stable

LADIES' LIST.

AN ALPHABETICAL LIST OF LADY RESIDENTS AT SHANGHAI, FOOCHOW, NINGPO, NORTHERN AND RIVERINE PORTS.

1884.

[Where the Name of the Place is omitted, Shanghai will be understood.]

ADA—BER.

Adams, Miss .... Am. Bapt. Miss., Kinhwa (Ningpo)
Air, Mrs. .... 11, Seward Road
Akers, Miss L. E., M.D., .. Meth. Episcopal Mission, Tientsin
Alabaster, Mrs. C. .... Hankow
Allcot, Mrs. G. .... Chinkiang
Allen, Mrs. H. J. .... H B M 's Consulate, Newchwang
Allen, Miss M.......... .... S. M. E. Mission 9, Woosung Road
Almeida, Mrs. C. M. d'... 9, Seward Road
Almeida, Mrs F. A. M. d' 9, Seward Road
Aleing, Mrs. Emma ...... Kiukiang
Amelunxen, Mrs. R.A von 18, Kiukiang Road
Ament, Mrs. W. S. ..... Peking
Anderson, Mrs. N P ... 1, Ma-ka-loo Terrace
Anderson, Mrs. R A. J.. 1, Chaou-foong Road (absent)
Anderson, Miss .... Am. Presbyterian Miss., Chefoo (ab.)
Anderson, Mrs. Arthur... Bubbling Well Road
Andrew, Mrs. G. .... China Inland Mission, Yunnan
Andrew, Mrs R. .... 10, Kiangse Road
Andrews, Miss M. E....... Am B. of C. for For. Mission, T'chow
Angus, Mrs. A. Forbes... Foochow
Anz, Miss...................... Chefoo Islands, Chefoo
Appleton, Mrs G. H. ... St. John's College
Aquino, Mrs. J F. d' ... 10, North Soochow Road
Aquino, Miss T. d'. ...... 7, Seward Road
Archenault, Sœur F. ...... Ningpo
Archibald, Mrs. John ... N. Bible Soc. of Scotland, Hankow
Archinti, Sister Teresa ... Roman Cath. Orphanage, Hankow
Arendt, Mrs. .... Peking
Armstrong, Mrs. O. ...... Tunkadoo Dock

Baessler, Mrs. .... 4, Peking Road
Bainbridge, Miss............ Am Presbyterian Mission, Chefoo
Balfour, Miss .... 13, Hankow Road
Baldwin, Mrs. A .... 2, Ming-hong Road
Baldwin, Mrs. C. C. ...... Foochow
Baldwin, Mrs. S. L. . .. Foochow (absent)
Baller, Mrs. F W .... China Inland Mission, Chefoo
Bamford, Mrs. A. J . . . 17, Kiangse Road
Bandinel, Mrs. J. J F.... Newchwang
Banister, Mrs.... .... Church Miss Society, Foochow
Bannerman, Mrs. J. ...... 42, Broadway, Hongkew
Barchet, Mrs. .... Am. Baptist Mission, Ningpo
Barnes, Mrs. .... 4, Amoy Road
Barr, Miss M. E..... ...... Am. Presbyterian Mission, Peking
Bartolini, Mrs. A. .... 11, Miller Road
Barton, Miss .... 7, Canton Road
Bates, Mrs. J.. .... Ningpo
Battat, Sœur Madeleine... Ningpo
Baumann, Mrs. A. .... 2, Hankow Road
Baxter, Mrs. A. G.. . ... Taku
Beckhoff, Mrs. E. .... 12, Hankow Road
Begg, Mrs C .... Hankow
Begley, Mrs C W .... . Foochow
Belbin, Mrs. E. .... 2, Ming-hong Road
Bell, Mrs F H. . ... 4, The Bund
Bello, Miss F F .... At Mrs. Markwick's, 21, W'poo Road
Belogolovy, Miss Pauline Tientsin
Belogolovy, Miss Anastasie Tientsin
Belogolovy, Miss Hope ... Tientsin
Benjamin, Mrs. D. D. .. 17, Yangtsze Road
Bergen, Mrs P. D . . Am Presb. Mission, Chinan-fu
Bernadès, Sœur . ... Peking
Bernasconi, Sister Giuditta Roman Cath. Orphanage, Hankow
Berry, Miss .... Am Presbyterian Mission, Chefoo

BIA—CAR.

Biancardi, Sister Giovanna	Roman Cath. Orphanage, Hankow
Bidwell, Mrs. H. S.	Bubbling Well Road
Biehl, Mrs. J. C.	Chefoo
Bielfeld, Mrs. Alex.	4, Canton Road
Billequin, Madame A.	Peking
Birt, Mrs. W.	3, Honan Road
Birt, Miss	3, Honan Road
Bisbee, Mrs. A. M.	41, Broadway, Hongkew
Blachford, Mrs. B. F.	Newchwang
Black, Mrs. H.	China Inland Mission, Kansuh
Black, Miss	China Inland Mission, Kansuh
Blair, Mrs. E. T.	Bubbling Well Road
Blodget, Mrs.	Peking
Bluntschli, Madame	8, Yang-king-pang, Fr. Concession
Bond, Mrs. W.	Taku
Boumboan, Madame	Municipalité Française
Bono, Mrs. C. V.	Kiukiang
Bonza, Sister Maria	Roman Cath. Orphanage, Hankow
Boodilin, Mrs. W. J.	Tientsin
Boone, Mrs. W. J.	St. John's College, Jessfield
Boone, Mrs. H. W.	4, Minghong Road
Borchardt, Mrs. F.	5, Whangpoo Road
Boswell, Mrs. J. D.	Central Hotel
Boswell, Miss	Central Hotel
Boswell, Miss Alice	Central Hotel
Botelho, Mrs. R.	7A, Miller Road
Boyd, Miss E. K.	Am. Episcopal Mission, Hankow
Boyd, Miss Fanny	China Inland Mission, Chehkiang
Bradfield, Mrs.	"Poplars," Bubbling Well Road
Bramfitt, Mrs.	Wesleyan Meth. Miss. Soc., Wusueh
Brand, Mrs. D.	10, The Bund
Bredon, Mrs.	Hankow
Brenan, Mrs. Byron	Chefoo
Brenan, Mrs. E. V.	Newchwang
Brereton, Mrs. J. G.	Chefoo
Brereton, Mrs. W.	Soc. for P'gation of the Gospel, P'king
Brewer, Mrs.	Wesleyan Meth. Miss. Soc., Wuchang
Brinkworth, Mrs. B. J. S.	29, Szechuen Road
Broumton, Mrs.	Ch. Inland Mission, Kwei-chau
Brown, Mrs. J. L.	3, Nanking Road
Brown, Mrs. Robert M.	Tientsin
Brown, Mrs. Thomas	1, Snukiang Road
Bruce, Miss M.	16, Peking Road
Bruce, Mrs.	Peking
Brunat, Mrs. Paul	33, Foochow Road
Bryant, Mrs.	London Miss. Soc., Hankow (absent)
Bryson, Mrs.	London Miss. Society, Wuchang (ab.)
Buchanan, Mrs. James	16, Canton Road
Buchanan, Mrs. W. C.	10, Szechuen Road
Buchheister, Mrs. J. J.	1, Ningpo Road
Burge, Mrs.	River Bank, 71, Broadway, Hongkew
Burkill, Mrs.	Bridge end, Bubbling Well Road
Burnett, Miss M. A.	Union Mission, Bridgman Home
Burns, Mrs. B. H.	18, The Bund
Burr, Mrs. W. A.	40, Broadway
Bush, Mrs. L. L.	36, Broadway
Buschendorff, Mrs. A. V.	Beach Hotel, Chefoo
Bushell, Miss Kate O., M.D.	Am. Meth. Episcopal Mission K'kiang
Butland, Miss	China Inland Mission, Si-chuen
Butler, Mrs. Geo.	Hotel des Colonies
Butler, Mrs. G. A.	Kin-le-yuen, French Bund
Butler, Mrs. J.	Am. Presbyterian Mission, Ningpo
Buyers, Mrs. Wm. B.	6, Nanking Road
Byrne, Mrs. E.	2, Whangpoo Road, Hongkew
Caldarola, Mlle. A.	Russell & Co.'s Silk Filature
Cameron, Mrs. Ewen	12, Yangtsze Road
Campbell, Mrs. D. C.	54, Broadway
Campbell, Mrs. Roderick	Agra Bank
Campbell, Mrs. Smollett	Chefoo
Campbell, Mrs. T. M.	Chefoo
Candlin, Mrs. G. T.	Meth. Missionary Society, Tientsin
Capp, Mrs. M. B.	Am. Presbyterian Mission, Tengchow
Cardwell, Mrs. J. E.	China Inland Mission, Kiangsi
Carion, Mrs. F. F.	10, Boone Road
Carion, Miss E.	10, Boone Road
Carlos, Mrs. B.	Newchwang
Carlson, Mrs. W.	52, Broadway
Carlson, Miss	52, Broadway
Carpenter, Miss M.	China Inland Mission, Chehkiang
Carpenter, Miss S.	China Inland Mission, Chehkiang
Carson, Mrs.	Newchwang
Carvalho, Mrs. A. H. de	25, Rue Montauban
Carvalho, Miss E. M. de	25, Rue Montauban

CAR—DUD.

Carvalho, Mrs. P. M. de	West Villa, Bubbling Well Road
Castelnuovo, Mlle. E.	Russell & Co.'s Silk Filature
Castillo, Mrs. S. P.	7, Miller Road
Castro, Mrs. G. B. A.	Tientsin
Cave-Thomas, Mrs.	Foochow
Cayrol, Sœur Joseph	Ningpo
Chapin, Mrs. O. H.	Am. Presbyterian Mission, S. Gate
Chapin, Miss J. E.	Am. B. of C. for For. Missions, Peking
Chapuis, Madame	Municipalité Française
Child, Mrs.	Peking
Christie, Mrs.	Newchwang
Clark, Mrs. C. D.	11, Hankow Road
Clark, Mrs. J. D.	3, Canton Road (absent)
Clarke, Mrs.	Ningpo
Clarke, Mrs. G. W.	China Inland Mission, Yunnan
Clavaud, Madame	50, Rue Montauban
Clements, Mrs. J. J.	47, Broadway
Clifford, Mrs. W. W.	11, Nanking Road
Clifton, Mrs.	1, Garden Villas, 5, Woosung Road
Cockburn, Mrs.	Church of Scotland Mission, Ichang
Coe, Mrs. F. E.	2, Mohawk Place
Colburn, Miss M. K.	Union Mission, Bridgman Home
Colgan, Mrs. James	54, Broadway, Hongkew
Colgan, Miss	54, Broadway, Hongkew
Collins, Mrs.	Tientsin
Collins, Mrs. W.	5, Chaou-foong Road
Compton, Mrs.	Wenchow
Cooper, Mrs. H.	Hunt's Wharf, Hongkew
Copp, Mrs. A.	American Bible Society, Chinkiang
Corbach, Mrs. H. W. B. von	8, Whangpoo Road
Corbett, Mrs.	Am. Presbyterian Mission, Chefoo
Cory, Mrs. J. M.	Bubbling Well Road
Costa, Miss M. A. G. da	8, Boone Place
Costa, Mrs. E. V. G. da	8, Boone Place
Costa, Mrs. F. G. da	8, Boone Place
Courtenay, Mrs. M. L.	2 and 3, Yuen-ming-yuen Road
Couto, Mrs. E. J. de	4, Quinsan Road
Couto, Miss	4, Quinsan Road
Coutts, Mrs. George W.	Bubbling Well Road
Cranston, Mrs. D.	1, Chaou-foong Road
Crawford, Mrs.	Am. South. Bap. Mission, Chefoo
Croft, Miss	Meth. Free Church Mission, Ningpo
Crowlie, Mrs.	Taku
Cushman, Miss C. M.	Am. Meth. Episcopal Mission, Peking
Dase, Mrs. I. M.	Chefoo
Dale, Mrs. H. W.	"Rose Cottage" Carter's Road
Dalrymple, Mrs. S. O.	44, Broadway, Hongkew
Dalziel, Mrs. J.	2, Seward Road
Danenberg, Mrs. J.	4, Seward Road
Darling, Mrs. D. A.	Trefancha
Dauverchain, Sœur G.	Ningpo
David, Mrs. D. M.	Chinkiang
Davis, Mrs. G. R.	Am. Meth. Episcopal Mission, Peking
Davis, Mrs. J. W.	Am. Presbyterian Mission, Soochow
Davis, Mrs. S. G.	Seventh Day Baptist Mission
De Bernières, Mrs.	The Hawthorns, Markham Road
Deegan, Mrs. E. J.	Astor House
Deighton-Braysher, Mrs.	4, Makaloo Terrace
Delastre, Mrs. E.	Hotel des Colonies
Denny, Mrs. O. N.	U. S. Consulate-General (absent)
Dermer, Mrs. Thos. M.	Foochow (absent)
Diament, Miss N.	Am. B. of C. for For. Mission, Kalgan
Diniz, Mrs. A. F.	13, Quinsan Road
Diniz, Mrs. A. J.	5, Seward Road
Dircksen, Mrs. H.	10, Whangpoo Road (absent)
Dodwell, Mrs. Geo. B.	East Villa, Bubbling Well Road
Donaldson, Mrs. C.	1, Lower Yuen-ming-yuen Road
Donnelly, Mrs. A. R.	Chefoo
Donovan, Mrs. J. P.	10, Kiangse Road
Douthwaite, Mrs. A. W.	China Inland Mission, Chefoo
Dowdall, Mrs. W. M.	21, Foochow Road
Downman, Miss	China Inland Mission, Si-chuen
Dowsley, Mrs.	Church of Scotland Mission, Ichang
Doyen, Sister	Peking
Doyle, Mrs. W. H.	14, Szechuen Road
Drage, Mrs. Z. B.	Bubbling Well Road
Drake, Mrs. S. B.	China Inland Mission, Shansi
Drew, Mrs. E. B.	9, Peking Road
Drummond, Mrs.	Bubbling Well Road (absent)
Ducoi, Sœur Marie	Kiukiang
Duchaix, Sœur	Peking
Ducourtyl, Sœur	Peking
Dudgeon, Mrs. J.	London Miss. Society, Peking (abt.)

DUF—GOL.

Duff, Mrs. T. .... Chinkiang
Duparc, Sœur Marie ...... Maison Saint Vincent, Ningpo
Du Jardin, Mrs. .... Chefoo
Duval, Mdme. .... French Municipality
Dyer, Mrs. Samuel .... 3a, Whangpoo Road

Eason, Mrs. A. .... China Inland Mission, Si-chuen
Easton, Mrs. G. F. ...... Ch. Inland Mission, Shensi
Ecclestone, Mrs. .... Tientsin
Ecuyer, Sœur J. .... Ningpo
Edkins, Mrs. .... Peking
Edwards, Mrs. J. .... 7, Quinsan Road
Edwards, Miss .... 7, Quinsan Road
Elberg, Mrs. J. .... Newchwang
Elias, Mrs. E. E. J. ...... 703, Nanking Road
Elwin, Miss Edith .... Hangchow
Elwin, Miss Rosie .... Hangchow
Elwin, Mrs. A. .... Hangchow
Emens, Mrs. W. S. ...... South Gate
Esteves, Mrs. F. M. ...... 27, Nanzing Road
Evans, Miss J. E. .... Am. B. of C. for For. Mis., T'ungchow
Evans, Mrs. H. .... Monck Sherbourne, 3, Minghong Rd.
Evans, Miss Mary .... China Inland Mission, Ganking
Everall, Mrs. H. .... "Eversleigh" Bubbling Well Road
Ezra, Mrs. J. .... 9, Soochow Road

Fabris, Mrs. E. A. .... Bubbling Well Road
Fairhurst, Mrs. T. .... Foochow
Farnham, Mrs. J. M. ...... Am. Pres. Mission, South Gate (abt)
Farnham, The Misses ...... Am. Pres Mission, South Gate (abt)
Faure, Sœur Adèle .... Maison Saint Vincent, Ningpo
Fausset, Miss A. L. ...... China Inland Mission, Si-chuen
Fauvel, Madame .... Hankow
Fearon, Mrs. .... "The Elms," Bubbling Well Road
Fearon, Miss .... "The Elms," Bubbling Well Road
Ferguson, Mrs. Geo. H. 40, Broadway, Hongkow
Ferguson, Mrs. R. .... Bubbling Well Road
Ferguson, Mrs. T. T. ... Belgian Consulate, Chefoo
Ferguson, Miss .... Belgian Consulate, Chefoo
Ferreira, Mrs. L. A. ...... 5, Quinsan Road
Figueiredo, Mrs. .... 8, Seward Road
Findlay, Mrs. J. .... Carter's Road
Fisher, Mrs. G. .... Tientsin
Fitch, Mrs. G. F. .... Soochow, care of Am. Presb. Mission
Flagg, Mrs. A. E. .... Central Hotel
Forbes, Mrs. William ...... Tientsin
Ford, Mrs. Thos. .... 74, French Bund
Forrester, Mrs. W. .... "Mayfair Lodge," Bubbling Well Rd
Foster, Mrs. A. .... Hankow
Fowler, Mrs. W. .... 12, Hankow Road
Foubert, Sister .... Kiukiang
Frandin, Mrs. Ete. .... Tientsin
Fryer, Mrs. H. G. .... 3, Miller Road
Fryer, Miss .... 3, Miller Road
Fryer, Mrs. John .... Kiangnan Arsenal
Fuller, Mrs. A. R. .... Shaouhing
Fuller, Mrs. W. R. ...... Beach House, Chefoo
Fuller, Miss .... Beach House, Chefoo
Fuller, Miss F. A. .... Beach House, Chefoo
Fullerton, Mrs. G. .... 10, Kiangse Road

Galbiati, Sister Regina ... Roman Cath. Orphanage, Hankow
Gale, Mrs. S. R. .... Shanghai Library
Galindo, Sœur .... Peking
Galles, Mrs. F. W. .... 30, Broadway, Hongkow
Galli, Sister Giuseppina ... Roman Catholic Orphanage, Hankow
Galpin, Mrs. Emily .... Meth. Free Ch. Miss. (Eng.) Ningpo
Gandini, Sister Florinda . Roman Catholic Orphanage, Hankow
Gardner, Mrs. F. E. ...... Glenrue House, Chefoo
Garretson, Miss E. M. ... Am. B. of C. for For. Miss., Kalgan
Garrett, Mrs. J. V. ...... 3, Boone Road
Gearing, Mrs. .... Chinkiang (absent)
Gilbert, Sœur P. .... Ningpo
Gilchrist, Miss Ella., M.D. Am. Meth. Episcopal Miss., K'kiang
Gilhodis, Sœur .... Peking
Gilmour, Mrs. D. .... 24, Kiangse Road (absent)
Gilmour, Mrs. J. .... London Missionary Society, Peking
Ginart, Mrs. M. .... 3c, Whangpoo Road
Giovanelli, Sœur Françoise Ningpo
Gipperich, Mrs. E. .... 5, Szechuen Road
Glover, Mrs. G. B. .... 6, Hongkong Road
Goddard Mrs. .... Am. Baptist Mission, Ningpo (abt)
Godwin, Mrs. Alfred A. ... 1, Quinsan Road
Goldie, Miss E. A. .... Church Miss. Society, Foochow

GOO—IGN.

Goodfellow, Mrs. H. S. ... South Villa, Bubbling Well Road
Goodfellow, Mrs. W. ...... Shanghai Gas Co.
Goodman, Miss C. S. ...... China Inland Mission, Ganking
Gould, Mrs. J. .... 3, Amoy Road
Grabe, Mrs. Otto .... Tientsin
Graham, Mrs. W. H. ...... 3a, Miller Road, Hongkew
Gram, Mrs. Chas. .... Pootung Custom Yard
Grant, Mrs. C. L. .... 4, The Bund (absent)
Graves, Mrs. .... Am. Episcopal Mission, Hankow
Green, Mrs. .... 25a, Nanking Road
Green, Miss .... 25a, Nanking Road
Grimmer, Mrs. .... 18, Nanking Road
Groom, Miss Annie L. ... China Inland Mission, Chefoo
Groves, Mrs. W. L. ...... Ningpo (absent)
Guillon, Sœur Vincent ... Ningpo
Gutterres, Mrs. D. M. ... 3, Seward Road, Hongkew
Gutterres, Miss R. .... 6, Quangse Road

Haas, Mrs. J. .... 20, Peking Road
Hall, Mrs. J. Ward ...... 35, Nankin Road
Hamlin, Mrs. W. P. ...... 34, Broadway
Hanisch, Mrs. F. O. ...... 10, Szechuen Road
Hanisch, Miss .... 10, Szechuen Road
Hanisch, Miss M. A. ...... 10, Szechuen Road
Hansen, Mrs. A. .... Chefoo
Harris, Miss Alice B. ...... Am. B. of C. for For. Mis., Foochow
Harris, Miss C. W. .... St. John's College
Harris, Mrs. .... 52, Broadway
Harris, Mrs. Wilmer ...... 4, Peking Road
Hart, Lady .... Peking
Harton, Mrs. W. H. ...... Foochow
Hartwell, Mrs. C. .... Foochow
Harvie, Mrs. J. Alex. ... Auklerwood, Hongkew
Haskell, Mrs. F. E. ...... 2, Soochow Road
Haven, Miss Ada .... Am. Bd. of C. for For. Miss., Peking
Hayes, Mrs. W. M. ...... Am. Presb. Mission, Tungchow
Henderson, Mrs. E. ...... 5, Hongkong Road (absent)
Henderson, Mrs. James ... Tientsin
Henderson, Miss Mary ... Tientsin
Henningsen, Mrs. J. ...... The Bund
Hertz, Mrs. Henry .... 17, Peking Road
Heuckendorff, Mrs. J. J. . Newchwang
Hickey, Mrs. P. S. .... Mulberry Cottage, near Ningpo Joss [House
Hill, Mrs. J. C. .... Taku
Hillman, Georginia M. ... Hankow
Hinds, Mrs. J .... Meth. Missionary Society, Tientsin
Hirsbrunner, Mrs. James .. 7, Siking Road
Hirth, Mrs., F. .... French Sikawei Road
Hitch, Mrs. Frederic D. ... 9, Szechuen Road
Hoare, Mrs. J. C. .... Ningpo
Hobson, Mrs. R. M. ...... Tientsin
Höflich, Mrs. A. .... The Hermitage, Sikawei
Hogan, Miss .... French School, Rue Montauban
Holbrook, Miss M. A., M.D. Am. B. of C. for For. Mis., Tungchow
Holcombe, Mrs. Chester. Peking
Holland, Mrs. W. .... Tientsin
Holmes, Mrs. .... Am. South. Bp. Miss., Tûngchow (ab)
Holt, Mrs. W. S. .... 18, Peking Road
Hopkins, Mrs. G. C. ...... 12, Soochow Villas
Horne, Miss .... China Inland Mission, Shansi
Horsburgh, Mrs. J. H. ... Hangchow
Hough, Mrs. T. F. .... 5, Miller Road (absent)
Houlbe, Sœur J. .... Ningpo
Howard, Miss L. A., M.D. Am. Meth. Episcopal Mis., Tientsin
Howard, Mrs. W. C. ...... The Palms, 43, Broadway
Howe, Miss Delia E. ...... Am. Meth. Episcopal Mis., Kiukiang
Howe, Miss Gertrude ...... Am. Meth. Epis. Mis., Kiukiang (ab)
Howes, Mrs. J. .... 3, Woosung Road, Hongkow
Howes, Miss L. .... 3, Woosung Road, Hongkew
Hübbe, Mrs. P. G. .... 28, The Bund
Huey, Mrs. B. E. .... 20, Broadway
Hughes, Miss K. .... China Inland Mission, Ganking
Hughes, Mrs. P. J. ...... H.B.M.'s Consulate
Hueslis, Mrs. B. N. ...... 3, Quinsan Road
Hunnex, Mrs. W. J. ...... Am. Bap. (Southern) Miss. Chinkiang
Hunt, Mrs. H. W. .... China Inland Mission, Kansuh
Hunt, Mrs. J. H. .... Kiukiang
Hunter, Mrs. S. A. D. ... Am. Presb. Mission, Chinan-fu
Hykes, Mrs. R. S. .... Am. Meth. Episcopal Mis., Kiukiang

Iburg, Mrs. I. C. H. ...... 19, North Soochow Road
Iffland, Mrs. A. .... 10, Whangpoo Road
Ignatio, Miss J. .... 7, Miller Road

IMB—LAW.

Imbault-Huart, Mrs. ...... French Consulate, Hankow
Imbert, Sœur Marie ...... Ningpo
Innocent, Mrs. J. .... Met. Missionary Soc. (Eng.), T'tsin.
Inveen, Mrs. Emma ...... Am. Baptist Mission, Ningpo
Isaac, Mrs. .... 20, Foochow Road
Isaac, The Misses .... 20, Foochow Road

Jack, Mrs. G. .... 12, Seward Road
Jack, Miss .... Newchwang
Jackson, Mrs. J. A. ...... China Inland Mission, Chehkiang
Jackson, Mrs. W. H ...... 5, Nanking Road
Jamieson, Mrs. .... Kiukiang
Jamieson, Mrs. R. A. ... 1A, Kiukiang Road
Jamieson, Mrs. W. D. ... Thistlewood, Bubbling Well Road
Jansen, Mrs. D. C. .... Astor House, Hongkew Bund
Jaurias, Rev. Mother...... Peking
Jenkins, Mrs. .... Am. Bap. Mission, Shaou-hing (abt)
Jennings, Mrs. T. C. ...... Chefoo
Jordein, Mrs. .... Hankow
Jessup-Clark, Miss......... 3, Canton Road
Jezowski, Mrs. J. .... Foochow
John, Mrs. Griffith......... London Miss. Society, Hankow
Johnson, Mrs. F............ Foochow
Jones, Miss Hannah ...... China Inland Mission, Kansuh
Jones, Mrs. Malcomb...... 34, Whangpoo Road
Jones, Mrs. Theo. F. ...... Foochow
Jorge, Mrs. H................ West Villa, Bubbling Well Road
Jorge, Miss .... West Villa, Bubbling Well Road
Jürgensen, Mrs. J. .... Newchwang (absent)
Joséphine, Sœur, ... Peking
Judd, Mrs. C. H. .... 2, Quinsan Road
Judd, Mrs. W. .... Bubbling Well Road
Judson, Mrs. .... Am. Presb. Mission, Hangchow
Julie, Sœur .... Peking
Jürgens, Mrs. H. .... 13, Szechuen Rd., corner F'chow Rd.

Kahler, Mrs. W. R. ...... 11, Dunbarton Terrace
Kelsey, Mrs. A. D. H., M.D. Am. Presb. Mission, Tengchow
Kerr, Mrs. Crawford ...... "Lawnside," Bubbling Well Road
Kerr, Mrs. J. D............. 23, Szechuen Road
Kerr, Miss C. M. .... Ch. Inland Mission, Kwei-yang (ab.)
Kierulff, Mrs. F............. Peking
Killeen, Mrs. C.............. 27, Broadway
King, Mrs. C. H. .... 27, Kiangse Road
King, Mrs. Paul H. ...... Hotel des Colonies
Kingsbury, Miss Emily... China Inland Mission, Shansi
Kingsmill, Mrs. T. W. ... "Windy Arbour," Markham Road
Kirchhoff, Mrs. .... 26, Whangpoo Road
Kirchner, Mrs. A. .... 10, Kiangse Road
Kirk, Mrs. J. C. H. ...... 49, Broadway
Kirkby, Miss A. E. ...... Union Mission, Bridgman Home
Kirkland, Miss H. .... Am. Presb. Mission, Hangchow
Kleinwächter, Mrs. F. ... Ningpo
Kluth, Mrs. .... Hongkew Police Station
Knights, Mrs. A. E. ...... 31, Szechuen Road
Knott, Mrs. R. .... 2, Miller Road
Kofot, Mrs. J................. Kiukiang
Koosnetzoff, Mrs. A. N... Tientsin
Kupfer, Mrs. L. E. ...... Am. Meth. Epis. Miss., Kiukiang

Lacote, Sœur V.............. Ningpo
Lagerheim, Mrs. O. de ... French Municipality
Laidler, Mrs. T. W. ...... 6, Miller Road
Laisun, Mrs. Tseng......... 11, Boone Road
Laisun, Miss Tseng......... 11, Boone Road
Laisun, Miss A. H.......... 11, Boone Road
Lalcaca, Mrs. E. P. ...... 4, Kiangse Road (absent)
Lambuth, Mrs. J. W....... 42, Corner of Kiangse & Peking Rds.
Lambuth, Mrs. W. R....... 42, Corner of Kiangse & Peking Rds.
Lambuth, Miss .... 42, Corner of Kiangse & P'king Rds.
Lamoud, Mrs. J. B. ...... 11, Soochow Road
Lancaster, Mrs. M. W. ... 57, Broadway
Land, Mrs. .... Kiukiang
Land, Miss .... Kiukiang
Lanning, Mrs. Geo. ...... 10, Upper Yuen-ming-yuen Road
Laracine, Sœur .... Peking
Lazarowicz, Sœur Augustine Maison Saint Vincent, Ningpo
Laughlin, Mrs. J. H ...... Am. Presb. Mission, Wei-hien
Laurence, Miss M. .... Church Miss. Society, Ningpo
Lavers, Mrs. .... 2, Sin Jaw Road, Bubbling Well Rd.
Law, Mrs. Alex. .... 2, Garden Villa
Law, Mrs. Robert .... 6, Chaou-foong Road
Law, Mrs. W. C. .... Rec.-ship "Corea"
Lawson, Miss S. E. ...... St. John's College

LEA—MIN.

Leach, Mrs. A. W........... 29, Broadway
Leclercq, Sœur .... Peking
Lees, Mrs. J.................. London Missionary Society, Tientsin
Leith, Mrs. A................ Hankow
Lethimonnier, Sœur E. ... Ningpo
Leyenberger, Mrs. .... Am. Presbyterian Mission, Chefoo
Liddell, Mrs. C. O.......... 17, Kiangse Road
Lightfoot, Miss F. D....... Am. Baptist Mission, Ningpo
Limby, Mrs. H. J.......... 3, Bubbling Well Road
Lind, Mrs. A. .... 24, The Bund
Lindsay, Mrs. .... 9, Kiangse Road
Little, Mrs. L. S. .... 10, Kiukiang Road
Little, Mrs. Robt. W. ... 14, Yuen-ming-yuen Road
Livingston, Mrs. Jas. ... Pagoda Anchorage, Foochow
Lloyd, Mrs. L. .... Foochow
Loam, Mrs. W. B. .... 2, Ewo Terrace
Locke, Mrs. .... Am. Episcopal Mission, Hankow
Longden, Mrs. W. C....... Chinkiang
Loup, Mrs. P. .... Tientsin
Louy, Sœur Stéphanie ... Ningpo
Low, Mrs. Edward G. ... 5, Sin Jaw Road, Bub. Well Road (ab)
Lowry, Mrs.................. Meth. Episcopal Mission, Peking
Lubeck, Mrs. H. .... 9, Boone Place
Lubeck, Mrs. L. A. ...... 13, Canton Road
Luca, Madame F. de ...... Italian Legation (absent)
Luscan, Sœur A............. Maison Saint Vincent, Ningpo

MacCallum, Mrs. Alex. ... Pootung
Machado, Mrs. F. G. ...... 7, Peking Road
Machado, Miss............... 7, Peking Road
Machado, Miss C. .... 7, Peking Road
Macintyre, Mrs. J .... Newchwang
Mackenzie, Mrs. James... 5, Nanking Road
Mackenzie, Mrs. J.......... Kiangnan Arsenal
Mackenzie, Miss .... Kiangnan Arsenal
Mackenzie, Mrs. Robert... "Elsanslea," Markham Road
Maclean, Miss R............. Chefoo
Maclean, Miss A. .... Chefoo
Maclean, Mrs. Peter ...... Fairfield House, Markham Road
Macleod, Mrs. Neil......... 9, Kiangse Road
Macpherson, Mrs. .... 30, Broadway
Mactavish, Mrs. .... 1, The Bund
Madaus, Miss .... 14g, Foochow Road
Maertens, Mrs. Aug. H... 25, Whangpoo Road
Maillard, Sœur .... Peking
Main, Mrs. Duncan ...... Hangchow
Malpass, Miss .... China Inland Mission, Chefoo
Marçal, Miss A. .... 3, Seward Road
Marçal, Miss M. .... 3, Seward Road
Marçal, Miss S. .... 3, Seward Road
Marie, Sœur .... Peking
Markwick, Mrs. R.......... 21, Whangpoo Road
Markwick, Miss M. A. ... 21, Whangpoo Road
Markwick, Miss J. M. ... 21, Whangpoo Road
Martin, Mrs. J. P.......... 15, Boone Road
Martin, Miss .... 15, Boone Road
Martin, Mrs. W. A. P. ... Peking
Martins, Mrs. R. F.... ... 7, North Soochow Road
Martins, The Misses ...... 7, North Soochow Road
Mason, Mrs.................. Am. Baptist Mission, Ningpo
Mateer, Mrs. C. W.......... Am. Presb. Mission, Tungchow
Mateer, Mrs. R. M. ...... Am. Presbyterian Mission, Wei-hien
Matheison, Mrs. A......... 10, Kiangse Road
May, Mrs. J. H............. 6, Quinsan Road
May, Miss.................... 6, Quinsan Road
May, Miss F. .... 6, Quinsan Road
May, Mrs. F. N............. Bubbling Well Road
McArthur, Mrs. .... 25, Broadway
McCoy, Mrs. A. P.......... Am. Presbyterian Mission, Peking
McCulloch, Mrs. .... Am. Southern Bap. Miss., Tungchow
McDougall, Mrs............. Engineers' Institute, Kiangse Road
McKean, Mrs................ Peking
McKee, Mrs. W. J. ...... Am. Presbyterian Mission, Ningpo
McLeod, Mrs. A. .... 10, Whangpoo
McLeod, Miss .... 10, Whangpoo
Meadows, Mrs. James ... China Inland Mission, Chehkiang
Meech, Mrs................... London Mission, Peking
Meier, Mrs. H. H. .... 11, Minghong Road
Mesini, Sister Santa ...... Roman Cath. Orphanage, Hankow
Mesny, Mrs. J. .... Hankow
Meurie, Sœur A............. Ningpo
Middleton, Mrs. O. ...... Old Ningpo Wharf
Mills, Mrs. .... Am. Presb. Mission, Hangchow
Minglederff, Mrs. O. G... S. M. E. Mission, 9, Woosung Road

MIT—PER.

Mitchell, Mrs. G. .... Taku
Mitchell, Mrs. J. .... 10, Kiangse Road
Mitchell, Mrs. J. A. ...... 4, Miller Road
Mobsby, Mrs. George ... 5, Chaou-foong Road
Moncrieff, Mrs. A. L. M... 16, Szechuen Road
Monteiro, Miss .... 10, Seward Road
Monteiro, Mrs. A. .... 10, Seward Road
Moon, Miss L .... Am. Southern Bap. Miss., Chefoo
Moore, Mrs. Andrew ...... 4, Boone Place, Hongkew
Moore, Mrs. J. M. .... Tientsin
Moore, Miss .... Tientsin
Moore, Mrs. C. F. .... Peking
Moorehead, Mrs. .... Newchwang
Moorehead, The Misses... Newchwang
Moorehead, Mrs. T. ...... Hankow
Moosa, Mrs. .... 6, Siking Road
Morse, Mrs. H. B. .... Tientsin
Morriss, Mrs. Henry ...... "Mohawk Lodge," Bub. Well Road
Moses, Mrs. J. .... 23, Foochow Road
Motchiyoski, Madame ... 21, North Soochow Road
Moule, Mrs. A. E. .... 18, Kiangse Road
Moule, Mrs. G. E. .... Hangchow
Moule, Miss J. .... Hangchow
Mouton, Mde. V. .... 3, Yuen-ming-yuen Buildings
Moutrie, Mrs. S. .... 59, Broadway
Mowat, Mrs. .... 32, The Bund
Muxham, Mrs. L. .... Old Ningpo Wharf
Muhlinghaus, Sœur Stéphanie, Ningpo
Muir, Miss Sarah .... China Inland Mission, Shansi
Murdock, Miss V. C., M.D. Am. B. of C. for For. Miss., Kalgan
Murray, Miss J. H. ...... China Inland Mission, Chehkiang
Murray, Miss E. .... Eng. Presb. Mission, Taiwan-fu
Murray, Mrs. J. .... Am. Presb. Mission, Chinan-fu
Muse, Miss A. E. .... S. M. E. Mission, 9, Woosung Road
Myres, Mrs. C. .... Tientsin

Nardon, Sister Erminia... Roman Cath. Orphanage, Hankow
Neal, Mrs. J. B. .... Am. Presb. Mission, Tungchow
Neller, Miss .... Kiukiang
Nelson, Mrs. M. .... 4, Chaou-foong Road
Nevius, Mrs. J. L. .... Am. Presbyterian Mission, Chefoo
Newman, Miss E. M. ...... Chefoo
Newman, Miss E. V. ...... Chefoo
Newman, Mrs. E. .... Chefoo
Newton, Miss Ella J. ...... Am. Board of For. Miss., Foochow
Nicoll, Mrs. Geo. .... China Inland Mission, Si-chuan
Nightingale, Mrs. .... Wesleyan Meth. Miss. Soc., Hankow
Noidans-Calf, la Countesse de, Peking
Nolting, Mrs. J. .... 10, Albany Gardens
North, Mrs. .... Wesleyan Meth. Mis. Soty., Wusueh
Nunes, Mrs. J. C. S. ...... 18 & 19, Chapoo Road
Nunes, Miss M. F. S. ... 18 & 19, Chapoo Road

Oberg, Mrs. G. L. .... 48, Broadway
Odell, Mrs. John .... Foochow (absent)
Oeltze, Mrs. C. .... Foochow
Ohlinger, Mrs. F. .... Foochow
Oliveira, Mrs. F. S. ...... 6, Upper Yuen-ming-yuen Road
Oliveira, Mrs. F. M. d'... 25 & 26, Peking Road
Olsen, Mrs. A. .... Hankow
Olsson, Mrs. A. .... 4, Shantung Road
Ord, Miss .... 32, Szechuen Road
Ord, Mrs. J. W. .... New Dock, Pootung
Orion, Madame .... French Post Office
Ortwin, Mrs. Wm. .... 3, Ming-hang Road
O'Shaughnessy, Miss ...... "Lawnside," Bubbling Well Road.
Ottaway, Mrs. .... Tientsin
Owen, Mrs. G. S. .... London Mission, Peking

Paleari, Sister Rachele ... Roman Cath. Orphanage, Hankow
Parada, Sœur E. .... Peking
Parker, Mrs. .... Southern Meth. Mission, Soochow
Parker, Mrs. G. .... China Inland Mission, Kansuh
Parker, Mrs. J. H. P. ... U.S. "Wellington"
Parkes, The Misses .... Peking
Parrott, Mrs. A. G. ...... China Inland Mission, Yangchow
Pearse, Mrs. E. .... China Inland Mission, Shensi
Penfold, Mrs. .... 8, Honan Road
Perboyre, Sœur G. .... Maison Saint Vincent, Ningpo
Percebois, Mrs. .... 34, Rue Montauban
Percebois, Miss L. .... 34, Rue Montauban
Percival, Miss .... 5, Upper Yuen-ming-yuen Road
Percival, Mrs. W. S. ...... 5, Upper Yuen-ming-yuen Road
Pereira, Miss A. J. .... 13 & 14, North Soochow Road

PER—ROU.

Pereira, Mrs. E. F. .... 25, North Soochow Road
Pereira, Mrs. J. F. .... 6, Seward Road
Pereira, Mrs. J. G. ...... 21, North Soochow Road
Perkins, Mrs. B. M. ...... 2, Bubbling Well Road
Perotta, Mdme. M. ...... Russell & Co.'s Silk Filature
Perrand, Sœur Augustine Ningpo
Perrin, Sœur Marie ...... Ningpo
Pestonjee, Mrs. R. .... 35, Kiangse Road
Petersen, Miss M. .... 18, Hankow Road
Petersen, Mrs. R. .... 18, Hankow Road
Philips, Mrs. C. J. A. ...... Kiukiang
Phillips, Mrs. Joseph ...... Foochow
Pinkoff, Mrs. E. J. ...... Hankow (absent)
Piccinelli, Sister Rosa ... Roman Cath. Orphanage, Hankow
Pichon, Madame .... 16, Peking Road
Pickwood, Miss .... Mohawk Lodge, Bubbling Well Road
Pickwood, Miss Blanche.. Mohawk Lodge, Bubbling Well Road
Pierson, Miss L. B. ...... Am. B. of C. for For. Missions, Pao-ting Fu
Pietra, Sister Natalina ... Roman Cath. Orphanage, Hankow
Pigott, Mrs. T. W. .... China Inland Mission, Shansi
Pilcher, Mrs. .... Meth. Episcopal Mission, Tientsin
Pim, Mrs. .... Foochow
Pinod, Mrs. T. .... 8, Tiendong Road
Platt, Mrs. A. R. .... Chefoo
Plumb, Mrs. N. J. .... Foochow
Poitevin, Mrs. L. .... 27, Nanking Road
Pollock, Mrs. .... Wuhu
Pond, Mrs. J. A. .... Hotel des Colonies [chuang
Porter, Miss Mary H. ... Am. B. of For. Missions, Pang-chia-
Porter, Miss Mary Q. ...... Meth. Episcopal Mission, Tientsin
Porter, Mrs. E. C. .... Am. B. of C. for For. Mission, P'ang-
Postlethwaite, Mrs. .... Foochow [chia (Shantung)
Price, Mrs. D. J. .... Chefoo
Primrose, Mrs. W. M. ...... 6, Yuen ming yuen Road
Pruitt, Mrs. C. W. .... Am. S. Baptist Mission, Chefoo
Pruyn, Mrs. Mary .... Union Mission, Bridgman Home
Purcell, Mrs. P. H. .... 4, Siking Road
Purdon, Mrs. J. G. .... 1, Hankow Road (absent)
Pyke, Mrs. .... Peking (absent)

Ramsay, Mrs. Hugh F. ... Hankow
Randle, Mrs. H. .... China Inland Mission, Chehkiang
Randolph, Mrs. A. E. ... Am. Presb. Mission, Hangchow (ab)
Rangel, Mrs. S. J. .... 9, Quangse Terrace
Rankin, Miss D. .... Southern Meth. Mission, Nanziang
Rankin, Miss L. .... Southern Meth. Mission, Nanziang
Reding, Mrs. J. E. .... 7, Nanking Road
Rees, Mrs. W. H. .... London Missionary Society, Peking
Reeves, Mrs. Geo. .... Chefoo
Rehders, Mrs. E. .... Tientsin
Reid, Mrs. .... Southern Meth. Mission, Soochow
Reifsnyder, Miss Elizabeth, M.D., Union Mission, Bridgman Home
Remedios, Miss C. M. ... 32, Chapoo Road
Remedios, Miss E. M. ... 32, Chapoo Road
Remedios, Mrs. S. A. dos. 5, Seward Road
Remedios, Mrs. S. B. dos. 32, Chapoo Road
Rendall, Mrs. .... China Inland Mission, Shansi
Riach, Mrs. John .... Eames' Bungalow (absent)
Ricaud, Sœur Vincent ... Maison Saint Vincent, Ningpo
Ricco, Mrs. .... French Municipality
Richardson, Mrs. F. R... 11, Seward Road
Ridez, Sœur J. .... Ningpo
Riley, Mrs. J. H. .... China Inland Mission, Si-chuan
Riley, Mrs. W. .... China Inland Mission, Chentu
Ritchie, Mrs. .... Eng. Presb. Mission, Tai-wan Fu
Ritter, Mrs. .... Tientsin
Roberts, Miss .... Am. Southern Baptist Mis., Chefoo
Roberts, Mrs. A. C. .... 28, Chapoo Road
Roberts, Mrs. O. L. ...... 12, Seward Road
Robertson, Mrs. H. J. ... Foochow
Robins, Mrs. .... 30, Kiangse Road
Robinson, Mrs. Alfred ... 1, Yuen-ming-yuen Buildings
Robinson, Mrs. J. .... Meth. Missionary Soc. (Eng.), T'tsin
Rocher, Madame L. ...... Hankow
Rocher, Mrs. E. .... 24, Whangpoo Road
Rodewald, Mrs. J. F. ..... Marienheim, French Sikawey Road
Roddier, Sœur L. .... Ningpo
Rodrigues, Mrs. J. ...... 7A, Miller Road
Rogerson, Mrs. J. M. ... Shanghai Gas Works
Rose, Mrs. J. .... 33, North Soochow Road
Ross, Mrs. J. .... Newchwang
Rossi, Mlle. E. .... Russell & Co.'s Silk Filature
Rouvière, Sœur M. .... Maison Saint Vincent, Ningpo

ROY—ST.

Royall, Mrs. .... 9, Woosung Road
Roye, Sœur .... Peking
Rom, Mrs. D. da .... Foochow
Rozario, Mrs. .... 3, Chapoo Road
Rozario, Mrs. C. E. do ... 3, Upper Yuen-ming-yuen Road
Rozario, Mrs. D. .... Foochow
Rozario, Mrs. F. P. ...... 8, Chapoo Road
Rudland, Mrs. W. D. ...... China Inland Mission, Chehkiang
Russell, Mrs. .... Ch. Missionary Society, Ningpo
Ryan Sister .... Kiukiang

Safford, Miss A. C. .... Am. Presbyterian Mission, Soochow
Sanchez, Mrs. C. A. ...... 5, Chapoo Road, Hongkew
Santos, Miss .... 6, Quangse Road
Santos, Miss A. A. dos ... 7, Miller Road
Sassoon, Mrs. E. E. ...... Corner of Nanking Road & Bund
Saunders, Mrs. J. C. ...... Foochow
Saunders, Mrs. Wm. ...... 3, Whangpoo Road, Hongkew Bund
Saylo, Mrs. T. H. .... Corner of Nanking & Szechuen Roads
Saylo, Mrs. W. J. .... Nowchwang
Sayres, Mrs. K. J. .... Am. Episcopal Mission, Wuchang
Sayres, Mrs. W. S. .... St. John's College
Schereschewsky, Mrs. S. I. J., St. John's College, Jessfield (ab.)
Schlichting, Miss .... 25, Whangpoo Road
Schlichtmann, Miss ...... 14a, Foochow Road
Schmidt, Mrs. P. .... Wright's Buildings
Schönfeld, Mrs. Louise... Foochow
Schultz, Mrs. H. Münster 8, Szechuen Road
Schultz, Mrs. J. H. ...... 5, Nanking Road
Scott, Mrs. B. C. G. ...... H. B. M. Consulate, Wuhu
Scott, Mrs. J. L. .... Bubbling Well Road
Seaman, Mrs. J. F. ...... Bubbling Well Road
Sears, Miss Annie B. ...... Am. Meth. Episc. Mission, Peking
Seed, Miss .... China Inland Mission, Chefoo
Senna, Miss M. R. de ... 21, North Soochow Road
Senna, Mrs. C. M. .... 21, North Soochow Road
Senna, Mrs. E. F. .... 34, North Soochow Road
Senna, Mrs. R. M. .... 13, Chapoo Road
Shann, Mrs. R. .... Ningpo
Sharland, Mrs. .... China Inland Mission, Chefoo
Shaw, Mrs. Ellen .... Pagoda Anchorage, Foochow
Shaw, Mrs. M. H. .... Am. Presbyterian Mission, Tungchow
Shaw, Mrs. T. .... 2, Balfour Buildings
Shaw, Mrs. R. W. .... "Mulberry Grove," Pootung
Shaw, Miss K. L. .... "Mulberry Grove," Pootung
Shaw, Miss L. B. .... "Mulberry Grove," Pootung
Shaw, Miss G. E. .... "Mulberry Grove," Pootung
Shaw, Miss F. D. .... "Mulberry Grove," Pootung
Shephard, Mrs. E. .... Bubbling Well Cottage
Sidford, Mrs. .... 45, Kiangse Road
Silas, Mrs. D. H. .... Bubbling Well Road
Sillom, Mrs. H. .... 30, Nanking Road
Silva, Mrs. A. M. da ...... 50, Rue du Consulat
Simoens, Mrs. J. R. ...... 18, Chapoo Road
Simoens, Mrs. N. .... 45, Rue Montauban
Simoens, Miss .... 45, Rue Montauban
Simpson, Mrs. C. Lennx. Kiukiang
Simpson, Mrs. James...... Corner of Carter & Bub. Well Roads
Sinnott, Mrs. P. .... 4, Upper Yuen-ming-yuen Road
Sinnott, Miss .... 4, Upper Yuen-ming-yuen Road
Sites, Mrs. Nathan ...... Foochow
Skinner, Mrs. G. L. ...... 3, Garden Villa
Smidt, Mrs. C. .... 34, Nanking Road. [chia (Shantung)
Smith, Mrs. E. D. .... Am. B. of C. for For. Mission, P'ang-
Smith, Mrs. J. D. .... Foochow
Smith, Mrs. T. G. .... 2, Peking Road
Smith, Miss G. .... Soc. for Female Education, Ningpo
Smith, Mrs. .... Peking
Smith, Mrs. .... The Deanery
Smith, Mrs. W. .... 20, Boone Road
Soares, Mrs. E. E. .... 27, Nanzing Road
Solomiac, Sœur L. .... Sup. Maison de Jesus-Enfants N'gpo
Solomon, Mrs. S. J. ...... 15, Szechuen Road
Sonne, Mrs. C. C. .... 63, Broadway
Souza, Mrs. .... 9, Boone Place
Souza, Mrs. B. de .... 10, Seward Road
Souza, Mrs. A. R. de...... 11, Quinsan Road
Souza, Mrs. V. B. de...... 11, Quinsan Road
Souza, Miss E. M. de...... 11, Quinsan Road
Souza, Miss A. R. R. de.. 11, Quinsan Road
Sowerby, Mrs. .... Am. Episcopal Mission, Hankow
Sparr, Miss Julie E., M.D. Am. Meth. Epis. Mission, Foochow
Spencer, Miss E. A. ...... St. John's College
St. Dominique, Sup. R.M. Institution St. Joseph, 25, Rue Mont.

ST—WAT.

St. Vincent, Mother ...... Institution St. Joseph, 25, Rue Mont.
Stanley Mrs. U. J. .... Am. B. of C. for For. Mis., Tientsin
Startseff, Mrs. A. D. ...... Tientsin [(absent)
Stenhouse, Mrs. .... Meth. Missionary Society, Tientsin
Stevens, Mrs. T. .... 50, Broadway, Hongkew
Stevens, Mrs. Edwin...... Ningpo
Stevenson, Mrs. .... Taku
Stewart, Mrs. J. A. ...... 4, Kiukiang Road
Stewart, Mrs. J. .... Tientsin
Stewart, Mrs. R. S. ...... Eng. Church Mission, Foochow
Stiles, Mrs. George W. ... 9, Quinsan Road
Stott, Mrs. G. .... China Inland Mission, Chehkiang
Stont, Mrs. .... 3, Chaou-foong Road
Strong, Miss F. M. .... Am. Presbyterian Mission, Peking
Stroud, Miss Fannie ...... China Inland Mission, Si-chuan
Suenson, Mrs. E. .... 62, Broadway, Hongkew
Sutton, Mrs. H. .... 20, Broadway, Hongkew
Swallow, Mrs. Alice ...... Meth. Free Church Mission, Ningpo
Swinney, Miss Ella F., M.D. Seventh-day Baptist Mission
Sylva, Mrs. H. .... 37, Szechuen Road

Taft, Mrs. M. L. .... Meth. Episcopal Mission, Chinkiang
Taillon, Mrs. L. .... Peking
Talpey, Mrs. A. H. ...... 3, Miller Road
Tarchini, Sister Carolina.. Roman Cath. Orphanage, Hankow
Tavares, Miss .... 13, Canton Road
Tavares, Miss Helena...... 13, Canton Road
Tavares, Mrs. P. J. ...... 690, Nanking Road
Tavares, Miss A. M. ...... 690, Nanking Road
Taylor, Mrs. C. H. .... Foochow Arsenal
Taylor, Mrs. F. E. .... 27, Szechuen Road
Taylor, Mrs. J. L. .... Am. Meth. Episc. Mission, Foochow
Taylor, Mrs. John T. ...... 8, Quinsan Road
Telien, Sister Eugenie ... Kiukiang
Thdron, Sister Marie ...... Kiukiang
Thirkell, Mrs. J. G. ...... 31A, Nanking Road
Thistle, Mrs. Mary .... 20, Peking Road
Thomas, Mrs. J. .... 10, Kiangse Road
Thomas, Mrs. W. E. ...... 12, Miller Road, Hongkew
Thomson, Mrs. E. H. ...... St. John's College (absent)
Thornley, Mrs. U. W. ...... Oliver's Hotel
Tisdall, Mrs. .... Hotel des Colonies
Titoushkin Mrs. .... Hankow
Tolliday, Mrs. T. .... 10, Kiangse Road
Tomalin, Mrs. E. .... China Inland Mission, Ganking
Towers, Miss .... 23, Szechuen Road
Trask, Miss S., M.D. ...... Am. Meth. Epis. Mission, Foochow
Trodd, Mrs. A. B. .... 5, Amoy Road
Trodd, Miss D. .... 18, Nanking Road
Tulloch, Miss F. J. C. ... 1, Miller Road
Twigg, Mrs. P. O'B. ...... 32, Szechuen Road
Tylor, Miss .... Chefoo

Unwin, Mrs. F. S. .... Nowchwang

Valantine, Mrs. B. A. ...... Bub. Well Rd., opposite Race Course
Vale, Mrs. T. Harold...... 5, Nanking Road
Valentine, Mrs. J. D. ...... Shaouhing
Van Ess, Mrs. .... Chefoo
Vandertak, Mrs. T. N. ..... 14, Mukalee Terrace, Kiangse Road
Vaperoau, Madame.......... Peking
Vawdrey, Mrs. .... 23, Szechuen Road
Veitch, Mrs. A. .... 12, Yangtsze Road
Vela, Madame M. .... 9, Miller Road
Verany, Sœur .... Peking
Vieira, Mrs. .... 843, Kiangse Road
Vincent, Sœur.................. Peking
Vismara, Mother Paula... Roman Cath. Orphanage, Hankow
Vita, Madame Vittoria.. 6, Whangpoo Road

Waddilove, Mrs. W. ...... 64, Broadway
Wadman, Mrs. .... Ningpo
Wadman, Miss Edith...... Ningpo
Waeber, Mrs. C. .... Tientsin
Walker, Miss .... Kin-loo-yuen
Walker, Mrs. .... Wesleyan Meth. Mis. Soc., Wusueh
Walker, Mrs. J. .... Am. B. of C. for F. Missions, Foochow
Walker, Mrs. W. S. ...... Southern Bap. Con. U.S.A., Soochow
Walkinshaw, Mrs. C. ...... Foochow
Walter, Mrs. Wm. .... Hankow
Warner, Miss S. A. ...... Am. Presbyterian Mission, Ningpo
Waters, Mrs. T. J. .... 30, Szechuen Road
Watson, Mrs. .... Wesleyan Meth. Miss. Soc., Wusueh
Watts, Mrs. J. .... Taku

WEA—ZUC.

Weatherstone, Miss ...... Hankow
Weatherstone, Mrs. T. . . Hankow
Webster, Mrs. .... Newchwang
Weeks, Mrs. C. D. .... Foochow
Weir, Mrs. Thomas.......... 60, Broadway, Hongkew
Welch, Mrs. J. .... Bubbling Well Road
Werner, Seour .... Peking
Westall, Mrs. A. C. ...... 24, Kiangse Road
Westwater, Mrs. A.......... U.Presb Ch. of Scot. Mission, Chefoo
Westwater, Mrs. A. M.... U.Presb.Ch. of Scot. Mission, Chefoo
Wetmore, Mrs. W. S. ... Bubbling Well Road
Wheelock, Mrs. T. R ... Bubbling Well Road (absent)
Wheen, Mrs. .... Sayle & Co , Nanking Road
Wheller, Miss F. .... Am.Meth.Episc. Mission, Sze-chuan
Wherry, Mrs. S. E. ...... Am. Presbyterian Mission, Peking
Wilkinson, Mrs. .... Ningpo
Whiller, Mrs. A. .... China Inland Mission, Chehkiang
White, Mrs. Robt. G...... Chinkiang (absent)
Whiting, Mrs. J. L. .... Am. Presbyterian Mission, Peking
Whitney, Mrs. L. S. ...... Foochow
William, Mrs. O. .... Bubbling Well Road
Williams, Miss L. O. ...... China Inland Mission, Ganking
Williams, Mrs. R. .... 1, Miller Road
Williams, Mrs. W. S. ..... 3, Ming-hong Road
Williamson, Mrs. .... Nat. Bible Soc. of Scotland, Chefoo
Williamson, Mrs. J. ...... China Inland Mission, Chehkiang
Willits, Mrs. O. W. ...... Am Meth Episc. Mission, Tientsin
Wills, Mrs. J. H. .... 9, Nanking Road
Wills, Mrs. W. A. .... 4, Shantung Road
Wilson, Miss .... China Inland Mission, Shensi
Wilson, Mrs. G. C. .... 10, Miller Road, Hongkew
Wilson, Mrs. J. .... Tientsin
Wilson, Mrs. O. .... 38, Broadway, Hongkew
Wisner, Mrs. J. H. ...... Bubbling Well Road (absent)
Wolfe, Mrs. J. R. .... Foochow
Wood, Mrs. .... Ch. of Scotland Mission, Ichang
Woodall, Mrs. G. W....... Meth. Episcopal Mission, Wuhu
Woodin, Mrs. S. F. ...... Foochow
Woodward, Mrs. .... Hankow
Woolston, Miss B. .... Am. Meth. Episc. Mission, Foochow
Woolston, Miss S. H. ... Am. Meth. Episc Mission, Foochow
Worley, Mrs. J. H. ...... Am. Meth. Episc. Mission, Nanking
Worley, Mrs. T. H. ...... Am. Meth. Episc. Mission, Chinkiang

Xavier, Mrs. C. A. .... 38, Chapoo Road, Hongkew
Xavier, Mrs. L. A. .... 1, Woosung Road, Hongkew
Xavier, Miss C. .... 1, Woosung Road, Hongkew

Yates, Mrs. .... French Concession, Old North Gate
Yates, Miss E. U. .... Meth. Episcopal Mission, Tientsin
Yeo, Mrs. Geo. J. .... Shanghai Gas Works
Yeomans, Mrs. .... Tientsin
Youd, Mrs. F. M. .... 4, The Bund (absent)

Zacharias, Mrs. .... 34, Szechuen Road
Zedelius Mrs. .... 11, Kiangse Road
Zuck, Mrs. James .... Tientsin (absent)

H.B.M. DIPLOMATIC AND CONSULAR SERVICE, CHINA.

PEKING—
Sir Harry S. Parkes, G.C.M.G., K.C.B., *Envoy Extraordinary, Minister Plenipotentiary and Chief Superintendent of British Trade*
C. T. Maude, *2nd Secretary*
E. C. Baber, *Chinese Secretary (absent.)*
W. C. Hillier, *Acting Chinese Secretary*
Do. *Assistant Chinese Secretary.*
C. W. Everard, *Acting Chinese Secretary*
S. W. Bushell, M.D., *Physician.*
A. E. Pirkis, *Accountant*
W. Brereton, *Chaplain.*
J. Scott, J. R. Coulthard, } *Assistants.*

AMOY—
R. J. Forrest, *Consul*
G. M. H. Playfair, *Assistant.*
K. Cockburn, *Acting Assistant.*

CANTON—
H. F. Hance, *Acting Consul.*
L. C. Hopkins, *Assistant*
P. O'Brien Butler, *Acting Assistant.*

CHEFOO—
Byron Brenan, *Consul.*

CHINKEANG—
E. L. Oxenham, *Consul.*

FOOCHOW—
C. A. Sinclair, *Consul.*
E. L. B. Allen, *Assistant*
E. H. Fraser, *Acting Assistant.*

HANKOW—
C. Alabaster, *Consul.*
H. B. July, *Acting Assistant.*

ICH'ANG—
C. T. Gardner, *Consul.*

KIUKIANG—
G. Jamieson, *Consul.*

KIUNGCHOW—
J. N. Jordan, *Acting Consul*

NEWCHWANG—
Herbert Allen, *Consul.*

NINGPO—
W. M. Cooper, *Consul.*
W. H. Wilkinson, *Acting Assistant.*

PAGODA ISLAND—
R. W. Mansfield, *Acting Vice-Consul.*

PAKHOI—
O. Johnson, *Acting Consul.*

SHANGHAI—
P. J. Hughes, *Consul*
W. R. Carles, *Acting Vice-Consul.*
——, *Registrar of Shipping.*
C. M. Ford, *Assistant.*
J. N. Tratman, *Acting Assistant.*
H. E. Fulford, ,, ,,
R. H. Mortimore, ,, ,,

SWATOW—
G. Phillips, *Consul. Officiating.*
G. Brown, *2nd Assistant.*
M. Fraser, ,,

TAIWAN—
T. Watters, *Consul. Officiating.*
P. F. Hausser, *Acting Assistant.*

TAMSUI—
A. Frater, *Consul. Officiating.*

TIENTSIN AND PEKING—
A. Davenport, *Consul.*
W. Holland, *Assistant.*

WENCHOW—
E. H. Parker *Acting-Consul.*

WHAMPOA—
——, *Vice Consul.*

WUHU—
D. C. G. Scott, *Consul.*

On Leave—*Consuls,* C. Allen, Gregory, Hewlett, Stronach, Watters; *Vice-Consul,* Giles; *Assistants,* Ayrton, Bourne, Bullock, Bristow, Hurst, Spence; *Students,* Brady, Warry; *Chinese Secretary,* E. C. Baber.
On Special Service.—A. Hosie (in Szechuen.)
Retirement during 1882.—None.
Death.—L. W. Heuley.

CHINESE GOVERNMENT DEPARTMENTS AT PEKING.—1884.

(Note.—An asterisk (*) is prefixed to the names of those officials who are members of the Yamên of Foreign Affairs, and a dagger (†) to indicate those who are also members of the Grand Council, in addition to their other functions.)

GRAND COUNCIL 軍機處.—This department, the actual Privy Council of the Sovereign, in whose presence its members daily transact the business of the State, is, like the *Tsung-li Yamên* or Office of Foreign Affairs, a Cabinet composed of Ministers holding various offices in the different Government Boards. It is composed at present of the following members:—

1.—The Prince of Kung.*
2.—Pao Yün.*
3.—Ching Lien.*
4.—Li Hung-tsao.*
5.—P'an Tsu-yin.
6.—Wêng T'ung-ho.

**Members also of the Tsung-li Yamên.*

GRAND SECRETARIAT 內閣.—This, once the Supreme Council of the Empire, has under the present dynasty been superseded in active importance by the Grand Council. It is composed of four *Ta Hsio-shih* or Grand Secretaries, and two *Hsieh-pan Ta Hsio-shih* or Assistant Grand Secretaries, of whom half are Manchu and half are Chinese. It constitutes the Imperial Chancery or Court of Archives, and admission to its ranks confers the highest distinction attainable by Chinese officials, although with functions that are almost purely nominal. Members of the Grand Secretariat are distinguished by the honorary title of *Chung T'ang*. The most distinguished Governors-General are usually advanced to the dignity of Grand Secretary whilst continuing to occupy their posts. The present members are the following:—

1.—Li Hung-chang, *Governor-General of Chihli.*
2.—*†Pao Yün, *Member of Grand Council, &c.*
3.—†Tso Tsung-t'ang, *Governor-General of Two Kiang.*
4.—Ling Kuei.
5.—Wên Yü, *President of Board of Punishments.*
6.—*†Li Hung-tsao, *President of Board of Civil Office.*
7.—Hsiang Lien.
8.—Chen Tê jun.
9.—Ching Shan.
10.—Ch'ên Pao ch'ên.

LI PU 吏部 Board of Civil Office.
Supervisor-General, *†Pao Yün.
1st President (Manchu), Kuang Shou.
2nd Do. (Chinese), Li Hung-tsao.
1st Vice-President, Ching Lien.*
2nd Do. Ch'i Shih-ch'ang.
3rd Do. K'un Kang.
4th Do. Hsü Ying-k'uei.

HU PU 戶部 Board of Revenue.
Supervisor-General (Vacant.)
1st President (Manchu), O-lo-ho pu.
2nd Do. (Chinese), Yen Ching-ming.
1st Vice-President, Fu K'un.
2nd Do. Sun Yi-ching.
3rd Do. Ching Hsin.
4th Do. Sun Chia-nai.

LI PU 禮部 Board of Ceremonies.
1st President (Manchu), Kn Chêng.
2nd Do. (Chinese), Hsü T'ung.
1st Vice-President, Kuei Ch'üan.
2nd Do. Li-ü Fu.
3rd Do. Kau Shên.
4th Do. T'ung Hua.

PING PU 兵部 Board of War.
Supervisor-General, Tso Tsung-t'ang.
1st President (Manchu), Jui Lien.
2nd Do. (Chinese), Pêng Yü lin.
1st Vice-President, Yueh Nian.
2nd Do. Huang T'i-fang.
3rd Do. Shih Tsêng.
4th Do. Liu Chin-t'ang.

HSING PU 刑部 Board of Punishments.
1st President (Manchu), Wên Yü.
2nd Do. (Chinese), Chang Chih-wan.
1st Vice-President, Sung Kuei.
2nd Do. Hsüeh Yün-shêng.
3rd Do. Kuei Hêng.
4th Do. Hsü Kêng-shên.

KUNG PU 工部 Board of Works.
Supervisor General, Ch'üan Ch'ing.
1st President (Manchu), Lin Shu.
2nd Do. (Chinese), Wêng T'ung-ho.
1st Vice-President, Hsing Lien.
2nd Do. Sun Yü-wên.
3rd Do. Ching Shan.
4th Do. Chang Chia-hsiang.

HAN LIN YÜAN 翰林院 Supreme College of Literature.
Chancellor (Manchu), *†Pao Yün.
Do. (Chinese), Hsü T'ung.

TU CH'A YÜAN 都察院 Court of Censors.
1st President (Manchu), Yün Hsü.
2nd Do. (Chinese), Pi Tao yüan.
1st Vice-President, Huai Ta-pu.
2nd Do. Hsü Kêng-shên.
3rd Do. Chung Lien.
4th Do. Tsêng Chi-tsê.

LI FAN YUAN 理藩院 Mongolian Superintendency.
Supervisor-General, Ling Kwei.
President, Wu-la-hsi-ch'ung-ah.
1st Vice-President, A-ch'ang-ah.
2nd do. do. Yueh Lin.
3rd do. do. Ko Tsu-k'o.

TSUNG-LI KOH KWOH SHE WU YAMEN 總理各國事務衙門 Office of Foreign Affairs.

(Composed of eleven members belonging to the other chief departments of State.)

1.—†Prince of Kung.
2.—†Pao Yün (*Grand Secretary, &c.*)
3.—†Li Hung-tsao, " "
4.—†Ching Lien, (*Vice-President Board of Civil Office.*)
5.—Lin Shu (*President, Board of Works.*)
6.—Ch'ên Lan-pin.
7.—Chou Chia-mei.
8.—Wu T'ing-fên.
9.—Chang P'ei-lun.
3 *Chief Secretaries.*
20 *Clerks.*

CHINESE REPRESENTATIVES ABROAD.

Great Britain:	Tsêng Chi-tsê.
France:	Do.
Germany:	Li Fêng-pao.
Spain, Peru, and United States:	Chêng Tsao-ju.
Japan:	Li Shu-ch'ang.

MASONIC.

LIST OF OFFICERS, 1884.

District Grand Lodge of Northern China.

R. W. District Grand Master..	R. W. Bro.	C. Thorne.
D. D. G. M.	W. Bro.	J. I. Miller.
D. G. S. W.	" "	W. H. Anderson.
D. G. J. W.	" "	W. C. Howard.
D. G. Treasurer	" "	W. H. Short.
D. G. Registrar	" "	E. P. Leicaen.
Pres. D. B. of G. P.	" "	C. J. Holliday.
D. G. Secretary	" "	A. Johnsford.
D. G. S. D.	" "	Rev. J. Innocent.
D. G. J. D.	" "	A. J. Allcott.
D. G. Supt. of Works	" "	J. M. Cory.
D. G. Direc. of Cer.	" "	J. Morris.
D. G. S. B.	" "	O. Middleton.
D. G. Organist	" "	Geo. B. Fentum.
D. G. Pursuivant	Bro.	J. Findlay.
D. G. Steward	"	J. Sullivan.
Do.	"	R. A. Gubbay.
Do.	"	J. Mackenzie.
Do.	"	J. Steward.
Do.	"	A. M. A. Evans.
D. G. Tyler	"	C. Merritt.

Royal Sussex Lodge, No. 501, E. C.

W. C. Howard	W. M.
E. P. Leicaen	I. P. M.
A. M. A. Evans	S. W.
J. Howell	J. W.
A. Johnsford	Treasurer.
G. M. Hart	Secretary.
R. Wm. Astill	S. D.
J. Clifton	J. D.
S. Gale	I. G.
E. Milbe	D. C.
T. Telliday	Steward.
J. Clark	do.
C. Merritt	Tyler.

Northern Lodge of China, No. 570, E. C.

J. M. Cory	W. M.
C. J. Holliday	I. P. M.
J. Findlay	S. W.
A. P. Macgregor	J. W.
Rev. F. R. Smith	Chaplain.
R. D. Starkey	Treasurer.
A. A. Krauss	Secretary.
J. Macmorran	S. D.
F. M. Gratton	J. D.
H. S. Goodfellow	I. G.
C. Merritt	Tyler.

Tuscan Lodge, No. 1027, E.C.

Osborne Middleton	W. M.
John Morris	I. P. M.
J. A. Sullivan	S. W.
R. A. Gubbay	J. W.
J. S. Ezekiel	Treasurer.
Thos. H. Vale	Secretary.
A. Alger	Organist.
James Jones	S. D.
S. Moutrie	J. D.
T. F. Hough	I. G.
Thos. P. Rae	M. of C.
J. M. Rogerson	Steward.
S. A. Nathan	do.
C. Merritt	Tyler.

Lodge Cosmopolitan, No. 428, S.C.

C. J. Holland	W.M.
T. Pemberton	I. P. M.
J. G. Thirkell	D. M.
J. Bannerman	S. M.
J. Gould	S. W.
T. S. Southey	J. W.
E. D. Meldrum	Treasurer.
W. Macfarlane	Secretary.
R. Phillips	S. D.
C. J. Tonkin	J. D.
C. M. Donaldson	I. G.
C. Merritt	Tyler.

Ancient Landmark Lodge, Mass. Const.

J. L. Hammond	W. M.
M. H. Cook	I. P. M.
Rev. W. S. Sayers	S. W.
C. Brown	J. W.
F. W. Galles	Treasurer.
A. Johnson	Secretary.
O. L. Skinner	S. D.
O. K. Bailey	J. D.
C. Merritt	Tyler.

Keystone Royal Arch Chapter.

J. L. Hammond	H. P.
N. P. Andersen	K.
J. O'Neil	S.
O. L. Skinner	C. H.
Chas. Brown	P. S.
Geo. Howard	R. A. C.
A. Mack	3rd V.
E. J. O. Rowland	2nd V.
A. Webster	1st V.
D. C. Jansen	Treasurer.
M. H. Cook	Secretary.
C. Merritt	Tyler.

Zion R. A. Chapter, No. 570, E. C.

Drummond Hay	Z.
John Morris	H.
C. J. Holliday	J.
T. W. Kingsmill	Treasurer.
J. M. Cory	Scribe E.
A. M. A. Evans	Scribe N.
Geo. R. Wingrove	P. S.
C. Merritt	Janitor.

Rising Sun Chapter, No. 129, S. C.

J. Bannerman	M. E. Z.
A. Johnsford	M. E. H.
W. C. Howard	M. E. J.
C. M. Donaldson	P. Z. Scribe E
J. G. Thirkell	Scribe N.
E. P. Leicaen	Treasurer.
C. J. Holland	1st S.
R. Phillips	2nd S.
H. Pestonjee	3rd S.
T. Pemberton	Dir. Cer.
C. Merritt	Janitor.

Celestial Preceptory.

H. M. Perkins	Emt. Preceptor.
W. Birt	Prelate.
F. W. Galles	Constable.
W. C. Howard	Marshal.
H. Evans	Treasurer.
M. H. Cook	Registrar.
A. Johnsford	Sub. Marshal.
R. A. J. Anderson	Capt. of Guard.
H. Peterson	1st Herald.
C. G. Balfour	2nd do.
C. Merritt	Equiry.

LIST OF

MARINE AND FIRE AND LIFE INSURANCE OFFICES

IN SHANGHAI, 1884.

OFFICES.	LIMITS.	AGENTS.
LOCAL MARINE.		
Canton Insurance Office (Limited)	....	Jardine, Matheson and Co.
China Merchants' Marine and Fire Insurance Co.	....	Ho Shun-chee.
China Traders' Insurance Co. (Limited)	....	J. R. Reiling.
Chinese Insurance Co. (Limited)	....	Melchers and Co.
North-China Insurance Co. (Limited)	....	J. Kennard Davis, Secretary.
On Tai Insurance Co. of Hongkong	....	Fung Hing Hong
Union Insurance Society of Canton (Limited)	....	Douglas Jones, Agent.
Yangtsze Insurance Association (Limited)	....	Russell and Co., Secretaries.
Yih-Wo Insurance Co.	....	C. M. S. N. Co.
LOCAL FIRE.		
China Fire Insurance Co. (Limited)	Tls. 75,000	Gibb, Livingston and Co.
Hongkong Fire Insurance Company (Limited)	Tls. 75,000	Jardine, Matheson and Co.
Shanghai Fire Insurance Co. (Limited)	....	Lee Chin-ping, Gen. Manager.
FOREIGN MARINE.		
Alliance Marine Assurance Company	....	Maitland and Co.
Alliance Marine Insurance Co.	....	Jardine, Matheson and Co.
American Lloyds' Association Capt. John P. Roberts, Surveyor.	....	Fraser and Co.
American Shipmasters' Association	....	Fraser and Co.
Assicurazioni Generali in Trieste	....	Gibb, Livingston and Co.
Austrian Insurance Company "Donau"	Tls. 40,000	Melchers and Co.
Austrian Lloyd	....	Melchers and Co.
Badische Schifffahrts-Assecuranz Gesellschaft, Mannheim	....	Melchers and Co.
Boston Board of Underwriters	....	Fraser and Co.
Bremen Underwriters	....	Melchers and Co.
British & Foreign Marine Insurance Co. (Limited)	....	Butterfield and Swire.
British Marine Mutual Insurance Association	....	Morris and Co.
Commercial Union Assur. Co. of London, (Marine)	....	North-China Ins. Co., Agents.
Consolidated Marine Insurance Co., Berlin	....	Eduard Schellhass and Co.
Düsseldorf Universal Marine Insurance Co. (Limited)	....	Siemssen and Co.
General Insurance Company, Helvetia	....	Melchers and Co.
General Marine Insurance Co., Dresden	....	Gepperich and Burchardt.
German Lloyd Marine Insurance Co. Limited	....	Siemssen and Co.
Germania Lloyd	....	Melchers and Co.
Globe Marine Insurance Company, (Limited)	....	Siemssen and Co.
Hamburg-Magdeburg Fire Insurance Co.	Tls. 25,000	Arnhold, Karberg and Co.
Home and Colonial Marine Insurance Co. (Limtd.)	....	Union Ins. Society of Canton.
Italia Società d'Assicurazioni Marittime Fluviali e Terrestri, Genova	....	Gibb, Livingston and Co.
Italia and Helvetia Marine Insurance Companies (Limited)	....	Gibb, Livingston and Co.
Java Sea & Fire Ins. Co. of Batavia (Mar. Branch)	....	Fraser and Co.
Joint Underwriters' Union, Amsterdam	....	P. Maclean and Co.
La Foncière Assu. Maritime	....	Coxon and Giraud.
La Grande Compagnie Société Anonyme d'Assurances Maritimes de Paris	....	Arnhold Karberg and Co.
La Suisse Company Assurances Maritimes	....	Sieber-Waser.
Lloyds	....	Gibb, Livingston and Co.
London and Provincial Marine Insurance Co., Ld.	Tls. 600,000	Drysdale, Ringer and Co.
Manchester Underwriters Association Limited	....	Holliday, Wise and Co.
Marine Insurance Company	‡	A. Lind.
Marine Insurance Co. of Basel	....	Melchers and Co.
Merchants' Shipping and Underwriters' Association of Melbourne	....	Gibb, Livingston and Co.
Mercantile Marine and Fire Insurance Company of South Australia	....	Adamson, Bell and Co.
Merchants Marine Insurance Company (Limited)	....	Mackintosh, Dudgeon and Co.
National Marine Insurance Association, Limited	....	Adamson, Bell and Co.
National Marine Insurance Co. of South Australia	....	Fraser and Co.
New York Board of Underwriters	....	Fraser and Co.
Ocean Marine Insurance Company	....	Lavers and Co.
Providentia Frankfort Insurance Co.	....	Melchers and Co.
Reliance Marine Insurance Co.	....	J. Alex. Harvie
Rhenania Versicherungs Actien Gesellschaft in Cöln a Rh.	....	E. Schellhass and Co.
Rhenania Versicherungs Actien Gesellschaft in Cologne	£10,000	Melchers and Co.
Royal Exchange Assurance Corporation	....	Alfred Dent and Co.
Samarang Sea and Fire Insurance Co.	....	Siemssen and Co.
Sverige Allmänna Marine Insurance Co. Ld., Gothenburg	....	Nils Möller.
South British Fire and Marine Insurance Co. of New Zealand	....	Primrose and Co.
South Australian Insurance Co.	....	Adamson, Bell and Co.
Straits Insurance Company (Limited)	....	Arnhold, Karberg and Co.
Thames and Mersey Marine Insurance Co., Limited	....	Adamson, Bell and Co.
Tokio Marine Insurance Company (Limited)	....	M. B. M. S. S. Co.
Transatlantic Fire Insurance Co. (Limited) Hamburg	....	Siemssen and Co.
Transatlantic Marine Insurance Co. (Limited) Berlin	....	Eduard Schellhass and Co.
Triton Insurance Company	....	Jardine, Matheson and Co.
Underwriting and Agency Association, London	....	Gibb, Livingston and Co.
Union Marine Insurance Co. (Limited) of Liverpool	....	Mackintosh, Dudgeon and Co.
Universal Marine Insurance Co. (Limited)	....	Evans, Pugh and Co.
Verein Hamburger Assecuradeure	....	Siemssen and Co.

‡ P. & O. S. N. Co.'s Steamer and M. M. Steamer, unlimited. Other steamer, £50,000

OFFICES.	LIMITS.	AGENTS.
FOREIGN FIRE AND LIFE ASSURANCE.		
Alliance Fire Assurance Company	Tls. 45,000	Jardine, Matheson and Co.
Caledonian Fire and Life Insurance Office	....	Mackintosh, Dudgeon and Co.
City of London Fire Insurance Co., Limited	....	Evans, Pugh and Co.
Commercial Union Assurance Co., (Fire)	Tls. 75,000	Lavers and Co.
Commercial Union Assurance Co. (Life Department)	....	Gibb, Livingston and Co.
Equitable Life Assurance Society of the United States	....	Wisner and Co.
Guardian Fire and Life Assurance Office	....	Fearon, Low and Co.
General Fire Assurance Co.	....	E. Schellhass and Co.
Fire Insurance Co. of 1877, Hamburg	....	Melchers and Co.
Fire Insurance Association, Limited	....	Gibb, Livingston and Co.
Imperial Fire Insurance Company of London	Tls. 50,000	Carlowitz and Co.
Hamburg-Bremen Fire Insurance	Tls. 30,000	H. Telge.
Hanseatic Fire Insurance Co.	Tls. 15,000	Coxon and Giraud.
La Foncière Assu. Feu	....	Carter and Co.
Lancashire Fire and Life Office	....	Adamson, Bell and Co.
Lancashire Insurance Company, Manchester	£10,000	
Lion Fire Insurance Company (Limited)	£10,000 or Tls. 40,000	Forrester and Co.
Liverpool and London, and Globe Fire Life Insurance Company	£10,000* or Tls. 30,000	Turnbull, Howie and Co.
London and Lancashire Fire Insurance Co.	Tls. 70,000	Butterfield and Swire.
London and Lancashire Life Assurance Co.	....	Melchers and Co.
London Assurance Corporation	£10,000	Holliday, Wise and Co.
London and Provincial Fire Insurance Co., Ltd.	....	Hyde, Hertz and Co.
Lubeck Fire Insurance Co.	Tls. 30,000	Eduard Schellhass and Co.
Manchester Fire Assurance Company	£5,000	Holliday, Wise and Co.
Magdeburg General Insurance Co., Limited	....	Eduard Schellhass and Co.
New Zealand Fire Insurance Co.	....	Fearon, Low and Co.
North British & Mercantile Insurance Company	£10,000	Russell and Co.
North German Fire Insurance Co.	Tls. 40,000	Melchers and Co.
Northern Assurance Fire and Life Co. — European	£20,000*	Turner and Co.
Northern Assurance Fire and Life Co. — Chinese	£4,000†	Turner and Co.
Norwich Union Fire Insurance Society — European	£10,000 or Tls. 40,000	Alfred Dent and Co.
Norwich Union Fire Insurance Society — Chinese	£2,000 or Tls. 8,000	Alfred Dent and Co.
Phoenix Fire Insurance Company	Tls. 35,000	Carter and Co.
Positive Government Security Life Assurance Co. (Limited)	£1,000	Drysdale, Ringer and Co.
Prussian National Insurance Co. of Stettin	....	Gepperich and Burchardt.
Queen Fire Insurance Company of Liverpool	£15,000	Fraser and Co.
Royal Exchange Fire Assurance of London	£5,000	Butterfield and Swire.
Royal Insurance Company of Liverpool	£15,000 or Tls. 60,000	Iveson and Co.
Scottish Imperial Insurance Co. — European	Tls. 40,000*	Dyce and Co.
Scottish Imperial Insurance Co. — One Life	£2,000	Dyce and Co.
Scottish Union and National Insurance Co.	....	White and Welsh.
Staffordshire Insurance (Limited)	Tls. 20,000	Adamson, Bell and Co.
Standard (Colonial) Life Assurance Company	£1,000	W. T. Phipps.
Sun Fire Office, London	£10,000	W. T. Phipps.

* On first class risks. † On Chinese buildings.

H.B.M. SQUADRON IN CHINA AND JAPAN.

Corrected to end of October Quarter, 1883.

All Officers whose names are printed in Italics are borne as Supernumeraries or Additional.

(G) against an officer's name denotes he is a Gunnery Lieutenant borne for Gunnery duties.

(T) that he is a Torpedo Lieutenant borne for Torpedo duties.

(N) that he is an Executive Officer borne for Navigating duties.

AUDACIOUS, 14, Double-screw, Iron Ship, Armour-plated.

6,010 (3,774) Tons. 4,830 (800) H.P.
Flag-Ship.

Vice-Admiral—George O. Willes, C.B. .... 3 Jan. '81
Flag-Lieutenant—Egerton B. B. Levett ...... 3 Jan. '81
Secretary—William W. Perry .... 3 Jan. '81
Clerk to Sec.—Francis C. Alton .... 3 Jan. '81
Francis E. Bennett .... 6 Dec. '82

Captain—Richard E. Tracey .... 3 Jan. '81
Commander—Auson Schomberg .... 5 Dec. '82
Lieutenant—Reginald A. Brock .... 5 Sept. '82
" George L. W. Adair............... 5 Sept. '82
" Thomas E. Cochrane .... 5 Sept. '82
" (G) John Casement............... 5 Sept. '82
" Hon. Harold A. Denison .... 5 Sept. '82
" (T) George L. King Harman ... Oct. '82
" *Thomas F. C. Dundas* ....29 June '83
Staff-Commander—Albert J. W. Neville ......24 Sept. '81
Capt. Marine—Edward A. M. Liardet .... 5 Sept. '82
Lieut. Marine—*John H. Plumbe* ....27 June '83
Chaplain—Rev. Henry D. Harper, B.A. ....13 Sept. '82
Fleet-Surgeon—Thomas S. Burnett .... 5 Sept. '82
Paymaster—Henry H. Wyatt .... 5 Sept. '82
Chief-Engineer—Thomas Edgar ....15 April '81
Nav. Instructor—(act.) Alfred T. Knight ... 3 Oct. '82
Sub-Lieutenant—Edward H. Martin ....30 Sept. '82
" John D. Hickley .... 5 Sept. '82
Surgeon—William E. Bennett .... 5 Sept. '82
Assist.-Paymaster—Reginald C. Hodder ...... 5 Sept. '82
" *Ernest E. Silk* .... 5 Sept. '82
Engineer—Henry E. Wingfield.................. 8 Oct. '81
" George Aborn ....31 Mar. '82
Assist.-Engineer—William T. Hocken .... 5 Sept. '82
Gunner—Edwin Bishop ....18 Aug. '81
Boatswain—John Thompson ....12 Aug. '81
" *George Hogg* ....28 Feb. '83
" *Alfred Nicholls* .... 4 Sept. '82
Carpenter—Edwin Edwards ....10 April '82
Midshipman—Charles J. T. Dormer............22 Nov. '82
" Lawrence de W. Satow ....15 Dec. '82
" Cecil E. E. Carey ....21 Oct. '82
" Walter Lumsden....................21 Oct. '82
" Edward A. Salwey................21 Oct. '82
" Graham S. P. Gwynn ....21 Oct. '82
" Henry I. W. Nevile ....15 Dec. '82
" Edwyn S. Alexander ....15 Dec. '82
" Ernest C. Hardy....................21 Oct. '82
" Charles B. Miller....................21 Oct. '82
" Henry O. Boger ....21 Oct. '82
Clerk—*Augustus H. Brigstocke* ....14 Sept. '83

The following officers are borne as additional for various special Services :—

Fleet-Surgeon—*Jonas W. Fisher*, M.D. .... 4 Nov. '81
For Sick quarters, Yokohama.
Assist.-Paymaster—*Chas. de H. Stewart* ......29 July '82
(In charge of Yokohama Depôt.)

(Commissioned at Devonport, 5th Sept. 1882.)

ALBATROSS, 4, Composite Screw Sloop.

940 (727) Tons. 640 (120) H.P.

Commander—Charles P. G. Hicks .... 8 Dec. '82
Lieutenant—Henry P. Routh .... 4 Dec. '82
" Albert F. Arthur .... 4 Dec. '82
" (N) Herbert N. Rolfe ....17 Jan. '83
Staff-Surgeon—Evelyn R. H. Pollard ....14 Dec. '82
Paymaster—Arthur S. C. Clarke ....12 Dec. '82
Chief Engineer—John W. Dupen ....14 Dec. '82
Gunner—Alphonso Styles .... 4 Dec. '82
Boatswain—Francis Hornibrook .... 4 Dec. '82
Carpenter—John S. Franckeiss .... 8 Dec. '82

(Recommissioned at Hongkong, 24th February, 1883.)

CHAMPION, 14, Screw Corvette.

Steel and Iron cased with Wood.
2,380 Tons. 2,340 H.P.

Will be recommissioned at Hongkong on arrival of *Orontes* with new crew, when Officers marked * will be re-appointed.

Captain—*Armand P. Powlett ....22 Aug. '83
Lieutenant—William L. H. Browne............ 1 Nov. '81
" (G) Francis G. Kirby .... 7 Dec. '80
" *(N) John C. Roughton ....13 Nov. '82
" Griffith G. Philipps ....15 Jan. '81
" Hugh F. Daubeny.................. 7 Dec. '80
" *James Erskine ....10 Jan. '83
Chaplain and Naval Instructor (act.)—Rev.
William J. Wilby, B.A. .... 7 Dec. '80
Staff-Surgeon—Valentine Duke, B.A., M.B. ... 7 Dec. '80
Paymaster—Dorisley Martin ....11 Jan. '81
Chief-Engineer—Robert Macaulay ....28 June '78
Sub-Lieut.—
Assist.-Paymaster—Montague Stephens ......30 Nov. '80
Engineer—Henry R. Marsden (*temp.*)......... 7 Dec. '80
Assist.-Engineer—*Frederick M. Cottam ... 5 Aug. '82
Gunner—Samuel H. E. Dawe .... 8 Sept. '80
Boatswain—Samuel J. Galley ....19 Aug. '79
Midshipman—Richard F. Phillimore ....23 Dec. '82
" David Bremner .... 6 Jan. '81
" *Frederick C. Learmouth ...... 6 Jan. '81
" Alexander W. Atkinson......... 6 Jan. '81
" Louis J. MacHutchin............ 6 Jan. '81

(Commissioned at Sheerness, 7th Dec., 1880.)

The following Officers have been appointed to the *Audacious* as additional for this Ship when recommissioned.

Lieutenant—Herbert A. W. Onslow............15 Sept. '83
" (G) William F. D. Walker ......15 Sept. '83
" Charles J. Briggs ....15 Sept. '83
" Arthur D. Ricardo ....15 Sept. '83
Staff-Surgeon—John C. B. Maclean, M.A., M.B. 15 Sept. '83
Paymaster—Francis J. P. Shapcote............15 Sept. '83
Chief-Engineer—*
Sub-Lieutenant—Robert H. Anstruther ......15 Sept. '83
Assist.-Paymaster—Thomas E. Phelps ......15 Sept. '83
Engineer—William J. Devan.......................15 Sept. '83
Gunner—Henry Arnold ....15 Sept. '83
Boatswain—William Jinks ....15 Sept. '83
" *James Barry* (act.)......................15 Sept. '83
Carpenter—William G. Withers ....15 Sept. '83
Midshipman—John F. Murray-Aynsley ......15 Sept. '83
" Frederick C. U. V. Wentworth.15 Sept. '83
" Alfred E. H. Morescnax ......15 Sept. '83
" Henry A. B. Shrubb ....15 Sept. '83

* Mr. George Swinney, now in *Wivern*, will be appointed to this Ship when recommissioned.

CLEOPATRA, 14, Screw Corvette,
Steel and Iron cased with Wood.
2,380 Tons. 2,610 H.P.
Will be recommissioned at Hongkong on arrival of *Orontes* with new crew, when Officers marked * will be re-appointed.

Captain—*Henry N. Hippisley .... 9 Sept. '82
Lieutenant—*George A. Primrose .... 9 July '82
" (G) Lewis D. Sampson ....24 Aug. '80
" *Frederick G. Stopford ....24 Aug. '80
" *(N) Francis W. Barrett.........15 Aug. '82
" Edward P. Powell ....24 Aug. '80
" *Scott W. A. H. Gray .... 9 Feb. '82
Chaplain and Naval Inst.—*Rev. William French, B.A. ....31 Dec. '80
Staff-Surgeon—William H. Stewart, M.D......24 Aug. '80
Paymaster—William E. P. Saer ....24 Aug. '80
Chief-Engineer—John Dunlop ....17 Oct. '79
Sub-Lieutenant—
Surgeon—*William G. O. Smith, M.D. ....19 Jan. '83
Assistant-Paymaster—Ralph B. Marwood ...24 Aug. '80
Engineer—John R. D. Johnson..................24 Aug. '80
Assistant-Engineer—Edwin K. Odam ....24 Aug. '80
Gunner—*George Norman........................14 May '83
Boatswain—*James Murphy ....31 Mar. '82
Carpenter—Benjamin Stoneman ....27 Aug. '78
Midshipman—Edmund C. P. Cooper ....24 Aug. '80
" Henry Thompson ....24 Aug. '80
" Frederick K. C. Gibbons ......24 Aug. '80
" Ernest F. De Chair ....24 Aug. '80
" Stuart St. J. Farquhar .... 2 April '83
Clerk—Paulin C. Cooke...............................24 Aug. '80

(*Commissioned at Devonport, 24th August* 1880.)

The following Officers have been appointed to the *Audacious* as additional for this Ship when recommissioned.

Lieutenant—(G) Arthur C. Woods ....15 Sept. '83
" Reginald P. Cochran ....15 Sept. '83
Staff-Surgeon—Joseph Wood, M.D. ....15 Sept. '83
Paymaster—Charles P. Skinner ....15 Sept. '83
Chief-Engineer—James Edmonds ....15 Sept. '83
Sub-Lieutenant—Phillip G. Tillard ....15 Sept. '83
Asst.-Paymaster—Percy T. M. Hughes ......15 Sept. '83
Engineer—John Fielder ....15 Sept. '83
Assist.-Engineer—Robert W. Donohue ......15 Sept. '83
Boatswain—Edward J. Case ....15 Sept. '83
Carpenter—Thomas E. Moore (act) ....15 Sept. '83
Midshipman—Algernon B. E. Greville.........15 Sept. '83
" Lionel F. W. Sanders............15 Sept. '83
" Edwin A. Day ....15 Sept. '83
" Allen T. Hunt......................15 Sept. '83
" Andrew P. Comber...............15 Sept. '83
" William O. Boothby ....15 Sept. '83

COCKCHAFER, 4, Screw Composite Gun-Boat.
465 Tons. 470 H.P.

Lieut. and Com.—Robert L. Groome .... 4 July '83
Lieutenant.—Godfrey H. B. Mundy............ 2 Jan. '83
(In lieu of Sub-Lieut.)
Sub-Lieutenant—(N) Algernon H. Lyons ... 9 Aug. '83
Surgeon—Samuel C. Browne...................... 2 Jan. '83
Assist. Paym. in Charge—George A. Hoskyn 2 Jan. '83
Engineer—John E. Chase .... 6 Feb. '83
Gunner—George S. Jennings ....25 Jan. '82

(*Commissioned at Devonport, 2nd January*, 1883.)

CURACOA, 14, Screw Corvette.
Steel and Iron cased with Wood.
2,380 Tons. 2,540 H.P.

Captain—George J. Anstruther...................28 Dec. '82
Lieutenant—Gordon Glennie.......................16 Dec. '82
" (N) Francis S. Ommanney ......16 Dec. '82
" William Hewetson.................16 Dec. '82
" Frederick R. W. Morgan ....16 Dec. '82
" Alfred E. Tizard ....11 July '83
" William G. Stewart ....11 July '83

Chaplain and Naval Instructor—Rev. John Dralmzon, M.A. ....27 Sept. '80
Staff-Surgeon—Charles C. Godding ....21 Dec. '82
Paymaster—Richard G. Chandler................ 8 Dec. '82
Chief Engineer—William Stewart...............14 Dec. '82
Sub-Lieut.—Cecil W. Ashby ....21 Sept. '82
Assist.-Paym.—George W. Whillier............ 8 Dec. '82
Engineer—George Parsons........................14 Dec. '82
Assist.-Engineer—Ernest J. Taylor ....14 Dec. '82
Gunner—Thomas Owens ....26 June '83
Boatswain—John Brock............................16 Dec. '82
" *Edward Bagge*.......................12 Nov. '81
Carpenter—John H. Johns......................... 8 Dec. '82
Midshipman—Thomas S. G. Newbold ....16 Dec. '82
" Carlton V. de M. Cowper ...... 5 Dec. '81
" Philip Walter ....16 Dec. '82
" Viscount Dursley ....16 Dec. '82
" George W. W. Dawes ....16 Dec. '82
" Ernest E. Lacy ....16 Dec. '82
" Archibald W. Shaw-Stewart...23 Nov. '81
" Archibald B. Purvis ....16 Dec. '82
Clerk—Joseph Willoughby ....15 Mar. '83

(*Recommissioned at Hongkong, 28th March*, 1883.)

DARING, 4, Composite Screw Sloop.
940 (727) Tons. 920 (120) H.P.
Will be re-commissioned at Hongkong on arrival of *Orontes* with new crew.

Commander—Francis J. J. Elliott.............10 Feb. '81
Lieutenant—Reginald Y. Smith ....10 Feb. '81
" (N) Henry Preedy ....13 Nov. '80
" Edward C. St. J. B. Neale ......23 Feb. '81
Staff-Surgeon—James B. Drew...................11 Feb. '81
Paymaster—John H. Cleverton..................10 Feb. '81
Chief Engineer—Thomas F. Hight ....19 Oct. '80
Gunner—Frederick Bryant .... 9 Dec. '80
Carpenter—Richard Taylor (act.)...............25 Feb. '81

(*Commissioned at Sheerness, 10th Feb.*, 1881.)

The following Officers have been appointed to the *Audacious* as additional for *Daring* when recommissioned.

Lieutenant—Peyton Hoskyns ....15 Sept. '83
" (N) Keppel Wade...................15 Sept. '83
" Henry V. W. Elliott...............15 Sept. '83
Staff-Surgeon—Alexander R. Joyce ....15 Sept. '83
Paymaster—Cornelius E. Grant ....15 Sept. '83
Chief Engineer—Hugh Burstow ....15 Sept. '83
Gunner—Charles E. Joy (act.) ....15 Sept. '83
Boatswain—Edmond Bride ....15 Sept. '83

ESK, 3, Double-Screw Iron Gunboat.
303 Tons. 340 H.P.
Hongkong.

Gunner—William Sledge (act.) .... 4 May '33

(*Borne in "Victor Emanuel."*)

ESPOIR, 4, Composite Screw Gunboat.
465 Tons. 470 H.P.

Lieut. and Com.—Edward H. Gamble ....11 Jan. '83
Lieutenant—(N) Henry R. Robinson ....11 Jan. '83
(In lieu of a Sub-Lieutenant (N)
Sub-Lieutenant—John M. de Robeck ....14 Aug. '83
Surgeon—Charles H. Wheeler, M.D. ....11 Jan. '83
Asst. Pay. in char.—William H. W. Markham11 Jan. '83
Engineer—John Fawcett ....14 Feb. '82
Gunner—Henry R. W. Ham (act.) ....11 Jan. '83

(*Commissioned at Devonport, 11th January*, 1883.)

FLY, 4, Double-Screw Composite Gun-Vessel.
603 (464) Tons. 400 (120) H.P.

Commander—John Hope ....25 Mar. '82
Lieutenant—George F. S. Knowling .... 5 June '82
" (N) Charles E. Pritchard.........22 Dec. '80
" Robert H. J. Stewart ....10 June '82

Paymaster—Frederick G. Farrow..............26 Mar. '81
Chief Engineer—John A. Lemon .... 7 Sept. '82
Surgeon—James B. Armstrong ....20 Mar. '81
Gunner—Andrew J. Bass ....22 Dec. '80
(Re-commissioned at Hongkong, 26th March, 1881.)

FLYING FISH, 4, Composite Screw Sloop.
940 (727) Tons. 840 (120) H.P.
Employed on Surveying Service.

Will be recommissioned at Hongkong on arrival of *Orontes* with new crew, when Officers marked * will be re-appointed.

Lieut. and Commander—Richard F. Hoskyn 26 Jan. '80
Lieutenant—Edward H. Dayly ....15 April '80
" (N) George Pirie ....15 April '80
" George W. Gubbins ....15 April '80
" *Henry Baker ....20 Oct. '81
" *Herbert A. Warren..* ....15 April '80
" *Cortland H. Simpson* ....16 Aug. '81
(*For Surveying Service.*)
Staff-Surgeon—Richard V. MacCarthy ......15 April '80
Paymaster—Henry C. Jenkins ....15 April '80
Engineer—*Edward Barrott .... 3 Mar. '83
Assist.-Engineer—John G. L. Baker........... 8 April '80
Boatswain—
(Commissioned at Sheerness, 15th April, 1880.)

The following Officers have been appointed to the *Audacious* as additional for this Vessel when recommissioned.

Captain—John F. L. P. Maclear ....15 Sept. '83
Lieutenant—Henry Harris.......................15 Sept. '83
" Gordon S. Gunn ....15 Sept. '83
" Henry E. Rooper ....15 Sept. '83
" William V. S. Howard...........15 Sept. '83
(In lieu of a Sub-Lieutenant.)
Paymaster—George Lawless ....15 Sept. '83
Surgeon—John Price ....20 Sept. '83
Boatswain—Richard Oliver ....15 Sept. '83

FOXHOUND, 4, Screw Composite Gunboat.
455 Tons. 470 H.-P.

Lieut. and Com.—John M. McQuhae ....24 Dec. '80
Lieutenant—(N) John P. Rolleston ....19 Nov. '81
(In lieu of a Sub-Lieutenant (N).)
Sub-Lieutenant—Lionel G. S. Hancock ......22 Dec. '80
Surgeon—William J. B. Bookey ....26 Mar. '81
Asst.-Paym.-in-charge—Horatio Howell ......22 Dec. '80
Engineer—Charles Allsop ....21 Nov. '82
Gunner—George A. Jennings (act.)............23 June '83
(Re-commissioned at Hongkong, 26th March, 1881.)

KESTREL, 4, Double-screw Composite Gun-Vessel.
610 (462) Tons. 830 (100) H.P.

Will be replaced by *Midge* when commissioned on arrival of *Orontes* with new crew, when Officers marked * will be appointed to the former Vessel.

Commander—*Edwin Hotham ....23 Aug. '82
Lieutenant—John E. Bearcroft ....24 June '81
" *Herbert W. Meredith.............20 Aug. '82
Nav.-Lieut.—Charles D. A. Marshead ....15 June '80
Engineer—William Olive ....24 Aug. '80
Surgeon—Thomas E. H. Williams ....15 June '80
Asst.-Paym.-in-charge—Bernard G. L. Evans10 Jan. '81
Gunner—Mark J. Delaney........... .. .. 6 Sept. '80
(Re-commissioned at Hongkong, 15th June, 1880.)

LINNET, 5, Double-screw Composite Gun-Vessel.
767 Tons. 1,050 H.P.

Commander—George W. Hill ....25 Sept. '83
Lieutenant—Watics Corbett ....21 Sept. '82
" (N) Edward P. Smythies......... 4 Aug. '80
" William H. W. Grove ....13 Dec. '82
Paymaster—Matthew Wellington................19 Sept. '82
Chief-Engineer—William H. Gulliver ....19 Sept. '82
Surgeon—Joseph Crowley, M.D. ....19 Sept. '82
Gunner—
(Commissioned at Chatham, 19th Sept., 1882.)

MAGPIE, 3, Double-screw Surveying-Vessel.
805 (665) Tons. 600 (160) H.P.

Commander—Hon. Foley C. P. Vereker ......15 Mar. '83
Lieutenant—Hugh R. Evans......................22 Dec. '80
" (N) Henry Bolam ....17 Dec. '79
" Henry H. Douglas ....18 Nov. '81
" *Andrew F. Balfour* ....24 Feb. '77
" *George O. Frederick* ....22 Dec. '80
Staff-Surgeon—Bernard Renshaw...............15 Oct. '81
Paymaster—Thomas F. Harrison ....22 Dec. '80
Chief-Engineer—Henry C. Stansmore.........15 Dec. '81
Boatswain—William Toner ....22 Dec. '80
Clerk—Charles J. Ferguson .... 1 Mar. '82
(Re-commissioned at Hongkong, 26th March, 1881.)

MERLIN, 4, Screw Composite Gunboat.
430 (295) Tons. 430 (60) H.P.

Lieut. and Com.—Reginald O. R. C. Brenton. 3 May '83
Lieutenant—(N) George H. King...............17 May '83
(In lieu of a Sub-Lieutenant (N)
Sub-Lieut.—Joseph R. Bridson...................12 May '83
Surgeon—George Smith.............. .... 3 May '83
Assist.-Paym.-in-charge—Francis F. Smith... 3 May '83
Engineer—Richard Harris.........................20 Feb. '83
Gunner—Richard P. Rivington (act.) .... 8 Feb. '83
(Commissioned at Devonport, 3rd May, 1883.)

MIDGE, 4, Double-screw Composite Gun-Vessel.
608 (464) Tons. 470 (120) H.P.

Will be commissioned at Hongkong to replace *Kestrel* on arrival of *Orontes* with new crew, when the Commander and Lieutenant from the former Vessel will be appointed to *Midge*.

Gunner—George J. Long .... 6 Sept. '81
(*Borne in "Victor Emanuel."*)

The following Officers have been appointed to the *Victor Emanuel* as additional to this Vessel when commissioned.

Lieutenant—Robert B. S. Wroy ....15 Sept. '83
" (N) Frank A. S. Farewell ....15 Sept. '83
Paymaster—Charles Farwell......................15 Sept. '83
Chief Engineer—John Kimber ....24 Aug. '83
Surgeon—Charles F. Newland ....15 Sept. '83
Gunner—William E. Pauley ....15 Sept. '83

PEGASUS, 6, Screw Composite Sloop.
1,130 Tons. 970 H.P.

Commander—Andrew K. Bickford .... 6 Dec. '82
Lieutenant—Charles S. Nicholson .... 5 Dec. '82
" (N) John F. Mills .... 5 Dec. '82
" Frederick A. Winter............... 5 Dec. '82
Staff-Surgeon—Herbert M. Ellis .... 6 Dec. '82
Paymaster—George F. M. Kent .... 7 Dec. '82
Chief Engineer—William M. Peak ....15 Dec. '82
Gunner—William Ferbrake (act.)... ....10 Nov. '82
Boatswain—Robert Harris......................... 5 Dec. '82
Carpenter—William Walkey .... 8 Dec. '82
(Re-commissioned at Hongkong, 24th February, 1883.)

SAPPHIRE, 12, Screw Corvette.
1,970 (1,405) Tons. 2,360 (350) H.P.

Captain—John R. T. Fullerton.................... 6 Dec. '82
Lieutenant—George H. Cherry..................18 Jan. '83
" Charles W. Thomas ....18 Jan. '83
" Edward E. Bradford ....18 Jan. '83
" Arthur E. Harford ....18 Jan. '83
Nav. Lieutenant—Walter Strugnell .... 2 Oct. '83
Chaplain and Nav. Inst.—Rev. Ebenezer T. Fyffe, B.A. ....29 Jan. '83
Staff-Surgeon—Edward E. Mahon ....18 Jan. '83
Paymaster—Charles J. Pawsey..................18 Jan. '83
Chief-Engineer—John Watson (*b*) ....24 Dec. '80
Sub-Lieut.—Henry Adair ....18 Jan. '83
Assist.-Paymaster—Edward D. Hadley ......18 Jan. '83
Engineer—Mathew W. Ellis ....18 Jan. '83

Assist.-Engineer—Henry S. Rashbrooke ......15 Dec. '82
Gunner—Frank Lewis .... 8 Nov. '82
Boatswain—John Howell ....12 Aug. '81
" *Philip Rodd*................................18 Jan. '83
Carpenter—Charles MacGregor.................. 8 Mar. '81
Midshipman—John E. P. Grenfell ....18 Jan. '83
" Edgar Lees ....18 Jan. '83
" Edward B. Kiddle ....18 Jan. '83
" George A. C. Ward ....18 Jan. '83
" Judge D'Arcy.................................18 Jan. '83
" Edwin V. Underhill ....18 Jan. '83
Naval Cadet—Henry D. Pelly ....18 Jan. '83
Clerk—*George Grant* ....14 July '83

(Commissioned at Devonport, 18th January, 1883.)

SWIFT, 5, Double-screw Gun-Vessel.
756 Tons. 1,010 H.P.

Commander—William Collins ....15 Mar. '81
Lieutenant—Vernon A. Tisdall..................15 Mar. '81
" Arthur H. Shirley ....15 Mar. '81
Nav.-Lieut.—Frank J. Harwood ....17 July '80
Staff-Surgeon—George B. Murray ....15 Mar. '81
Paymaster—Francis R. C. Whiddon ....15 Mar. '81
Chief Engineer—Peter Colquhoun ....21 July '81
Engineer—John W. Hole ....15 Mar. '81
Gunner—Michael King ....17 July '80

(Commissioned at Chatham, 15th March 1881.)

TWEED, 3, Double Screw Iron Gunboat.
363 Tons. 340 H.P.
Hongkong.

Gunner—John Blampey (act.) ....23 Sept. '80

(Borne in "Victor Emanuel.")

VICTOR EMANUEL, 2, Ship.
5,157 (3,087) Tons.
Receiving Ship at Hongkong.

Captain—William H. Cuming .... 2 May '81

(Commodore of the 2nd Class.)

Secretary—Sidney W. Wright ....22 Apr. '79

Commander—Edward H. M. Davis ....25 May '83
Lieutenant—Robert T. Wood .... 6 Mar. '82
Nav.-Lieutenant—George W. Balliston ......21 Feb. '81
Staff-Surgeon—Robert Turner, M.D. .... 7 July '80
Paymaster—Edwin B. S. Sandys ....26 May '82
Surgeon—Alexander L. Christie, M.D. ....15 Sept. '82
Assist.-Paymaster—Henry J. Ollard............14 June '83
Assist.-Engineer—*William F. Pamphlett* ......10 Mar. '83
Gunner—John Armstrong ....19 Dec. '81
Boatswain—Edward W. Austin ....17 Jan. '79
Carpenter—George B. Mahon ....20 Aug. '81

The following Officers are borne for various services:—

Lieutenant—(T) *Douglas A. Gamble* ....17 July '83

(For service with "Wivern" and Torpedo boats.)

Staff-Comm.—*Frederick A. Johnston* .... 5 Dec. '82
Inspector of Machinery—*Harry Williams* ...... 5 May '82
Engineer—*William H. Rock* ....16 Aug. '81
" *Charles Lane* ....19 Nov. '81
Boatswain—*Job Adams* .... 9 Apr. '92

(For Hongkong Yard.)

Engineer—*Caleb J. North* ....17 July '83

(For re-venting heavy Guns.)

Chaplain—*Rev. Charles M. Vaughan L. Th.* ... 7 Sep. '81

(For Hongkong Hospital.)
New Books opened 1st January 1881.

VIGILANT, 2, Paddle Despatch Vessel.
1,000 (835) Tons. 1,230 (250) H.P.

Lieut. and Commander.—Thomas B. Maxwell 4 July '83
Lieutenant.—(N) Francis A. A. G. Tate ......22 Dec. '80
Paymaster—Abraham Turner .... 5 Jan. '83

Chief Engineer—Joseph A. Smith ....22 Dec. '80
Sub-Lieut.—George S. Shuckburgh ....13 Mar. '82
Surgeon—Richard E. Biddulph B.A., M.B.......28 Aug. '83
Assist.-Engineer—John G. Stevens .... 4 Aug. '80
Boatswain—James R. Gibbs ....22 Dec. '80

(Re-commissioned at Hongkong, 26th March, 1881.)

WIVERN, 4, Screw Iron Turret Ship, Armour-plated.
2,750 (1,899) Tons. 1,450 (350) H.P.
Hongkong.

Chief Engineer—*George Swinney ....22 Dec. '82
" John Hobbs ....15 Sept. '83
Gunner—John Shea ....23 June '83
Carpenter—Charles Young .... 5 May '83

(Borne in "Victor Emanuel.")

*This Officer will be appointed to the *Champion* when re-commissioned.

ZEPHYR, 4, Screw Composite Gunboat.
438 (308) Tons. 530 (60) H.P.
Will be recommissioned at Hongkong, to replace *Kestrel*, on arrival of *Orontes* with new crew. Officers marked * will be re-appointed.

Lieut. and Comm.—George N. A. Pollard ... 6 Oct. '80
Sub-Lieutenant—*Edmund P. E. Jervoise ... 5 June '82
Surgeon—William Hayes ....29 Oct. '81
Assist.-Paym.-in-charge—Richard H. Clark... 6 Oct. '80
Engineer—*William S. Stribbling ....11 July '83
Gunner—Frederick J. Bishop .... 6 Aug. '80

(Commissioned at Sheerness, 6th Oct., 1880.)

The following Officers have been appointed to the *Audacious* as additional for the *Zephyr* when re-commissioned.

Lieut. and Commander—Charles K. Hope ...15 Sept. '83
Sub-Lieutenant—(N) Godfrey Hubbard ......15 Sept. '83
Surgeon—William M. Lory ....15 Sept. '83
Asst.-Paym.-in-charge—Joseph W. Chaster...15 Sept. '83
Gunner—Edward H. Purkis (*act*)...............15 Sept. '83

U.S. SQUADRON IN CHINA & JAPAN.

RICHMOND, 2nd rate. 14 Guns. 2,000 Tons.
Flag Ship.

Commander-in-chief—Admiral John Lee Davis.
Aid-Lieutenant—A. E. Marix.
Fleet Surgeon—A. S. Oberly.
Do. Engineer—Chief-Engineer P. Inch.
Do. Marine Officer—Captain F. H. Corrie, U.S.M.C.

Captain—J. S. Skerrett.
Executive Officer—Lieut.-Com. C. O'Neil.
Navigator—Lieut.-Com. E. S. Houston.
Watch Officers—Lieutenants J. J. Hunker, F. H. Delano, H. H. Barroll, and F. E. D. Veeder.
Ensign—G. W. Denfield.
Paymaster—E. N. Whitehouse.
Passed Asst.-Surgeons—B. F. Rodgers and S. H. Dickson.
Passed Asst.-Engineers—W. W. Heaton and R. R. Leitch.
Assistant Engineers—A. H. Hunt and J. M. Pickrell.
Second Lieutenant, Marines—C. Mercer.
Mate—A. F. Callender.
Boatswain—Wm. Manning.
Gunner—Geo. Fouse.
Carpenter—D. W. Perry.
Sailmaker—J. S. Franklin.
Pay Clerk—D. Mowat.

ENTERPRISE, 3rd rate. 615 Tons.

Commander—Albert S. Barker.
Lieutenant Commander—George M. Book.
Lieutenants—George A. Norris, Hugo Osterhaus, M. A. Shufeldt and H. M. Hodges.

Ensigns—N. J. L. T. Halpine, Edward Lloyd, jr., R. F. Lopez and L. J. Clark.
Surgeon—Horation N. Beaumont.
Passed Assistant Paymaster—Jas. A. Ring.
Chief Engineer—H. D. McEwan.
Passed Assistant Engineer—C. J. Habighurst.
Assist.-Engineers—George W. McElroy and J. H. Baker.
Second Lieutenant of Marines—T. J. Fillette.
Pay Clerk—H. D. Alexander.

ESSEX, 3rd rate. 615 Tons.

Commander—A. H. McCormick.
Lieutenants—M. R. S. Mackenzie, William H. Parker, Wainwright Kellogg, Karl Rohrer, Corwin P. Rees, and W. M. Irwin.
Ensigns—W. E. P. Muir and A. Bitler.
Surgeon—M. L. Ruth.
Passed Assistant Paymaster—Louis A. Yorke.
Chief Engineer—Daniel P. McCartney.
Passed Asst.-Engineer—F. J. Hoffman.
Assistant Engineer—Martin Bevington.
First Lieutenant of Marines—O. C. Berryman.
Pay Clerk—James.

JUNIATA, 3rd rate. 928 Tons.

Commander—P. F. Harrington.
Lieutenants—Samuel Belden, E. H. C. Leutze, Richard Rush, Richard Mitchell and C. H. Lyman.
Ensigns—Ridgley Hunt, P. W. Hourigan, Stokeley Morgan, F. J. Haeseler, A. N. Mayer, T. Worthington, H. B. Ashmore and F. A. Hountoon.
Surgeon—G. W. Woods.
Assistant-Surgeon—J. C. Baker.
Paymaster—I. Goodwin Hobbs.
Chief Engineer—P. A. Renrick.
Passed Assistant Engineer—Asa M. Mattice.
Assistant Engineer—C. R. Salisbury.
First Lieutenant of Marines—H. H. Coston.

MONOCACY, 3rd rate. 6 Guns. 747 Tons.

Commander—F. J. Higginson.
Executive Officer—Lieut.-Com. A. J. Iverson.
Navigator—Lieutenant A. B. Wyckoff.
Lieutenants—L. P. Jouett and V. L. Cottman.
Ensigns—W. G. Hannum and W. J. Sears.
Paymaster—H. C. Machette.
Passed Assistant Engineer—W. L. Nicholl.
Passed Assistant Surgeon—C. Biddle.
Assistant Engineers—H. S. Ritteffer and F. M. Bennett.
Pay Clerk—C. M. Ostrander.

PALOS, 4th rate. 6 Guns. 306 Tons.

Lieut. Commander—J. D. B. Gliddon.
Lieutenant—W. P. Conway.
Ensigns—H. C. Poundstone and J. H. Rohrbacker.
Passed Assistant Surgeon—A. C. Cabell.
Assistant Paymaster—W. B. Wilcox.
Assistant Engineer—G. W. Snyder.

U. S. Naval Hospital, Yokohama.

Medical Director—J. S. Dungan.
Passed Assist.-Surgeon—M. H. Simons.
Assistant Paymaster—J. A. Mudd.

U. S. Naval Store-House, Nagasaki.

Passed Assistant Paymaster—J. C. Sullivan.
Pay Clerk—D. Farrell.

EVENTS CONNECTED WITH CHINA.

YEAR.
B.C.
2700 Chinese first Cycle.
208 or 211 Great Wall of China completed.
A.D.
420 Nanking the Capital of China.
1260 Seat of Government transferred to Peking.
1275 Marco Polo introduced Missionaries.
1517 Europeans first arrived at Canton.
1536 Macao granted to the Portuguese.
1617-1647 The Tartars conquered China.
1660 Tea sent to England.
1662 General Earthquake, 300,000 buried at Peking
1680 East India Co. begin to trade with China.
1719-1727 Commercial relations with Russia.
1731 Another earthquake, Peking and suburbs, loss 180,000.
1793 Sept. 14 Earl Macartney's Embassy arrived at Peking.
„ Oct. 7 He was ordered to depart.
1816 Feb. 8 Lord Amherst's Embassy to China.
1822 Nov. 1 Burning British Factories, Canton.
1832 May 31 First number *Chinese Repository* published.
1834 Apr. 22 The exclusive rights of the East India Company ceased.
Opium dispute commenced.
1834 Apr. 25 Free trade ships sailed for England.
„ Nov. 7 Opium trade interdicted by Chinese.
1835 Feb. 23 Opium burnt at Canton.
1836 Dec. 14 Captain Elliot Chief British Commissioner.
1839 May 24 Captain Elliot and Brit. residents left Canton.
„ June 3 Opium destroyed by Chinese.
„ Aug. 23 Hongkong taken.
1840 Jan. 5 Emperor's Edict interdicting all trade with England for ever.
1841 Jan. 21 Hongkong taken possession of by the British.
„ Feb. 20 Bogue Forts taken by Sir G. Bremer.
„ May 31 Canton ransomed for 6,000,000 dollars.
„ Sept. 14 Bogue Fort destroyed.
„ Oct. 1 Chusan retaken.
„ 10 Chinhai taken.
„ 13 Ningpo taken.
1842 June 19 Shanghai taken.
„ Aug. 29 Nanking Treaty signed on board the *Cornwallis*, Chinese to pay 21,000,000 dollars.
1850 Aug. 3 First number of *North-China Herald* issued.
1853 Jan. 12 Woochang taken by Insurgents.
„ Mar. 19/20 Rebels take Nanking.
„ May 19 Rebels take Amoy.
„ June 14 Chinkiang unsuccessfully attacked by Imperialists.
„ Sept. 7 Rebels take Shanghai.
1854 Jan. 4 Insurgents attacked at Tah-lew.
„ Apr. 19 Irruption of Rebels into Pechili.
„ July 30 Coins of 1000, 500, 400, 300 and 200 cash, abolished by Imperial decree.
1855 Feb. 17 Insurgents evacuated Shanghai.
1856 Feb. 20 Kiman taken by the rebels.
„ Oct. 8 Outrage on Brit. lorcha *Arrow*, Canton river.
„ Dec. 14 European Factories at Canton burned.
1857 Jan. 15 A-lum poisoned the bread at Hongkong.
„ Mar. — Lord Elgin appointed Envoy.
„ July 1 Hakodadi, Kanagawa and Nagasaki opened.
„ Aug. — Blockade of Canton.
1858 Jan. 5 English and French enter Canton.
„ Jan. 5 Yeh sent prisoner to Calcutta, died April 9, 1859.
„ May 20 Allies take Peiho Forts.
1859 Apr. 26 Suez Canal commenced.
1860 Aug. 12 War begins, English under Sir Hope Grant; French, General Montauban.

1881	April	19	Savings Bank opened at Shanghai, in connection with Hongkong and Shanghai Banking Corporation
,,	April	29	German barque *[illegible]* attacked by pirates between Hongkong and Amoy.
,,	April	30	Launch of the s.s. *Tai-wo*, third boat of Messrs. Jardine, Matheson & Co.'s Yangtsze line
,,	May	15	Ratification at Peking of Treaty between Russia and China
,,	May	16	C.M.S.N Co.'s s.s. *Hankwang* stranded on S E. Shantung Promontory, and became a total wreck
,,	May	28	British steamer *Elgin* lost on a voyage from Saigon to Hongkong, struck on Bombay Shoal, during a gale, and became a total wreck. Crew and passengers put to sea in three boats, and were eventually rescued; only three lives being lost
,,	June	2	German barque *Musoo* foundered near the Ladrones; crew took to boats and make their way to Hongkong.
,,	June	21	Fire at Foochow, four lives lost, and 517 houses destroyed
,,	June	28	British steamer *America* struck on an island on the S.W. coast of Corea, and was afterwards abandoned at sea, the Captain failing in his attempt to bring her on to Shanghai, crew saved.
,,	July	10	Earthquake in Kansuh; great loss of life.
,,	July	11	Shanghai Tramway Scheme sanctioned at Meeting of Ratepayers
,,	July	14	British barque *Aberdonian* lost in typhoon in Chusan group, Captain and 19 of the crew lost.
,,	July	16	American barquentine *Annie S. Hall* lost in same typhoon near Taichow Island; Captain and crew saved.
,,	July	19	Ratification at Peking of the Treaties of Commerce and Emigration between the United States and China concluded in 1880.
,,	July	22	Arrival in Hongkong of the Chinese gunboats *Iota*, *Kappa*, and *Lambda* from Newcastle-on-Tyne
,,	Aug.	6	Fire at Ningpo; 120 houses destroyed.
,,	Aug.	20	Ratification of the amended Russo-Chinese Treaty at St. Petersburg.
,,	Aug.	26	Severe typhoon at Foochow; great damage ashore and afloat, three European sailors and over eighty Chinese drowned in the river.
,,	Aug.	26	Charter granted to the British North Borneo Company
,,	Aug.	27	Loss of the Danish barque *Flensborg* on Table Island, Pescadores; crew saved.
,,	Aug.	28	Typhoon and Flood at Shanghai. In surrounding district whole villages were swept away; great loss of life in native population
,,	Sept.	16	Convention between Germany and China ratified in Peking
,,	Sept.	20	Meeting of Committee of Shanghai Chamber of Commerce to discuss the feasibility of organising a system of Meteorological reports from the China coast.
,,	Sept.	26	Typhoon on Japan coast, British steamer *Ash* supposed to have been gone down with all hands, when one day out from Nagasaki, on a voyage to Shanghai; twenty-six Europeans and several natives lost.
,,	Sept.	26	The British barque *Nouveau Mondelli* on a voyage from Keelung to Shanghai, is supposed to have been lost in the same storm.

1881	Sept.	30	Wreck of the British ship *Bolton Abbey* on the Pratas Reef, China Sea, four of the crew lost in attempting to reach land
,,	Oct	3	Treaty between Brazil and China signed at at Tientsin
,,	Oct.	4	Wreck of the British ship *Geraldine Paget* on the Pratas Shoal, one man drowned, the rest of the crew saved.
,,	Oct.	5	The German steamer *Quinta* driven ashore on Taichow Island while on the passage from Hongkong to Saigon, and afterwards destroyed by fire
,,	Oct.	5	Disastrous typhoon at Haiphong and district, over one thousand lives lost and immense damage to property
,,	Oct.	5	The British steamer *Pakhoi* stranded on Brown's Rock when entering the Amoy harbour, and subsequently slipped off a bank into deep water
,,	Oct.	8	Opening of two Chinese Hospitals at Tientsin.
,,	Oct	10	Wreck of the E. and A. steamer *Brisbane* near Port Darwin.
,,	Oct.	20	The Chinese gun-vessels *Chao Yung* and *Yang Wei* arrived in Hongkong from Newcastle-on-Tyne.
,,	Oct.	23	The American ship *Humboldt* was wrecked on the Paracel Reef and three of the crew drowned when attempting to land on the rocks.
,,	Oct.	27	Wreck of the American barque *New Era* near Bojendor, in the Philippines, while on the voyage from Hongkong to San Francisco; no lives lost
,,	Oct.	31	Funeral of the late Empress Tsze An, widow of the late Emperor Hien Fung.
,,	Nov.	13	Death of Mr G. French, Chief Justice of H.B M.'s Supreme Court for China and Japan, at Hiogo.
,,	Nov.	13	British barque *Lydia* left Newchwang, but has not since been heard of, vessel supposed to have gone down with all hands.
,,	Dec.	1	The *Northern Post*, daily paper, started at Tientsin.
,,	Dec.	1	Wreck of the British barque *Forward Ho* near Nambu, Japan; no lives lost.
,,	Dec.	2	Princes Albert Victor and George of Wales arrived in Shanghai.
,,	Dec.	4	The German barque *Pallas* went ashore on Quemoy Island, near Amoy, and became a total wreck
,,	Dec.	24	The Imperial Chinese Telegraph line from Shanghai to Tientsin opened.
,,	Dec.	26	German barque *Walkyre* wrecked near Bootan while on a voyage from New York to Hongkong
1882	Mar.	7	Departure from Hongkong of Sir John Pope Hennessy
,,	Mar.	13	Extensive fire in the native city; upwards of 300 houses burnt down.
,,	Apr	1	Masonic Club opened.
,,	Apr.	1	Arrival of the French expeditionary force at Haiphong
,,	Apr.	1	Wreck of the Spanish lorcha *King-doo-foo* about 70 miles from Woosung
,,	Apr.	19	Death of Li Hung-Chang's mother at Wuchang.
,,	Apr.	21	Wreck of the British barque *Oaenstang* in Hainan Straits
,,	Apr.	21	Extensive fire in Foochow.
,,	Apr.	21	Telegram received stating that Mr. Robert Hart had been appointed a K C M.G.
,,	Apr	21	Imperial Decree promulgated instituting the Order of Shuang-lung Pao-shing or Double Dragon to be conferred on foreigners.

1882 Apr. 25 Capture of the Citadel of Hanoi by French troops.
„ Apr. 30 Attack by a Corean mob upon a Japanese shooting party near Gen-shan-shin; one Japanese killed and two wounded.
„ May 1 Destructive fire in Ningpo; upwards of 200 houses burnt down.
„ May 12 H.E. Chang Shu-sheng, Viceroy of the Two Kwang, visited Hongkong *en route* to Tientsin.
„ May 15 Heavy gale in Shanghai; several minor accidents in the river.
„ May 16 List of Applications of the Shanghai Electric Company closed, when there was a great demand for shares.
„ May 18 First number of *Hu Pao* published.
„ May 22 Treaty between United States and Corea signed at Rensan, Corea, by Commodore Shufeldt and the Corean authorities.
„ May 22 Funeral of Li Hung-Chang's mother at Wuchang.
„ June 3 Treaty between Brazil and China ratified at Shanghai.
„ June 6 Treaty between Great Britain and Corea signed at Rensan, Corea, by Admiral Willes and the Corean authorities.
„ June 7 H.E. Tso Tsung-Tang, Viceroy of Nanking, arrived in Shanghai.
„ June 9 His Excellency Tso Tsung-Tang left for Woosung.
„ June 9 Strike amongst the builders' *employés* in Shanghai; the volunteers called out.
„ June 15 Shocking outrage on the Abbé Cornaux at Hu-lau in Shing-king.
„ June 16 Loss of Am. barque *Dirigo* on the island of Video; crew all saved.
„ June 22 The Am. barque *Benjamin Aymar* went ashore at Amakusa, Japan, but was subsequently got off.
„ June 30 Treaty between Germany and Corea signed at Rensan, Corea, by Herr Von Brandt and the Corean authorities.
„ July 15 Typhoon in the East Coast of China; much damage done to shipping.
„ July 23 Attack upon the Japanese Legation at Seoul, Corea, by a Corean mob; eight members of the Legation killed.
„ July 26 Electric Light first exhibited in Shanghai.
„ July 30 British barque *Empress* wrecked at the entrance of the river.
„ Aug. 3 British ship *Jessie Burrill* burnt near Tung-ying Island.
„ Aug. 6 Loss of the s.s. *Hongkong* in the Haitan Straits.
„ Aug. 20 Attack on Messrs. Sassoon's premises at Foochow, by *lekin* officials.
„ Aug. 28 Collision in the Yang-tsze between the s.s. *Pekin*, the tug *Ewo* and the ship *Hattie E. Tapley*.
„ Aug. 29 Fall of a block of houses in the Hankow Road, Shanghai, burying several of the Chinese workmen.
„ Sept. 2 Sir Thomas Wade left Shanghai for England.
„ Sept. 4 Loss of the s.s. *Europe* near the mouth of the river Min.
„ Sept. 15 The s.s. *Yorkshire* went aground on the Thalia Bank, near Amoy and was subsequently towed off without injury.
„ Oct. 19 Serious affray between British and German men-of-war sailors in Shanghai.
„ Oct. 29 Collision in the Yang-tze between the s.s. *Hanyang* and the lorcha *Annie*; the former totally lost.
„ Oct. 30 Convention between Japan and Corea ratified by the Mikado.

1882 Nov. 7 Great fire in Canton; 800 houses destroyed.
„ Dec. 9 Horrible murder of a Japanese boy in Hongkow.
„ Dec. 13 Great fire in Canton; 100 shops burnt.
„ Dec. 26 Horrible murder and subsequent fire in Quang-se Road.
„ Dec. 26 Extraordinary meeting of the Hongkong and Shanghai Banking Corporation in Hongkong, to vote an increase of Capital from $5,000,000 to $7,500,000.
1883 Jan. 1 The port of Jenchuan, Corea, opened to Japanese trade.
„ Jan. 5 First number of *Star in the East* issued.
„ Jan. 6 The C.N. Co.'s steamer *Wuhu* went ashore at Langshan Crossing in the Yangtsze, and became a total wreck.
„ Jan. 9 The Ching-yung-shing silk hong failed; liabilities Tls. 540,000.
„ Jan. 9 The Chu-sen-huo lorcha hong failed; liabilities Tls. 200,000.
„ Jan. 15 Steamship *Sherard Osborne*, with E. E. A. I. & China Tel. Co.'s cable, arrived.
„ Jan. 20 Death of the Ex-Regent of Siam, at Ratbhuree, Siam.
„ Jan. 21 Sir R. T. Rennie, Chief Justice, arrived at Shanghai.
„ Jan. 22 Several Chinese hongs failed.
„ Jan. 24 Loss of the Norwegian steamer *Odin* on rocks at the east end of Tung Ying island; crew saved.
„ Jan. 27 Police raid on Tientsin rowdies in Fohkien Road.
„ Jan. 27 The British steamer *Carisbrooke* took fire and was scuttled in Hongkong harbour.
„ Jan. 30 Loss of the Norwegian barque *Henrik Ibsen* on the Pescadores; crew saved.
„ Feb. 2 Steamship *Kenmure Castle* lost in Bay of Biscay.
„ Feb. 5 New Mixed Court opened.
„ Feb. 5 Wreck of *Wuhu* sold at Tls. 780.
„ Feb. 9 Fire in the French Concession, Shanghai, seven houses destroyed.
„ Feb. 13 Death of Monsenhor Calderon, Vicar Apostolic of Fohkien.
„ Feb. 15 Sir R. T. Rennie took his seat as Chief Justice at the Supreme Court.
„ Feb. 18 Loss of the U.S. corvette *Ashuelot* on the East Lammock Rock; eleven lives lost.
„ Feb. 26 Loss of the C.M.S.N. Co.'s steamer *Meli* on the bar at the mouth of the Huó river; chief mate and seven of the crew drowned.
„ Mar. 6 *Hacan* first steamer to Tientsin this year.
„ Mar. 9 The Tug Boat Association's boats transferred to English flag.
„ Mar. 10 H.E. Tso Tsung-tang visited Shanghai.
„ Mar. 10 Steam dredger *Anding* arrived.
„ Mar. 11 New Organ for the Cathedral arrived.
„ Mar. 13 News of Minister Bourée's re-call reached Shanghai.
„ Mar. 14 "Ward" claims finally settled.
„ Mar. 16 Fall of a row of Chinese houses near Maloo; three lives lost.
„ Mar. 18 Fire at Tung-ka-doo; seven lives lost.
„ Mar. 20 Great Fire at Bangkok; 600 buildings destroyed and thousands of persons rendered homeless.
„ Mar. 27 Bombardment and capture of the Citadel at Namdinh, Tonquin, by the French forces.—Attack by Annamites and Chinese on the Citadel at Hanoi.
„ Mar. 27 Two Corean Princes arrived at Shanghai from Tientsin.
„ Mar. 30 Arrival of Governor Sir George Bowen, G.C.M.G., in Hongkong.

1883 Apr. 1 The Dutch schooner *Malanan* driven on shore on the Pratas Shoal and looted by Chinese, captain and two of the crew reached Hongkong in a small open boat.

" Apr. 2 Murder of the Rev. Père Terrasse, a French priest, and several native converts in Yunnan.

" Apr. 2 Outrage on a houseboat party at Hung-jao

" Apr. 2 H.E. Li Hung-chang arrived at Woosung.

" Apr. 6 The Li Kang Bank failed, liabilities Tls. 300,000.

" Apr. 8 Imperial Chinese Telegraph line from Shanghai to Canton commenced.

" Apr. 10 Loss of the steamer *Mound Castle* on a rock off Chungchow, near Hongkong.

" Apr. 12 Steamship *Golconde*, the pioneer vessel of the Compagnie Marseillaise de Navigation à Vapeur arrived at Shanghai.

" Apr. 14 The Shanghai Volunteers inspected by Major Hajnhan from Hongkong.

" Apr. 19 Loss of the steamer *Carnarvonshire* in Siugo Bay, near Oshima, Japan, all hands saved.

" Apr. 22 Arrival in Macao of Senhor da Roza, the new Governor of that Colony.

" Apr. 29 New Organ at the Trinity Cathedral used for the first time.

" May 1 Panic at Hankow.

" May 4 Emeute at the Kiangnan Arsenal.

" May 8 Announcement telegraphed by Reuter of the appointment of Sir Harry Parkes as British Minister to China.

" May 10 *Kolstrop* lost on Dyer's Island.

" May 10 H.H. the Maharajah of Johore arrived in Shanghai.

" May 16 The steamship *Breconshire* ran into the Yokohama Lightship and sank it.

" May 19 Disastrous surprise and defeat of a French sortie led by Commandant Rivière, near Hanoi, and death of that officer together with other officers and about 80 rank and file.

" May 19 Ratifications of the American Treaty with Corea exchanged at Seoul.

" May 22 Yacht for Li Hung-chang launched at Boyd's Yard.

" May 23 The Eastern Extension Telegraph Co.'s new cable to Shanghai opened.

" May 28 H.E. Li Hung-chang arrived at Shanghai.

" May 28 Volunteer Review.

" May 28 Collision near Chefoo of the C.M.S.N. Co.'s steamer *Hing-shing* and the British schooner *Catherine Marden*, loss of the steamer and six of her crew, the schooner much damaged.

" June 6 M. Bourée arrived at Shanghai on his way home.

" June 6 M. Tricou, to replace M. Bourée, arrived at Shanghai.

" June 11 Cartridge explosion on the French Concession; seven persons injured.

" June 15 Fire on the French Concession; sixty Chinese stores destroyed.

" June 18 Outrage on foreigners on the French Sicawei Road.

" June 25, 26, 27, 28 Market Riots in the Maloo.

" July 4 Negotiations between M. Tricou and Li Hung-chang on the Tonquin question suspended.

" July 5 Li Hung-chang returned to Tientsin.

" July 9 The Canton Kowloon telegraph line formally opened to traffic.

" July 14 Farewell banquet given to Sir Harry Parkes at Tokio.

1883 July 16 Telegraphic communication between Bangkok and Saigon established

" July 16 The Detective Si-yung sent into the city

" July 18 Prospectus of the North Borneo Steamship Company issued

" July 18 Death of Tu Duc, King of Annam, at Hué, his capital.

" July 19 Defeat of the Annamites outside Namdinh by Colonel Badens.

" July 20 Death of H.E. Iwakura Tomomi, Udaijin of Japan, at Tokio.

" July 21 Si-yung restored to the custody of the Municipal Police. Preliminary trial at the Mixed Court.

" July 21 Loss of the steamer *Spark* off Cape Cami, Hainan Straits.

" July 23 New building for the entertainment of distinguished foreign guests at Tientsin formally opened by the Viceroy of Chihli.

" July 25 Swatow declared "infected" and quarantine restrictions imposed at Shanghai on vessels from the former port.

" July 26 Fire in Canton Road; one life lost

" Aug. 1 Si-yung surrendered to the city authorities.

" Aug. 4 The Mih-ho-loongs chartered the *Kiang-teen* for a picnic to Pootoo.

" Aug. 5 Murder, robbery and arson at Lo-ka-woi

" Aug. 5 & 6 Severe typhoon at Shanghai and Ningpo.

" Aug. 6 The Danish barque *Carl Wilhelm*, which had sprung a leak on the 5th, was abandoned by crew when about 30 miles from the Saddles.

" Aug. 7 Severe defeat of the Annamites outside Namdinh by the French under Colonel Badens.

" Aug. 7 A jinricsha coolie murdered by an unknown foreigner on the Soochow Creek.

" Aug. 10 The str. *Foochow* went ashore on Finger Rock, outside Chefoo, in a thick fog, and became a total wreck.

" Aug. 12 Fracas between some of the Customs employés and natives at Honan, Canton; a Chinese boy shot dead by J. H. Logan.

" Aug. 13 Attack on the Bubbling Well Cottage by 200 beggars.

" Aug. 15 Capture of Hai Duong, in Tonquin, by the French forces.

" Aug. 15 Important engagement near Hanoi between the French under General Bouet and the Black Flags; the French obliged to retire.

" Aug. 15 Tremendous rise of the river at Songkoi, Tonquin; enormous loss of life and property.

" Aug. 18 Loss of the British brig *Brenda* near the Goto Islands while on the passage from Shanghai to Nagasaki.

" Aug. 16 Bombardment of Hué by the French commenced.

" Aug. 20 Capitulation of Hué to the French.

" Aug. 22 Great fire at Foochow; two hundred houses destroyed, and seven lives lost.

" Aug. 22 Severe gale at Ningpo.

" Aug. 23 *Pladda* went ashore near Lightship.

" Aug. 23 Mr. A. E. Reynolds, "the oldest resident" in China, died at Shanghai.

" Aug. 24 Violent storm at Shanghai and Chinkiang.

" Aug. 24 Farewell address presented to Sir Harry Parkes at Yokohama.

" Aug. 25 Treaty of Peace between France and Annam signed at Hué.

" Aug. 27 Fatal accident on the river, Mr. Darg drowned.

1883 Sept. 1 Terrific electric storm at Shanghai.
„ Sept. 1 Severe three days' engagement between French under General Bouet and the Black Flags outside Hanoi.
„ Sept. 6 Sir Harry Parkes arrived at Shanghai.
„ Sept. 7 Sir George Bowen, Governor of Hongkong visited Shanghai.
„ Sept. 8 Death of the Infant Princess Masu, daughter of the Mikado of Japan, at Tokio.
„ Sept. 10 Riot at Canton; the foreign settlement on Shameen attacked by a native mob, and sixteen houses sacked and burned.
„ Sept. 20 The trial of Logan, for shooting a Chinese boy at Honam, commenced, before Chief Justice Rennie at Canton.
„ Sept. 25 A post boat attacked by robbers on the Sicawei creek and Tls. 3,000 stolen.
„ Sept 25 Extensive robbery of telegraph cable from Woosung.
„ Sept. 27 Conclusion of the Logan trial at Canton; verdict of manslaughter; prisoner sentenced to seven years' penal servitude.
„ Oct. 4 Collision between the *Kiangtsen* and *Yangtsze* on the river.
„ Oct. 6 Fire near the Arsenal at Foochow; about fifty houses destroyed.
„ Oct. 8 The Sun Tai and Tai Loi Banks suspended payment; liabilities Tls. 150,000.
„ Oct. 11 Old Woosung railway plant brought back to Shanghai from Formosa.
„ Oct. 16 Fire at Ningpo; 30 houses burned down.
„ Oct. 21 Tso Tsung-tang visited Shanghai.
„ Oct. 25 Sir Geo. Bowen returned to Hongkong.
„ Oct. 26 Earthquake at Chefoo.
„ Nov. 5 The heads of three of the Quangse Road murderers suspended outside the city walls.
„ Nov. 8 His Worship Chên retired from the Mixed Court after twenty years of service and forty years intercourse with foreigners.
„ Nov. 13 First monthly exhibition of the Shanghai Art Society.
„ Nov. 23 Telegraph cable between Japan and Fusan, Corea, laid.
„ Nov. 23 Great fire at Foochow; over 300 houses destroyed and three lives lost.
„ Nov. 25 The Taotai's police occupied Hogg's village.
„ Nov. 25 Tsao Si-yung sent to Soochow.
„ Nov. 26 Treaties between Great Britain and Corea, and Germany and Corea signed at Seoul by Sir Harry Parkes and Mr. Zappe.
„ Nov. 29 Riotous attack on Tax Collectors on the Yangtsze-poo Road.
„ Dec. 7 Attack by a native mob on the French Consular Yamên at Canton.
„ Dec. 16 Capture of Sontay by the French forces, and signal defeat of the Black Flags.
„ Dec. 24 Loss of the Douglas steamer *Albay* off Tower Point, near Swatow; third officer and several Chinese passengers lost.
„ Dec. 1 Suspension of the Vow Kong Bank.
„ Dec. 1 The Taotai's police occupied Li Hongkow.
„ Dec. 16 Outrage on a Sikh at Pootung.
„ Dec. 29 Loss of the *Hwaiyuen* off Haeshin, and 250 lives lost.

Chinese Emperors.

1627	Chwang-lei.	1795	Kea-king.
1644	Sung-che (Tsing dynasty.)	1820	Taou-kwang.
1662	Kang-he.	1850	Kien-fung.
1723	Yung-chin.	1861	Tung-chi.
1736	Keen-lung.	1875	Kwang-sü.

CHINESE PRONUNCIATION

OF

FOREIGN HONGS

IN SHANGHAI, 1884.

ALPHABETICALLY ARRANGED.

A-C

威化阿
Ah-hwa-weng.
RODEWALD & Co.

刺加呵
Ah-ka-leh.
AGRA BANK, Limited

廠板杉頭下
Ao-dou-san-pan-tsang.
LOWER BOAT HOUSE.

B

噸吧
Ba-tun.
BARTON, Capt. Z.

衛德畢
Bat-teh-way.
BIDWELL, R. S.

場球抛內場馬跑
Bau mo zang-nei pau jeu-zung.
SHANGHAI CRICKET CLUB.

利倍
Bay-lee
BAILEY, JNO.

畢斯碧
Be-sz'-be.
BIGSBY, W. E. D.

猕來孛
Beh-lay-t'a.
BRANDT, O.

發別
Bih-fah.
KELLY & WALSH.

和平
Bing-oo.
BIRT, W., & Co.

C

堂會酒戒
Cha-chew-whei-tang.
TEMPERANCE HALL.

C

納耶札
Chah-lang-na.
CRONNER, A.

利長
Chang-le.
BISSET, J. P., & Co.

豐兆
Chaou-foong.
HOGG, E. JENNER

行洋昌啟
Che-chong.
WONG, C. T., & Co.

四高之
Che kao-ss.
YANG-TSZE-POO ROAD —POINT.

行洋泰乾
Chi'en-ta.
BIELFELD, ALEX.

生醫盛興
Chin-zing-e-sung.
ROGERS & PERKINS, Drs.

隆晋
Ching loong.
MUSTARD & Co.

隆晋
Ching-loong.
INDEPENDENCE PILOT Co.

明精
Ching-ming.
COMINS, C.

局報電國中
Chung kwok tin-pau-kuk.
IMPERIAL CHINESE TELEGRAPHS.

院書西中
Chung-si-shu-yuen.
ANGLO-CHINESE COLLEGE.

吉用堂善種
Chung-sien-tang-yung-chih.
MOTOHIYOSHI, M.D., S.

www.ingramcontent.com/pod-product-compliance
Lightning Source LLC
Chambersburg PA
CBHW021528270326
41930CB00008B/1154
* 9 7 8 3 3 3 7 3 7 2 6 7 5 *